THE INTERNATIONAL LIBRARY OF PSYCHOLOGY, PHILOSOPHY AND SCIENTIFIC METHOD

Edited by C. K. OGDEN

An Examination of Logical Positivism

By JULIUS RUDOLPH WEINBERG, Ph.D.

About the Series

THE PURPOSE of *The International Library* is to give expression, in a convenient form and at a moderate price, to the remarkable developments which have recently occurred in Psychology and its allied sciences. The older philosophers were preoccupied by metaphysical interests which, for the most part, have ceased to attract the younger investigators, and their forbidding terminology too often acted as a deterrent for the general reader. The attempt to deal in clear language with current tendencies, has met with a very encouraging reception, and not only have accepted authorities been invited to explain the newer theories, but it has been found possible to include a number of original contributions of high merit.

LITTLEFIELD, ADAMS & CO.
Paterson, New Jersey

INTERNATIONAL LIBRARY OF PSYCHOLOGY, PHILOSOPHY AND SCIENTIFIC METHOD

Edited by C. K. OGDEN

AN EXAMINATION OF LOGICAL POSITIVISM

By

JULIUS RUDOLPH WEINBERG, Ph.D.

Cornell University

1960

LITTLEFIELD, ADAMS & CO.

Paterson, New Jersey

THE INTERNATIONAL LIBRARY OF PSYCHOLOGY,
PHILOSOPHY AND SCIENTIFIC METHOD

Edited by C. K. OGDEN

1960

PUBLISHED BY LITTLEFIELD, ADAMS & CO.
Reprinted by arrangement with Humanities Press, Inc.
For sale only in the U.S.A., its possessions, and territories.

Dedicated to my Mother

●

First published in the English language by Routledge and Kegan Paul, Ltd., London, in 1936 and reprinted in 1950. Cloth edition available from Humanities Press, Inc., New York, in the United States of America.

CONTENTS

PART I. LOGICAL FOUNDATIONS

PART II. THEORY OF SCIENTIFIC METHOD 105

PART III. THE ELIMINATION OF METAPHYSICS 173

PART IV. RADICAL PHYSICALISM 227

PART V. CONCLUSION

PREFACE

I wish to express my gratitude to the members of the Sage School of Philosophy, especially Professors Burtt, Sabine, and Church, for their kindness in making many helpful suggestions and criticisms. I am also indebted to Dr. Rudolf Carnap for the explanation of several difficult points of logical syntax, and because he has allowed me to read an unpublished manuscript on the subject of meaning and verification. Finally, I wish to thank Professor Henry Bittermann, of Ohio State University, for reading the manuscript, and Mr. Manley Thompson, Jr., for reading the proof and preparing the indices.

J. R. W.

AN EXAMINATION OF LOGICAL POSITIVISM

INTRODUCTION

I

The philosophy of the Viennese Circle has undergone so many radical changes since its formal organization in 1928 that a statement of its aims is likely to include too much or to omit too much to be very informative. Nevertheless, the first statement of its official programme is sufficiently general to avoid misunderstanding.

In this official statement [1] the principal aims are set out as follows : first to provide a secure foundation for the sciences, and second to demonstrate the meaninglessness of all metaphysics. The method used to realize these aims is the logical analysis of all concepts and propositions. There have been other philosophical movements devoted to similar purposes, among which nineteenth century positivism and pragmatism may be mentioned. Likewise other philosophical movements have exclusively employed logical analysis to demonstrate their doctrines. The various contemporary realistic philosophies are specific instances. The unique characteristic of the philosophy of the Viennese Circle is the exclusive use of logical analysis to demonstrate positivistic theses.

The two most fundamental doctrines of Logical Positivism are (1) that propositions of existential import have an exclusively empirical reference, and (2) that this empirical reference can be conclusively shown by logical analysis. The empiristic doctrine is thus to be proved by a logical method. This calls for an account of logic consistent with

[1] " Wissenschaftliche Weltauffassung." *Der Wiener Kreis*, Wien, 1929, s. 15 ff.

such a thorough-going empiricism. At first sight this would seem to present a difficulty. Philosophical systems which employ logical methods almost exclusively would undoubtedly be expected to produce non-empirical results. If, however, logic is taken simply as a method of connecting meanings it is not difficult to reconcile logical methods with empirical results. If logical formulæ, in other words, assert nothing about the meanings of propositions, but simply show how such meanings are connected, then an empiricism based on a logical analysis of meanings is not inconsistent. This is what the Logical Positivists have attempted to do.

Their work then naturally falls into two parts : the foundations of a scientific method free from metaphysics, and the elimination of pseudo-concepts introduced by metaphysics into science and philosophy.

The distrust of metaphysics is almost as old as metaphysics itself. The rise of the great schools of ancient philosophy was followed by critical reactions in the form of scepticism. In the Middle Ages, although outspoken criticism of official metaphysics was prohibited, there is no doubt whatever of the widespread existence of radical anti-metaphysical movements in the schools. In modern times each great philosophic system has had an equally great critic. It is beyond the compass of this work to chronicle the history of these various attempts to demolish the great metaphysical systems. Nevertheless, some of the more prominent of them should be mentioned because they constitute the intellectual heritage of the contemporary form of positivism, with which this study is concerned.

In his criticial work Hume is the first great positivist. It was he no less than Kant who was responsible for the death-blow to deductive metaphysics. The discovery that the sphere of deductive reasoning is closed to statements about matters of fact (because deduction is no more than a complicated transformation occurring solely within the sphere of concepts) was known long before Hume wrote his great work. Hume's virtue was the thoroughgoing and relentless application of the discovery to all forms of abstract reasoning and, in particular, to metaphysics. Furthermore, the attempted reduction of statements about matters of fact to statements solely concerned with experience was the second great preparation that Hume made for the subsequent development of positivism. On the critical side, therefore, Hume is the positivist *par excellence*.[1] Nevertheless, he cannot be considered positivistic in the present sense of the term, since he seemed frequently to assume the existence of the trans-empirical world and to justify this assumption on the grounds of belief. It is not difficult to show that a thoroughgoing application of Hume's principles need not lead to scepticism. If scepticism is not the inevitable consequence of Hume's critical principles, then there is no *necessity* of introducing belief. On the other hand, the idea of belief as a method of description or explanation leads to as much metaphysics as before, so that there is no appreciable advance.[2] The use of psychological analysis, particularly in the case of belief, but elsewhere as well, is what principally distinguishes Hume from his positivistic descendants, just as the logical analyses of his works form the connecting link between them.[3] Many, if not all, of the principal doctrines of contemporary positivism derive from Hume. In almost all respects Hume is intellectually closer to the philosophy of the Viennese Circle than is the author of the *Cours de la Philosophie Positive*. The empiristic trend of Logical Positivism may safely be traced, I believe, to Hume. The logical foundation of Positivism must, nevertheless, be distinguished from the particular logical method employed to establish Hume's foundation. It is, therefore,

---

[1] Cf. "Wissenschaftliche Weltauffassung," op. cit., p. 17, apropos the two sources of the errors of metaphysics with Hume's *Enquiry concerning Human Understanding*, sec. xii, part iii.

[2] Hume realized this difficulty very clearly, but did not, it seems to me, take the obvious way out of it. See Appendix to his *Treatise of Human Nature*.

[3] Thus, for example, where Hume traced every idea to a corresponding impression or group of impressions, Logical Positivists reduce the meaning of every proposition to atomic facts.

necessary to look to Leibniz for the requisite methods. The structure of the propositions of logic has been thoroughly analysed only in recent times. Leibniz made the first great advance in this direction. He clearly distinguished between truths of reason and truths of fact, and he emphasized one fundamental property of logical truths. This was the doctrine that analytic propositions were unconditionally true because they possessed a certain formal property, namely the fact that the predicate of every analytic proposition can be shown to be contained in the subject. The division of propositions into truths of reason and truths of fact, together with the first approximation to an analysis of the former, places Leibniz among the sources of Logical Positivism. This, however, is not to say that Leibniz and the positivists have used this discovery for the same purposes, or even to say that the discovery is interpreted in the same way. The positivists are simply indebted to Leibniz for this discovery and for the use of logical analysis in philosophy.

At first sight it seems strange to include Immanuel Kant among the precursors of contemporary positivism. The point of departure of the Critical Philosophy is a reaction against the extravagances of empiricism as well as those of rationalism, the method of investigation adopted in the exposition of the system is far from empirical (being a composition of analytic and *a priori* synthetic reasoning, the former predominating [1] at times), and thus many of the results of the Critical Philosophy are completely in conflict with anything that might be called positivism. On the other hand, the presence of an *a priori* method in the system connects it with similar methods in contemporary positivism. These are details, however, and obscure the more intimate connection between positivism and the Critical system.

The real links are to be found in the common aims of the two philosophies. Both positivism and criticism desire to render the foundations of mathematics and natural

---

[1] Cf. Vaihinger, H., *Kommentar Zu Kant's Kritik*, pp. 412 *et seq.*

science absolutely secure and free from extraneous elements of a metaphysical character. Both positivism and criticism reject transempirical and deductive metaphysics. There is little doubt that the Kantian philosophy played its part in the development of positivism. Indeed, the famous Kantian refutation of the proofs for the existence of God is, in the main, in the exact spirit of contemporary positivistic thought.

Another aspect of the Kantian philosophy may have been of even greater influence than its anti-metaphysical direction. I refer to the phenomenalistic tendencies which characterized the second edition of the *Critique of Pure Reason*. Even though Kant was never a complete phenomenalist, the tendencies which guided the second edition were explicitly used by such positivistic thinkers as Avenarius and, in our own time, Schlick. From the logical point of view a strict adherence to phenomenalism on the terms of Kant's philosophy should lead to an abandonment of the transcendental object, on the one hand, and of the transcendental unity of apperception on the other. The phenomenalism thus produced is a close approximation to positivism in the contemporary sense of the word.

Hume, Leibniz, and Kant may, therefore, be regarded as the most influential precursors of positivistic thought. To these philosophers should be added those of the French Enlightenment. Generally speaking, the methods of the Enlightenment were almost as uncritically dogmatic as those of Continental rationalism and whatever of scholasticism remained. The general spirit of the Enlightenment was not genuinely anti-metaphysical and experimental, and is, therefore, not to be considered as a preparation for the positivism of the present day in any direct sense. This much, however, can be said. The reaction against the persistent elements of dogmatic theology and psychology that had characterized Continental thought probably paved the way for a more profound reaction against all metaphysics, including that of the Enlightenment itself, and so made a

genuine appreciation of the experimental method possible.
It was, then, not so much what the philosophers of the
Enlightenment said or believed, but rather what they did,
that provided the possibility of a positivistic philosophy.

The beginnings of positivism, as far as the philosophies
which go by that name are concerned, are found in the first
half of the nineteenth century. Three names stand out here
as fundamentally important : Cournot, Germain, and Comte.
The briefest outline of their essential methods and results
will suffice to show what relationship these bear to the
contemporary positivism of the Viennese Circle. From what
immediately follows it will be clear that the connection is
not as direct and intimate as might be supposed.

The Positive Philosophy of Comte has three distinctive
marks, only one of which is retained in the contemporary
doctrine of the Viennese Circle. It has, above all, a practical
turn, that is the value of knowledge for human concerns
is the principal criterion of what is truly scientific. Next
in emphasis the historical approach to problems of thought
is given primary importance. Finally the omnipotence of
empirical method is asserted and defended with great force.
Only this last-named characteristic constitutes a bond of
connection with Logical Positivism. This connection, it
must be admitted, is not very great.

Metaphysical assertions are regarded as hypotheses,
somewhat less tangible than the hypotheses of theology.
They have led to insoluble problems, and thus have out-
lived their period of utility. They are to be rejected on this
ground. Such is the attitude toward metaphysics taken
by the Positive Philosophy of Comte. The result is naturally
a restriction of hypotheses to the empirically verifiable
realm. Logical Positivism rejects metaphysics for quite
another reason. Metaphysical assertions are not simply
useless or indemonstrable ; they are nonsensical. There is
no question of a significant assertion which cannot be
verified. Utility does not concern the contemporary
positivist of the Viennese Circle in any way. Hence the

attitude toward metaphysics taken by Comte and that taken by the Viennese are by no means identical. There is, however, no great leap from the one to the other. "Do not concern yourself with assertions that are indemonstrable for such a concern is useless," leads quite easily to "Do not concern yourself with indemonstrable assertions, for such a concern is as senseless as the assertions which occasion it." There is a natural development from Comte to the Viennese Circle, but this development was not the one actually followed. With the exception of Mach and a very few others, most of the nineteenth century positivists regarded metaphysics as a set of significant but indemonstrable and useless assertions.

The contemporary form of positivism has little use for the historical analysis of thought forms which plays so great a role in Comte's system. For Comte something was to be learned about concepts from their historical setting. The Viennese Circle, however, prefers to treat all concepts on the same level. Herein lies another essential difference. The sole criterion of the value of concepts is, for the Viennese Circle, that of logical significance. Comte, on the other hand, seemed to give metaphysics a significant position in the development of thought.

The only direct connection between the older and the contemporary positivism is the insistence on empirical method as the sole source of truth. As we have observed, the reason for this faith differs in the two cases. The latter group alone claims a purely logical ground for its insistence on the primacy of empirical data.

The subsequent history of positivistic thought, so far as it concerns the present study, involves the development of empiricism in England and the scientific philosophers of Germany. John Stuart Mill and Herbert Spencer are usually reckoned as being in the direct line of descent from Comte. Of these two, Mill alone was a fairly consistent empiricist, but his psychologism in logical theory together with the tinge of realism which colours his ideas concerning matter are radical departures from Comte as well as off the direct historical path leading to Logical Positivism.

In order to take up the course of development of this school it is best to turn to the work of Mach, Avenarius, Hertz, and Popper-Lynkeus. (There are many others, but these are the most significant names.)

The work of these thinkers consisted largely in an attempt to relieve physics and psychology from metaphysics, Mach [1] in particular attempted to show how the absolute conceptions of physical reality were unverifiable and quite dispensable in physical inquiry. In this way the metaphysical idea of an objective world was vigorously attacked. At the same time Mach wanted to remove all metaphysics from psychology by showing that the psychological (or subjective) world as well as the objective physical world could be regarded as derivatives of the neutral elements of experience.

The chief difficulty with Mach's views seems to have been that his claim to neutrality in regard to metaphysical issues was not completely justified. There are, in fact, two aspects of his argument against metaphysics which are difficult, if not impossible, to disentangle. First there are the logical objections to the assumption of the existence of objects which, by definition, lie beyond the range of scientific investigation ; for example, absolute space, material substance, and the ego. Certain purely logical and methodological objections against such concepts could be presented with great force without any alternative hypotheses for the explanation of the world. Mach sometimes argued in this simple logical way. But, in the second place, he suggested that all the metaphysical explanations of the concepts just mentioned could be replaced by the hypotheses of diverse arrangements of the neutral elements of experience. This somehow gave the impression that the logical objections to metaphysical ideas in science rested on the empirical hypothesis of " elements ". This impression, rightly or

[1] *Beiträge zur Analyse der Empfindungen*, Jena, 1886.

wrongly conceived, was responsible in large part for the unfavourable reception of Mach's views. It certainly had less telling effect on metaphysics than if he had argued against metaphysical ideas on purely logical grounds.

Aside from this Mach is more closely allied with Logical Positivism than perhaps any previous thinker. If we try to discover the reason for the failure of Mach and his positivistic contemporaries to construct a consistent and absolutely neutral scientific philosophy, we must remember that the logical theory in the last quarter of the nineteenth century had not advanced to the point necessary to provide a logical method of antimetaphysical thought. There were, in the last decade of the century, several contributions to logic of the utmost importance (those of Pierce, Frege, Peano, Schroeder), but the influence of these contributions was not felt, and so it is not surprising that positivism did not make much headway among philosophers.

The contemporary positivistic thought of the Viennese Circle is a combination of the empiricism of the nineteenth century and the logical methods developed since that time. This combination makes it possible for positivists to adopt a genuinely neutral point of view and to avoid making decisions about matters which are beyond the scope of analysis. In this way their conclusions rest upon purely logical analyses and are not vitiated by unjustified pronouncements about empirical questions which philosophy cannot answer.

The empiricism of Hume, the logical methods of Leibniz, the critique of metaphysics by Hume and Kant, and finally the anti-metaphysical doctrines of Mach in respect of physics and psychology, prepared the way for Logical Positivism in so far as these systems contained the general methods and results. The specific logical technique has a somewhat different history, for the most part unrelated to the great philosophical systems.

Discounting the early investigations in symbolic logic, the first important studies were made by George Boole and

Augustus de Morgan in the first half of the nineteenth century. These investigations were followed by the development of the logic of relations by Charles Pierce and Ernst Schroeder. The logical foundation of mathematics was investigated about the same time by Giuseppe Peano and Gottlob Frege. The results of these labours were, I believe, the beginnings of a radically new method in philosophy.

Leibniz hoped for the time when two philosophers would "calculate" rather than discuss the outcome of a philosophical issue. The creation of a new method in logic seemed to realize his dream. The principal result of the work in symbolic logic in the nineteenth century was, in fact, applicable to many philosophical problems. I shall mention only a few of them here.

While many philosophers had clearly realized that propositional form and propositional inference frequently have relational structure (in contradistinction to the subject-predicate structure of the traditional form), the rigorous treatment of relational forms in terms of a logical calculus was not possible until Pierce's and Schroeder's work had been done. In so far as relational inference and the relational structure of propositions have any bearing on philosophical problems, this work was of fundamental significance.

Frege's treatment of the class-concept provided a theory of logic which seemed to demonstrate the nominalism of earlier empiristic philosophies. Now it is one thing to provide arguments of a philosophical or psychological nature for nominalism, and another to provide a demonstration of this doctrine in a rigorous mathematical way. Frege, and later Russell, attempted and, to some extent, succeeded in the latter. The elimination of abstract universals is an essential part of Frege's doctrine.

Finally, although the complete elucidation of the nature of analytic propositions was not accomplished until Wittgenstein's work on this subject was written, the formulation of logic and mathematics in symbolic notation made it possible to show (1) that all analytic reasoning falls

[relation between propositions - building or relating general to simple]?
use planet example - W.H. vs. Carnap's "construction"

into a system, and (2) that all analytic reasoning has some
common element of structure. Leibniz and Kant had clearly
explained the nature of analytic propositions of the subject-
predicate form.   Their explanation is correct for those
propositions, but for propositions of relational form it has = ?
no significance.   A complete explanation of the nature of
an analytic proposition should apply to analytic propositions
of whatever form. It was necessary to exhibit all these forms
and the deductive principles which govern them before the
essential analytic property common to all could be shown.

In general the development of symbolic logic provided
a new method of investigation in philosophy and justified
in part Hume's nominalistic empiricism and the Leibnizian
distinction between truths of reason and truths of fact.

II

The development of logic, especially the logic of relations,
was responsible for the rise of present positivistic tendencies.
The logical theories of Frege and Russell, culminating in the
Principia Mathematica, are the principal source of the
methodology of Logical Positivism.   I shall, therefore,
devote some space to Russell's doctrines as given in the
Principia Mathematica.

The principal business of the *Principia Mathematica* is
the deduction of logic and pure mathematics from a small
number of premises all presumably of logical character.
A premise is of logical character, according to Russell, if
it is unconditionally true ; more exactly if it is always true,
absolutely general, and contains no constants except logical
ones. A logical constant is one of the following : " and,"
" or," " implies," " equivalence," " not both," " neither-
nor," " not," " all," " there exists," etc.

Russell assumes certain ideas as undefined (not indefinable)
within the limits of his system. These ideas are introduced
in connection with the groups of axioms which determine
their uses.

The calculus of propositions requires three undefined ideas, " proposition," " negation," " disjunction," symbolized by means of a kind of notation which is now in general use. The following dictionary will explain the essentials of this notation.

p, q, r . . . stand for propositions.

v is a binary operation involving two (or more) terms.

Thus "pvq" means " at least one of the two propositions is true ".

$\sim$ is a unary operation involving one term or one complex of terms.

Thus $\sim p$ means "p is false" and $\sim(pvq)$ means "p or q is false".

All the logical constants (excepting generalization and particularization) are definable in terms of " $\sim$ " and " v ". Thus p and q, p implies q, etc. :

$$p.q = df. \quad \sim(\sim pv \sim q)$$

[" p and q are true " is the same as saying " It is false that p is false or q is false."]

$$p \supset q = df. \quad \sim pvq = \sim(p.\sim q)$$

[" If p then q " is the same as saying " Either p is false or q is true " which is the same as " It is false that p is true and q is false."] This may be a strange definition for implication but it serves the two purposes for which implication is used in logic and science. In logic implication is used in the proof of proposition as follows : If A is a truth of logic, and if $A \supset B$, then B is a truth of logic. It is necessary only that the truth of the antecedent depend on the truth of the consequent in order that the implication obtain.

In material inference we say if A is factually true and if $A \supset B$ is factually true, then B is factually true. This fails only when A is true and B is false. The *Principia* definition of " $\supset$ " thus serves these purposes well.

$$p \equiv q = df. \quad p \supset q.p \supset q$$

[" p and q are equivalent " means " p implies q, and q implies p ". Equivalent propositions are, in general, not identical. If $p = q$ then obviously $p \equiv q$, but if $p \equiv q$ we cannot generally infer $p = q$.]

With this dictionary we can state a set of axioms from which all the recognized principles of the logic of propositions may be deduced.

The Russell set of axioms (primitive propositions) is as follows :—

1. $pvp . \supset . p$ (tautology)
2. $p . \supset . pvq$ (addition)
3. $pvq . \supset . qvp$ (permutation)
4. $pv(qvr) . \supset . qv(pvr)$ (association)
5. $p \supset q : \supset . (pvr) \supset (qvr)$ (summation)

Some of these axioms are not independent, so we may use a set of three axioms.[1]

1. $p . \supset . \sim p \supset q$ which is the same as 2 above.
2. $\sim p \supset p . \supset . p$ which is the same as 1 above.
3. $p \supset q : \supset . q \supset r . \supset . p \supset r$ which is the same as 5 above.

For the purpose of proof, some nonformal axioms are required. It is not necessary to give them all here. The rules of inference and substitution suffice to show the character of such axioms.

Substitution. In any formula a symbol p may be replaced by a symbol q if the replacement is complete. E.g.

$$p . \supset . \sim p \supset q (\frac{p}{q}) = p . \supset . \sim p \supset p ([\text{``}\frac{p}{q}\text{''}] = \text{`` replacing } q \text{ by } p \text{''}).$$

Inference. If A is a truth of logic, and if $A \supset B$ is a truth of logic, then B is a truth of logic. E.g. (1), (2), (3) are truths of logic and (1), (2), (3) . $\supset . p \supset p$; therefore $p \supset p$ is a truth of logic.

All logical proof for the logic of propositions proceeds by the application of such non-formal rules to the axioms. It is not necessary to give an example of such a proof because the procedure is self-explanatory.

It is clear that a system of axioms could be arranged in

[1] Lukasiewicz, J., Bernays, P., and Nicod, J., have proved this.

such a way as to generate all the consequent theorems mechanically. This is, of course, the ideal of procedure in logic.

The logic of functions of one or more variables ntroduces many new primitive ideas. A propositional form is often asserted to be true for all or some instances satisfying that form. Thus " all x has ϕ " and " some x has ϕ ". This involves the ideas of (1) a propositional function, (2) the quantifiers " $(\exists x)$ " . . ., " (x) " . . ., (3) the apparent variable, and (4) the logical type.

A propositional function of one variable is a formula with one undetermined constituent such that an admissible determination of the constituent in question produces a proposition. Thus " $\phi \hat{x}$ ", when a is inserted in the " $\hat{x}$ ", becomes " ϕa ", which is a complete proposition.

In order to assert that all values of the " $\hat{x}$ " are true values of the function, the universal quantifier " (x) . . . " must be introduced. Thus " $(x)\phi x$ " means " every x has ϕ " where ϕ is any predicate of x. Similarly the assertion that at least one value satisfies $\phi \hat{x}$ involves the particular quantifier, " $(\exists x)$ . . ." Thus " $(\exists x)\phi x$ " means " at least one x has ϕ ".

The " x " in " ϕx " is a real variable since the scope of x's variation is not limited. However, in " (x) . . ." or in " $(\exists x)$ . . ." the scope of x's variation is fixed by tne prefixes " (x) . . ." or ("$\exists x)$ . . ." Here x varies only apparently, and therefore is an " apparent variable ".

The use of the idea of a propositional function involves a limitation on the kind of values which the function can assume. Thus " man $(\hat{x})$ ", i.e. " $\hat{x}$ is a man " cannot assume any arbitrary kind of entity as a value. Three distinct cases arise ; (1) the value of a function may be a false proposition ; (2) the value of a function may be a true proposition ; (3) the function, when certain things are inserted as values, may become nonsense. In order to avoid case (3) certain rules must be introduced so as to limit the significance of propositional functions.

These rules constitute the theory of logical types. A

logical type is the range of significance of a propositional function, i.e. the range of values of " $\phi\hat{x}$ " for which " $\phi x \mathrm{v} \sim \phi x$ " obtains. The theory of types can be stated as follows : Under all circumstances it must be assumed to be non-significant :—

(1) for a function to be a value of itself or for a function not to be a value of itself. E.g. " $\phi(\phi)$ " and " $\sim \phi(\phi)$ " are both nonsense.

(2) for a function to be a value of another function, both of which have the same kind of object for values.

(3) for a function to be a value of a function of a higher order than itself when the degree of difference in order is greater than one.

(4) for a function to be a value of a function of lower order than itself.

It is possible to show that a vicious-circle paradox can be deduced from any violation of the typal rules. The most familiar of these paradoxes is the one about impredicable functions. If it is asserted that a function is not a value of itself, such functions as are not self-applicable may be defined as follows :—

Impr. (F). $\equiv \sim F(F)$, i.e. " a function F is impredicable " is equivalent to " F is not F ". Now either $F(F)$ or $\sim F(F)$ for every F (by the law of excluded middle). Hence Impr. (F) or $\sim$ Impr. (F). Substitute Impr. for F, i.e. Impr. (Impr.). But *ex hypothesi* Impr. (Impr.). $\equiv$. $\sim$ Impr. (Impr.). This is a contradiction. There is only one way to eliminate such a contradiction, and that is to assume that both $F(F)$ and $\sim F(F)$ are nonsense. This limits the possible values of functions and thus the theory of types results.[1]

Now the theory of types has two parts, which are usually called the simple theory and the extended theory. The simple theory states that it is non-significant to suppose that a function can or cannot be a value of its own argument.

[1] Cf. Carnap, Rudolf, " Die Antinomien und die Unvollständigkeit der Mathematik," *Monatshefte für Mathematik und Physik*, Leipzig, 1934, 41. Band, 2 Heft, p. 264.

A hierarchy of types results from the theory. In order to understand this hierarchy it is necessary to introduce the notion of classes and relations or incomplete symbols.

In the *Principia Mathematica* propositional functions are treated separately according as they contain one or more than one argument-places.

A function of one argument, $\phi\hat{x}$, determines a range of values for which it is significant. Any function which determines the same range of values as another function is said to be formally equivalent to the latter function. Any set of formally equivalent functions forms a class and, conversely, if there is a class its members are values of a propositional function or of all formally equivalent functions. A class is the extension (i.e. the range of significant values) of a propositional function and of all the functions formally equivalent to this function.

Similar considerations obtain for functions of more than one argument, e.g. $\phi(\hat{x}, \hat{y})$. The problem here is more complicated. In the first case where functions of one argument were involved it was easy to define equivalent functions. Here, however, there is a greater complexity, since for the function $\phi(\hat{x}, \hat{y})$ there are many more propositions resulting from generalization. There are, in fact :—

$$(x)\ (y)\ \phi(x,y)\ ;\ \ (x)\ (\exists y)\ \phi(x,y)$$
$$(\exists x)\ (\exists y)\ \phi(x,y)\ ;\ \ (\exists y)\ (x)\ \phi(x,y).$$

If y is a constant, i.e. if $y = a$, then there are more propositions, viz. :—

$$(x)\phi\ (x,a)\ ;\ \ (\exists x)\ \phi(x,a).$$

If x is a constant, i.e. if $x = b$, then $(y)\ \phi(b,y)\ ;\ (\exists y)\ \phi(b,y)$.

There are thus eight different propositions formed by generalizing on the function $\phi(\hat{x}, \hat{y})$. Functions of three, four, etc., arguments would yield even more complicated kinds of generalization.

It is clear that functions of two arguments are formally equivalent if and only if they are satisfied by the same values.

A dyadic relation is the extension of all formally equivalent functions of two arguments.

A logical type is determined by a set of all classes which have the same kinds of members or all things which are members of the same kinds of classes.

Individuals form the first type, usually designated by "$type_0$". Classes of individuals form the second type. Classes of classes of individuals form the third type, and so forth. There is thus a hierarchy of types of the following structure :—

$$t_0 \qquad t_1 \qquad t_2 \qquad t_3$$

The structure of any functions of whatever type must, therefore, be $t_n (t_n - 1)$, i.e. functions of type t_n must take arguments of the next lower type and only such arguments. There will be an infinity of types and in each such infinity there will be an infinity. This is clear for the following reason. If we begin with the type of individuals we can form classes, classes of classes, and so on without end. The dyadic relation of individuals, the classes of such relations, classes of such classes, and so on constitutes another infinity. In every case, then, there will be hierarchy of types containing infinitely many types and there will be an infinity of hierarchies of this kind.[1]

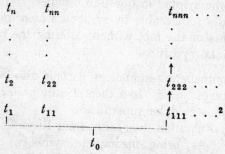

[1] Russell and Whitehead disallow the possibility of infinitely many hierarchies and infinitely many types, but this would seem to be an arbitrary limitation imposed by their somewhat " realistic " interpretation of the axiom of infinity.

[2] This representation of the typal hierarchy is, I fear, over simplified. It conveys the general idea, however erroneous the details may be. The principal difficulty is that I have not indicated the place of heterogeneous relations, i.e. relations among terms of different type.

By means of certain conventions classes of heterogenous type may be constructed without contradiction.

We cannot have a class consisting of individuals and classes, but we can, under certain conditions, have a class of classes of individuals and relational couples. So much for the theory of types.

What are classes? Russell recognized that the vicious-circle paradoxes arose from two related fallacies; (1) the supposition that a function could be a value of its own argument; (2) the supposition that a class (the extension of a function) was somehow a thing. These fallacies are eliminable by (1) the theory of types and (2) the related theory that classes are logical fictions. According to the second theory, a class symbol can only be defined in certain uses and is thus eliminable by application of the definitions. A class-symbol is therefore an incomplete symbol which does not directly represent *anything*. It is a notational convenience which seems necessary for the construction of logic and mathematics. The strict definition of an incomplete symbol may be given in the following form :—

A symbol is incomplete : (1) if it does not represent any constituent of the fact symbolized by the proposition in which the symbol in question occurs ; and (2) if it is theoretically replaceable by symbols which do represent constituents of the fact without altering the meaning of the original proposition.

In the nominalistic terminology it could also be said that classes are mere words. In a theoretically perfect language class-symbols would be superfluous.

An unusual paradox thus arises from Russell's treatment of classes. As being incomplete symbols, classes are theoretically eliminable from any symbolic system *salve veritate*. Yet, as being the foundation of arithmetic, the theory of classes seems to be an indispensable part of mathematical logic. This is because cardinal numbers are defined as classes of similar (i.e. bi-uniquely correspondent) classes and because ordinal numbers are defined as classes of ordinally similar relations.

It might be supposed that a functional notation could be substituted for the class notation so that the use of incomplete symbols would be avoided. This, in fact, is not the case. The latter notation requires implicit definitions which involve incomplete symbols in the very same manner as the class theory.

This would seem to entail a distinction between two kinds of incomplete symbols, namely, those which are eliminable by application of definitions, and those which are not eliminable by this method. It is then open to logicians to pursue one of two possible methods of symbolic construction. On the one hand a system may be constructed in which no implicit definitions occur. On the other hand, an extension of the theory of definition may be devised so as to allow for implicitly defined terms.

An extension of the theory of types involves a further difficulty. According to Russell, functions have orders as well as types. A function of one argument, e.g. $\phi\hat{x}$, in which no function occurs as an apparent variable, is a first order function (also called " predicative functions " or " matrices "). Functions of the second order are those in which functions of the first order occur as apparent variables. Thus, if $\phi!\hat{x}$ [1] is a first order function, $\phi_2\hat{x}$ (e.g. $(\phi!)\phi!x$) is a second order function. For example, if " $(\phi!)\ \phi!x$ " means " Napoleon had all the characteristics of a great general ", then any one of these properties, $\phi!$, is a predicative function of Napoleon, but the property of possessing a set of properties is not predicative. In this particular case it is clear that the second order property is reducible to the first order properties, i.e. $\phi_2x \supset \phi_1x$, since the range of values of ϕ_1 is manifestly contained in that of ϕ_2. In general, however, it is not evident that $\phi_1x \supset \phi_2x$, $\phi_2x \supset \phi_1x$, or more generally still, it is not clear that $\phi_nx \supset \phi_{n+1}x$, $\phi_{n+1}x \supset \phi_nx$. An axiom is, therefore, required to insure the formal

[1] " $\phi!\hat{x}$ " means " ϕ is a predicative function ".

equivalence of higher and lower functions. The axiom must show that :—

$$(1) \quad \phi_n + _1 \equiv \phi_n, \text{ and that}$$
$$(2) \quad \phi_n \equiv \phi_1.$$

The need for this axiom is evident in two places in *Principia Mathematica*. The definition of identity of individuals reads : Two individuals are said to be identical if they possess all predicative properties in common. This depends on the axiom (2) which assures us that higher order properties are reducible to predicative properties, for individuals might otherwise share all predicative properties and yet differ in higher order properties. (The axiom (2) and the definition are equivalent to Leibniz's " identity of indiscernibles ".) The axiom is also required in the foundation of the theory of real numbers. This phase of the problem will not be examined here.

There are still other axioms required for the foundation of mathematics. The first of this last group is the axiom of infinity which is equivalent to the assertion that there is an existent class for every inductive cardinal number, i.e. that there are infinitely many individuals.

The second axiom is required for the theory of infinite series. It states that, given a class of distinct and existent classes,[1] there exists a class composed of at least one member of each of the aforementioned classes. This is the multiplicative axiom.

The principal axioms of the *Principia* may be grouped as follows :—

A. Formal axioms of ungeneralized propositions :—

$$p . \supset . \sim p \supset q$$
$$\sim p \supset p . \supset . p$$
$$p \supset q : \supset . q \supset r . \supset . p \supset r.$$

B. Formal axioms of propositions involving apparent variables :—

---

[1] Distinct classes are classes without common members ; existent classes are classes with at least one member.

$(x) \ \phi x . \supset . \phi u$ (Whatever holds of all, holds of any).

$\phi u . \supset . (\exists x) \phi x$ (Whatever holds for one holds for some).

C. Existence axioms.

1. Axiom of Reducibility: For every function of whatever order, there is a formally equivalent predicative function.

2. Axiom of Infinity: If A is an inductive cardinal number, then the cardinal successor of A exists.

3. Multiplicative axiom: For every class of existent classes, there is a class composed of at least one member of each of the aforementioned classes.

In addition to these formal axioms there are certain non-formal rules for manipulating the system. In particular, these rules are: The rule of substitution, the rule of inference, and the theory of types.

The existence axioms of the *Principia* are not formally certifiable, i.e. are not unconditional truths of logic, and hence may only be introduced as uncertified hypotheses. They seem to be required for the foundation of mathematics, but are, nevertheless, of a character quite unlike the other axioms of the *Principia* system.

The non-formal rules are also open to objection on the ground that they are not sufficiently segregated from the formal rules, and on the ground that they, too, require a kind of justification. A reason must be given, that is, for the fact that from truths of logic we can produce truths of logic by means of substitution and inference. And thus a formalization of these rules which are non-formal in respect of the *Principia* system would seem to be required. The presence of existence axioms and of unexplained rules of manipulation are recognized defects in *Principia Mathematica*.

For the purposes of this study the four most significant aspects of the logical system of *Principia Mathematica* are :—

    1. The theory of types.

    2. The theory of classes.

3. The theory of definition.
4. The theory of deduction.

Together these theories make possible the construction of a logical language with the following characteristics :—

1. Every sign in the language is either an undefined sign or an abbreviation for a group of signs which are themselves undefined or lead back to a group of undefined signs (theory of definition). A defined sign can always be replaced by the signs by means of which it is defined (substitution).

2. Transformations are allowed from one group of signs, which signify in a certain way, to another group of signs which signify the same things in a different way without altering the meanings (theory of definition and deduction).

3. Signs may be introduced which serve as notational conveniences but which do not, properly speaking, signify anything (theory of classes). It is thus possible to employ signs in a language without attributing an ontological reference to them.

4. The construction of complex signs from simple ones produces a hierarchy of signs which determines the place of every function or class (theory of types and orders). This makes it possible to determine the significance of signs by the mode of their construction and to avoid contradictions. A number of philosophical problems disappear by this method, and certain other problems can be solved without any trouble simply by indicating the method in which certain ideas are formed (i.e. the way certain sign-complexes are constructed).

5. All these aforementioned characteristics of the logical language serve to provide a means by which the meaning and verification of any proposition is determinable. In this way complex problems of meaning and truth are reducible to the simplest ones. All undefined signs can be listed in this language, and all complex defined signs are derivable, in various ways, from the simple undefined signs by quite explicit rules. The application of such rules solves

the problem of meaning and truth so far as complex signs are concerned. The meaning of the simple signs and truth of propositions constructed exclusively from such simple meanings are not determinable within the *Principia Mathematica* (or any similar system).

These are the reasons why Logical Positivism adopts a method of logical analysis for the foundation of science and the elimination of metaphysics. It should be observed that psychological analysis plays absolutely no rôle in this programme. The whole procedure involves simply the application of certain logical rules.

This stands in direct contrast to the methods not only of older positivistic thought but also of most philosophical investigation of the past and present. There is either a wholly psychological approach to problems (as in Pragmatism), or an admixture of logic and psychology without a clear distinction between the two methods (as in realism) in most discussions of philosophical issues.

The logical and mathematical theory of the *Principia Mathematica* forms the basis for the logical methods pursued by the Viennese Positivists. However much it leaves in question the *Principia Mathematica* was, at the time of its publication, undoubtedly the most advanced single body of logical doctrines which had appeared.

There is much in the *Principia Mathematica* which is unquestionably neutral as regards any specifically philosophical issues. However, there are many doctrines presented there which could not possibly be fitted into a rigorously consistent empiricism.

For an example of the possibility of logical analysis of meaning, no better can be found than Russell's theory of description. Russell defined the use of descriptive phrases as follows : " The so-and-so exists (' the ' in the singular) " means " there is one and only one thing possessing the characteristic called ' so-and-so ' and that thing is identical with some specific entity." Symbolically,

$$E! \, (\imath x) \, (\phi x) = df. \, (\exists c) \, \phi x \, . \equiv_x . \, x = c$$

The advantage of this definition cannot be immediately grasped without a knowledge of the problems which it was designed to solve. Nevertheless, two important results for philosophy follow from it. First, it is impossible to speak of the existence of an object named but not described. Second it is always possible to assert true propositions about objects described which do not exist, without assuming some universe of discourse in which those objects are somehow real but non-existent. This is an example of the use of logical analysis in philosophical problems. All significant uses of the word " existence " are accounted for by Russell's method. Equivocal uses of the word are eliminated. These two results constitute a rigorous demonstration of the line of argument in Kant's refutation of the alleged proofs for the existence of a Supreme Being. They also effectively dispense with the distinction between existent and subsistent reality without confusing what philosophers have frequently called essence and existence. Russell's verbal explanation of his doctrine may have occasioned confusion on some of these points. His symbolic theory is utterly free from such confusion. This, then, is a capital illustration of logical analysis in philosophy.

The neutral portion of the *Principia* deals largely with the logic of elementary propositions. The portion which cannot apparently be fitted into an empirical philosophy is concerned with the realistic interpretation of infinity and the general proposition. By suppressing this portion of the work the *Principia* can be used as a point of departure for an empirical philosophy which attempts to reduce all meanings to empirical meanings by means of a purely logical (analytical) reduction of all concepts to empirical concepts. The doctrine of the Viennese Circle is a combination of logical analysis largely patterned after the *Principia Mathematica*, with a radical empiricism. I shall try to explain how this is possible and how it came about.

III

Not long after the publication of the *Principia Mathematica* philosophers and logicians became aware that it required some radical alterations to be a satisfactory foundation for logic and mathematics. It was equally evident that some premises of logic and mathematics, which had long been unconsciously assumed, had been brought to light by the *Principia*.

One of the critics of this work was a pupil of Russell, Ludwig Wittgenstein. Realizing the tremendous value of the *Principia* as a sign language, he also realized that some essential connection between logic and experience must be established in order to insure the significance and applicability of logic to experience without sacrificing its truth. This led to an investigation of the nature of propositions in general and the nature of the propositions of logic in particular. The result of this was the *Tractatus Logico-Philosophicus*.

Wittgenstein's work may be regarded as an attempt to construct the rules of an exact language. It is a criticism of the *Principia Mathematica* in so far as he treats that work as a first approximation to the theoretically perfect language. It is a criticism of metaphysics in so far as he regards metaphysics as a mistake arising from the misunderstanding of the logic of language.

The Viennese Circle as an organized group was formed in 1928 with Moritz Schlick at its head. Prior to that time the ideas of the members of the group had been derived from various sources, particularly Mach, Avenarius, and Josef Popper. The development of symbolic logic and its critical analysis by Wittgenstein and others showed that empiricism could be founded on logical rather than psychological analysis.

Thus the philosophy of the Viennese Circle is an empiricism established by logical methods. Briefly stated, it is established by showing that under analysis the meaning of concepts and propositions is, in every case, ultimately empirical. Propositions which are not ostensibly empirical in reference are therefore either reducible to empirical propositions or are simply nonsense. A proposition is shown to be nonsense by demonstrating that its analysis leads (1) to contradiction, (2) to propositions with certain constituents for which no determinations can be given, i.e. irreducibly indeterminate propositions, or (3) propositions which have forms violating the rules of logical syntax. There are propositions which must be treated as special cases because they are not empirically determinable and, nevertheless, seem to have some significance. These are the propositions of logic and mathematics themselves. An empiricism developed and demonstrated exclusively by logical methods must find a place for logic. Otherwise it is not a complete system, since it would fail to account for itself. Logical propositions are treated as part of the apparatus of symbolism without having any symbolic reference. They are part of the schematism for the description of empirical reality but do not, as such, describe anything.

The philosophy of the Circle, in so far as it follows the theory I have just outlined, is little more than a series of extended comments on the fundamental *early* work of Wittgenstein. In so far, however, as it departs from Wittgenstein, the work of the Circle must be separately treated, first as a reaction against Wittgenstein, and second as the construction of an independent philosophy.

The reaction came about in this way. Wittgenstein's empiricism leads to several difficulties. Every proposition of existential import is shown to be empirical in reference. Its meaning is determined by the method of its verification, i.e. by the fact which would make it true. The relation between meaning and reality, however, cannot be expressed by language. (Later I shall try to show how this comes about.) It is inexpressible. But then all logical syntax, that is, all the rules which lead us to reduce all propositions to empirical propositions, are inexpressible. The result is that the logical method contains something that cannot be analysed and must, therefore, be non-empirical.

Another difficulty of equal importance results from the ultimately empirical reference of all propositions. Reality is limited by the empirical data and by the true propositions describing the data. It is impossible to assert significantly (1) the existence of anything which cannot be described in experiential terms, and (2) the existence of something that can be described in experiential terms but that, presumably, is not described in terms of " my " experience. This leads to a kind of solipsism. It makes an intersubjective science impossible.

These and similar difficulties produced a reaction against the doctrines of Wittgenstein. Another philosophy, which is known as Radical Physicalism, thus arose and divided the Viennese group. This new system may be regarded both as an attempt to correct the errors and difficulties of Logical Positivism and as a wholly independent system. Logical Positivism, as I have tried to point out, has a definite connection with empiristic philosophies of the past. Radical Physicalism, on the other hand, has no historical antecedent in the realm of philosophy. Its only source of ideas is the science of physics in a logically organized form.

Radical Physicalism dispenses with all absolutism. There are no ultimate propositions, and there is no connection between the propositions and the " empirical data " in the physicalistic version of Positivism. Both doctrines contain vestiges of metaphysics which must be eliminated. Both lead to undemonstrable assertions. The doctrine of ultimate propositions leads to a logically absolute realm of atoms of discourse which is not open to further analysis. The doctrine that these ultimate propositions are connected in an inexpressible manner with the empirical data lying beyond the realm of discourse leads to a dualism of language and data which cannot be bridged. Radical Physicalism

proposes to conduct all logical and experimental investigation *within* the realm of language. There is no inexpressible
residue of " data " or " experience " left to be dealt with
by non-logical methods. Such is the programme of
Physicalism as presented by its founder, Otto Neurath. The
problems which follow from Wittgenstein's doctrine do not
arise in the physicalistic theory.

The critic of the Viennese philosophy is, therefore, faced
with a dual task. He must examine the alleged difficulties
in the theory of Logical Positivism and try to discover, at
the same time, whether Physicalism, in overcoming these
difficulties, is free from objection on its own account.

Radical Physicalism effectively overcomes some of the
difficulties of Logical Positivism, but encounters some
problems peculiar to itself which seem to be irresoluble on
the terms of the theory. The objections to Physicalism,
therefore, do not apply to Positivism, and it is incorrect to
consider the two systems in the same terms.

*   *   *   *

In the course of this study I shall expound and criticize
the theories and methods of Logical Positivism in an order
of presentation which seems best suited to represent them
with utmost fairness.

Logical Positivism has two principal tasks before it : to
present a consistently empirical account of scientific method
and to demonstrate the meaninglessness of metaphysics.
Both of these are to be accomplished by logical analysis.

I shall present the logical foundation of Positivism first.
Then the applications of the method of analysis to
mathematics and natural science will follow. Next I shall
treat of the elimination of metaphysics and the consequence
of this. All this will be preparatory to the consideration of
a specific case of positivistic analysis which presents a theory
of knowledge free from metaphysics. This is the *Logischer
Aufbau der Welt* of Rudolf Carnap. It will serve our purposes
chiefly as an attempt to avoid the solipsism which seems to

be an inevitable consequence of the logical theory. I shall try to show how utterly this fails.

Then I shall present the doctrine of Physicalism as a separate philosophical system. The reasons for rejecting Physicalism as a scientific philosophy will be presented in some detail in these chapters.

The study will be concluded by a theory of language which seems to me to overcome the difficulties of both Logical Positivism and Radical Physicalism. I have included this as an alternative theory, and its principal value is simply to show what consequences follow from premises which are the proper contradictories of positivistic and physicalistic doctrines. This, at least, will show the reader what he probably must accept if he finds both Positivism and Physicalism to be unsatisfactory solutions of philosophical and scientific problems.

PART I

LOGICAL FOUNDATIONS

CHAPTER I

WITTGENSTEIN'S THEORY OF MEANING

The new logic, developed by Boole, Schroeder, Pierce, Peano, and Frege (to mention only the most important names) was made into a well-organized system by Russell and Whitehead in the *Principia Mathematica*. A definite logical theory underlies this work. The *Principia Mathematica* is, nevertheless, incomplete or erroneous in at least three respects. This incompleteness or erroneous character could be explained somewhat paradoxically by saying that (1) there is too much theory, (2) there is not enough theory, and (3) there is no theory whatsoever. There is too much theory in the sense that a purely symbolic system, purporting to be logically autonomous, should not require any verbal or non-formal instruction for its manipulation and should not require any theoretical basis not contained in the formal paraphernalia of the system, whereas *Principia* must be explained at every step by non-formal instruction and theories, etc. On the other hand, it is no objection, but rather a logical demand, that whatever theory can be formalized within a formal system should be so formalized, and that whatever cannot be formalized should not occur at all within the system. In this sense, *Principia* does not contain enough theory. Finally, whatever deserves the name of " theory of a formal system " should be organized in a completely articulate manner, such that no part of the theory does not have a well-defined connection with the theory as an organized whole. In this sense *Principia* has no theory at all.

An axiom which is not formally expressed, but which is integral to *Principia*, is the so-called axiom of Extensionality. This axiom states that every function of functions is an extensional function. It is not necessary to inquire whether " function *f* is extensional " is an exception to this axiom. The important thing is that the axiom is apparently violated almost at the outset by the introduction of the proposition connecting real and apparent variables. For instance $(x)\ \phi x \supset \phi u$, which is roughly translated as " whatever holds of all, holds of any ", should be an extensional function by the axiom of extensionality. Now $(x)\ \phi x$ is evidently an extensional function of $\phi \hat{x}$ whereas ϕu is apparently not an extensional function of the propositional function, since the idea of " any " is equivalent neither to that of " all " nor to that of " this individual one ". The idea of " any ", therefore, has no place in the system, and its introduction indicates the absence of a theory in *Principia*.

Again, the theory of types may be considered. A type is the range of significance of all propositional functions which take the same objects as values of their arguments, i.e. of all equivalent functions. The theory, or, better, axiom of types, states : Arguments of a given function are all of the same type. This theory cannot be formulated within the system of *Principia* because the idea of " any " possible argument of a given function is not an extensional idea. There are other reasons why this idea cannot be formulated, one of which is that constant expressions occurring in mathematical logic are limited to the logical constants, and because " type " is a constant expression, but not a logical constant, it cannot occur in the formal system of *Principia*. This much for the theoretical difficulties of *Principia*, considering it solely from the formal point of view.

From the broader standpoint of general philosophy, other difficulties arise which are of greater interest here. The explicit purpose of the *Principia* was to demonstrate that the concepts and assertions of mathematics are entirely derivable from the concepts and assertions of symbolic logic. From many essays of the authors (particularly Russell), as well as from the fact that certain sections have an especially philosophical interest, it is revealed that another equally important purpose also guided the construction of the *Principia*. The construction of an exact logical language is to serve in solving philosophical problems and in presenting a complete schematism for representing the structure of the world of science and experience.

This construction can occur in two ways, each of which stands in subtle opposition to the tenets of Logical Positivism, but seems none the less to be demanded by those tenets. The first method of construction is to introduce the set of forms of all elementary propositions as a complete group of primitive forms of all facts which can occur in science or experience. Thus, if $x, y, z \ldots$ represent the constituents of a fact and R_n represents the component, then the forms of all facts would be illustrated by the following schema :—

$$R_1 (x) \quad \text{`` Quality-individual '' form}$$
$$R_2 (x, y), \quad \text{`` binary '' relational form}$$
$$R_3 (x, y, z) \text{`` ternary '' relational form.}$$

In general :—

$$R_n (x_1 \ldots x), \text{`` } n\text{-adic '' relational form.}$$

From the purely notational point of view this schema could be simplified by treating all forms as classes or as predicates.

$$\phi (x)$$
$$\phi ((x), (x, y))$$
$$\phi ((x), (x, y), (s, y, z)), \text{ etc.}$$

Philosophically these schemata are indefensible because they neglect the fundamental distinction between classes and relations. But could not the same criticism be levelled against the treatment of an n-adic and an $n+1$-adic relation which neglects the fundamental distinction between n-ads and $n+1$-ads ? The difference between two relations with different numbers of terms is not simply the difference of number. On the one hand the whole structure of a fact is different according to the number of constituents of the fact. A general sequence of propositional forms has, therefore, only a notational value, but tells us nothing about the world's structure. The attempt to set forth all possible forms of propositions is required by Logical Positivism. Its principal instrument of investigation is logic, for logic alone can express the syntax of language. The example above shows that the syntax of language cannot be formulated except from an arbitrary standpoint. On the other hand, this conclusion would seem to follow from the empiricism of Logical Positivism. Only those forms of propositions which have genuine counterparts in the empirical world are to be admitted in the logical schematism of admissible (i.e. significant) concepts.

The second method of construction involves no *a priori* decision concerning the possible forms of all propositions. The structure of propositions is related to the structure of facts ; if new kinds of facts cannot be foreseen, their possible forms cannot be anticipated in discourse. A strict and thorough-going empiricism would have to concede that new kinds of facts cannot be foreseen. The second method, therefore, is simply concerned with the logical treatment of propositional forms already known to have objective counterparts in the empirical world. Logical analysis can, therefore, be applied only to what is already known to be significant, because discovered in the empirical world. Here, logical analysis would, except in a few cases, be superfluous because the genuine value of logical analysis consists in its application to those assertions which have hitherto not been examined. Elimination of pseudo-concepts of science by means of logical analysis seems to demand a schematism of admissible conceptual forms. An empirical criterion of meaning and verity seems to make the construction of such a schematism impossible. This is the problem inherited by Logical Positivism from its empiristic and logistic forbears. The *Principia Mathematica* seems to favour the construction of a schematism such as has been set out above. Its logical theory, which is only implicit as we have seen, must be altered for the purposes of analysis in the positivistic sense. Wittgenstein's logical theory may, from this point of view, be conceived as a criticism and alteration of the logical language of *Principia Mathematica*.

With these remarks I shall proceed to develop the logical theory of Wittgenstein.

I

The fundamental characteristic of Wittgenstein's philosophy is the relationship which he attempts to establish between language and the world. By language, in this usage, is meant the totality of significant assertions (as contrasted, e.g., with language as used in the emotive sense). The totality of significant propositions is related to the totality of objectives of those assertions, and this is the world. " The world " is thus a phrase with a denotation but without connotation.

Wittgenstein calls the objectives of significant assertions " facts ". Facts are what make propositions true, or, alternatively, propositions assert the existence or non-existence of facts. Since facts are the fundamental parts of the world, it would be impossible to define " fact " without circularity. A fact may be described as a combination of objects. This differs from the Aristotelian conception of fact only in so far as a fact may be of any conceivable structure in Wittgenstein's philosophy, whereas any Aristotelian philosophy (for metaphysical reasons) limits facts to the " inherence of something in something else ". An object is whatever can occur as the constituent of a fact. Now, if facts are taken as fundamental, and hence indefinable, an object could be variously defined. (*a*) It may be defined as the set of facts in which it occurs, i.e. as the set of facts which possess at least one feature of absolute similarity to one another. For example, the facts of " blue colouring the sky at time t_o " and of " blue colouring this book at time t_n " have one feature, " blue," of absolute similarity. (b) Or an object can be defined as whatever is a distinguishable element of a fact. Thus, by exhaustively enumerating all the distinguishable elements constituting a fact, it is possible to isolate all the objects composing the fact in question.

The fact is an independent entity, for whatever dependence may mean in the strictly logical sense, it is reserved for objects, i.e. for entities obviously requiring completion. Facts, being self-sufficient, require no completion, and so are, in the logical sense, independent of one another. Objects are independent, too, in the sense that an object is not restricted to occurrence in one fact rather than another, but they are dependent in the sense that they must occur in some fact or other.

For the purpose of clarity and without doing too much violence to Wittgenstein's theory, examples of facts may be taken from the perceptual experience of an individual. Thus " coloured-spots," " relations among spatial figures such as black spots on white paper," etc., may be used as illustrations.

The relation between the colour and the object coloured, between two tones in order of temporal succession—in general, among objects which go to make up a fact—is not a further element of the fact over and above the objects related. The relation is the structural, the articulate, feature of the fact. But it is nothing beyond the objects which are related in a specific manner. In other words, the objects combining to form a fact do so by internally combining with one another. In short, the structure of the fact is not an element of the fact ; rather objects are only elements of given fact in so far as they enter into the fact in some specific mode of combining with one another. Structure, accordingly, cannot be isolated and designated by a single term of discourse, that is, structure cannot be named.

In my opinion, this part of Wittgenstein's analysis is his

first important contribution to philosophical logic. The conclusions which are drawn from it are not unquestionable, but the importance of the emphasis on structure must not be overlooked. Those problems which depend on the nature of *relation* should find the key to their solution in the preliminary recognition that the structure of things and facts is represented in language and thought in an entirely different way from the way in which things themselves are represented. The notion of structure, which will presently be further elucidated, is of fundamental importance. I shall return to it frequently, for it is the basis both of the valid and the invalid deductions that are made by Logical Positivism.

In current usage, " fact " has a very vague significance. " Facts " are spoken of and the expression " it is a fact that . . ." is frequently used. It cannot be over-emphasized that " fact " is used by Wittgenstein in a technical sense which is somewhat uncommon among other philosophies, and which does not normally occur in discourse at all. At the same time, it is fairly clear that the philosophers who use " fact " in this way mean that facts are what make propositions significant and true. Now, this is somewhat paradoxical, because, while we can use " fact " correctly in sentences, and while, if we thought about it at all, all of us probably would come to explain " fact " in approximately similar ways, it is, nevertheless, true that we ordinarily use " fact " without knowing exactly what we mean. I believe this difficulty has two sources. In the first place, we speak of true and false propositions, and of the existence and non-existence of facts. These terms seem to be correlative, but since a " non-existent fact " is obvious nonsense, it is clear that the correlation is only apparent. There is not in ordinary language an adequate terminology to explain the relationship of propositions and facts. The second source of confusion results from the first. The introduction of the required terminology can occur only by way of a complicated theory, and none such is at our disposal. Hence, when an attempt is made to understand Wittgenstein's conception of fact, the following must be borne in mind : (1) it is a technical idea ; (2) it is, nevertheless, connected with ordinary usage, if that usage be exactly fixed ; (3) speaking of " facts " violates the rules of logical syntax in Wittgenstein's theory, and serves only an elucidatory purpose, to be dispensed with as soon as the ideas have become clarified.

As a technical idea, a fact is simply a combination of formal entities ; that is, a combination of objects. As indicated above, this is not a definition, because it would then be circular, since facts are the indefinables. Objects are distinguishable elements of facts. This again is not a definition, for it entails the definition of " being the same object as " and " sameness " in Wittgenstein's theory is likewise indefinable. Moreover, objects are named or described rather than defined. At the very best, one can indicate only what constitutes being an object by pointing it out or by enumerating the facts of which it is a possible constituent.

With these preliminary remarks I shall proceed to develop the fundamentals of Wittgenstein's theory.

The world is the totality of independent atomic facts. An atomic fact is a fact which is not compounded out of other facts. Since facts are ultimately independent of one another all compound facts are reducible to atomic facts. Which facts are atomic and which are not cannot be determined *a priori*, but must, in any case, be discovered by direct inspection. That atomic facts must exist as a demand of logical theory is, according to Wittgenstein, an abstract necessity capable of demonstration. This supposed demonstration will later be shown to be fallacious.

Atomic facts are composed of objects in immediate combinations. The way in which the objects are combined is called the structure of the fact. The possibility that objects may combine together in a definite way so as to constitute an atomic fact is called the form of the object. The form of the object is, therefore, the possibility of the structure of the fact. Since " possibility " is a logical concept and not an ontological one, " object " is a formal reality requiring completion in order to exist, and only conceivable as being completable in a given set of ways. The totality of ways in which an object may acquire completeness or materiality is, as noted above, the form of the object.[1]

Wittgenstein also believes that the object must be an absolutely simple entity. This belief is supposed to be capable of logical demonstration. The fallacy which can be found in the demonstration of atomic facts occurs in this one also. It is advisable to present these proofs in their rightful place.

II

The realm of propositions is far richer, perhaps infinitely so, than the realm of objects and facts. Instead of the simple totality of atomic facts, there are positive and negative propositions, conjunctions, and disjunctions of propositions. There must also be added the different ways of expressing the same proposition. The complexity of the world is outdone by the greater complexity of symbolism. How, then, can a relationship be established between them ? Wittgenstein attempts to do this in a simple, but amazingly forceful, analysis. There are two essential parts to this analysis, the explanation of the relation between propositions and facts, and second, the explanation of the interconnection of propositions among themselves.

One of the most commonly expressed opinions of the first mentioned relationship is · the relation between propositions and facts is an agreement when the propositions are true and a disagreement when they are false. " Agreement " is a somewhat vague term, and requires a precise definition in order to serve the purposes of exact analysis.

Wittgenstein conceives agreement between propositions and facts to consist of a pictorial relation. The proposition is a picture of the fact. If the pictorial relationship is

---

[1] I have explained " possibility " more fully in Chapters II and VI.

concealed, this is because of the use of an arbitrary system of notation, the rules of which are not known. The pictorial character of the proposition consists in the circumstance that it is itself a fact which possesses certain features in common with the other fact which it pictures. These common features between the two facts by virtue of which one can picture the other are : (*a*) a common logical form, (*b*) a one-one correlation between the objects comprising the respective facts. Wittgenstein believes that this relationship cannot be further explained. In Russell's logic, however, it is possible to express the community of structure of two facts. Let x, y and z,w be two pairs of objects, the first united in an R-way and the second in an S-way, thus xRy and zSw. Now the necessary and sufficient conditions that R and S possess the same structure are : There is a correlator P whose domain is the field of R and whose converse domain is the field of S, such that the relative product $P \mid S \mid \breve{P} = R$. Thus the structure of a fact, for Russell, would be the class of all facts structurally similar to a given fact. For Wittgenstein, however, structure is not further analysable. It must be presupposed. I introduced the definition, nevertheless, in order to enable the reader to understand what Wittgenstein intends to convey by the terms " structure " and " having a common structure ".

The necessary and sufficient condition for picturing one fact by another is community of structure. This does not mean that of any two facts possessing the same structure, one will be a picture of the other, for " being a picture of a fact " involves that which, by arbitrary convention, is decided upon to be so used. Nevertheless, it is not the arbitrary decision, but the possession of a certain structure, which makes the picturing of facts possible.

Propositions, then, are pictures of facts. The proposition which pictures a given fact is a fact in its own right. It may be a psychological process, a set of marks, a vocal utterance or the like. It is noteworthy that two or more facts may be used to represent the same objective fact. In this case, another complication arises. When two or more facts are so used they must all have something in common, for they all express the same sense. It is then necessary to distinguish between the essential and the unessential features of the propositions. The unessential features of a proposition are those characteristics of a particular language or mode of expression which disappear when the proposition is translated from one language to another, or when the proposition is expressed vocally and then written. The essential features are those which remain constant throughout all transformations of this kind. Wittgenstein claims that the logical form is the common invariant feature of the various modes used to express a proposition. Therefore, several facts differing in many particulars may be used to express the same sense, i.e. to picture the same objective fact, if they enjoy community of form. Thus it is necessary to amend the definition of a proposition. A proposition is a fact used to picture another fact, or a class of facts used to picture another fact. In the first case the structure of the propositional fact is identical with the structure of the other fact. In the second case the class of facts enjoys a common structure, and this structure is identical with the structure of the fact represented.

This emendation introduces a further property of the proposition. We may speak of the proposition as sign and of the proposition as symbol, or alternatively, of the external and of the internal features of the proposition, or, again (as above), of the unessential and the essential features of the proposition. Regarded as a sign, or externally considered, the proposition is a fact in its own right. As symbol or internally considered, it remains a fact in its own right, but is not so regarded. It is used, to represent (i.e. to picture) another fact. When so used it exists solely for representative purposes, and it is no longer an object of contemplation. As Russell, in explaining Wittgenstein's theory, has said, no mention is made of it, but by means of it mention is made of something else. The external feature of the proposition disappears from view and the internal symbolic properties alone are contemplated in so far as they represent another fact. Again, the symbolic internal properties are the characteristics of structure.

Wittgenstein calls the structural properties of the proposition its form of representation. It is in virtue of this form that the proposition expresses a sense. *The sense of the proposition is the possibility of the fact which it represents.* It is necessary to distinguish between the sense of a proposition, the truth of a proposition, and the proposition itself. The delineation of the concept " sense " shows this very clearly. That which the picture represents is its sense. The proposition neither is identical with its sense nor does it contain its sense. The possibility of expressing the sense is all that is to be found in the proposition. The sense of a proposition is, therefore, distinct from the proposition as such. For two propositions may express the same sense, e.g. " Cæsar loves Brutus " and " Caesar amat Brutum ". Likewise " Brutus is loved by Cæsar " expresses the same sense as " Cæsar loves Brutus ", yet they are two different propositions. The truth and the sense are distinct, because the former consists of the actual agreement of sense with reality, whereas the latter is simply the possibility of agreement. Thus a proposition can be understood without knowing whether it is true.[1]

In this exposition I have tried as far as possible to allow the author to speak for himself without interrupting with criticisms. It is necessary to have a fuller comprehension of the theory before introducing critical considerations. I shall anticipate two points here which will perhaps aid in the understanding of the theory.

The first is that the ultimate reference of all propositions which have a sense for us is the empirical realm. The atomic facts, therefore, are experiential facts. The sense of propositions is to be found in experience and experience

---

[1] Wittgenstein, L., *Tractatus Logico-Philosophicus*, London, 1922, prop. 3.13, 4.031, 4.2.

alone. The second is that the ordinary conception of the proposition as written, spoken, or thought, leads to another view than the one outlined above. There are at least three reasons for this contrary opinion. The general proposition, the descriptive proposition, and many propositions which are neither general nor descriptive seem to be understandable without reference to any experience. Likewise, the propositions of logic and arithmetic seem to be independent of experience. Wittgenstein must show, therefore, that general propositions are reducible to elementary propositions, that descriptions are transformable into representations, that representations, i.e. elementary propositions, are simply and exclusively concerned with empirical reality, and finally that logic and mathematics can be treated in such a way as to avoid an a-prioristic interpretation. All of these considerations save one must await the treatment of general propositions. At present I shall simply discuss the question " If elementary propositions are not ostensibly pictures of facts of experience, how can they be shown actually to be pictures ? " [1]

The theory that elementary propositions, and thus thoughts of a certain kind, are pictures of reality is not new. In one sense it is a translation into logical language of Hume's theory of ideas as copies of impressions. The important difference lies in the fact that the nature of psychological processes does not enter into consideration in the present theory. None the less, certain objections to the former theory may be reiterated with regard to the present one.

Certainly the proposition in its external form does not resemble the fact for which it stands, save in rare instances, e.g. *in the case of a map*. The great majority of propositions does not appear to be remotely like the thought or the fact. Schlick, who now accepts Wittgenstein's theory, formerly

---

[1] For opposite views see : Frank, Phillipp, " Was bedeuten die gegenwärtigen physikalischen Theorien," usw., *Erkenntnis*, Bd. I. Gätschenberger, R., *Zeichen, Die Fundamente des Wissens*, Stuttgart, 1932. Schlick, M., *Allgemeine Erkenntnislehre*, 2 Auf. Springer, 1925.

criticized similar doctrines. Thus he wrote : " In ordinary language agreement simply means likeness. Two tones, two colours, two proportions, two opinions, agree if they are alike. The word is obviously not to be taken in this sense here, for the judgment is something completely different from that which is judged, . . . it is not like that which is judged, and this can only be contested from the standpoint of adventurous metaphysical systems which equate thought and being in general, and about which we should waste no words here."

" If agreement here does not mean likeness, perhaps it could mean similarity. In what sense are our judgments similar to facts ? Similarity must mean at least partial likeness, hence it must be possible to find certain moments of the judgment which are revealed in the facts themselves. In purely conceptual truths where the object judged, as well as the judgment, consists of purely ideal forms, likeness might be found in both sides under certain circumstances, but that cannot be the essential requisite for truth, for propositions about real things also make claim to truth— here, indeed, the nature of truth first becomes a problem— but in both one will seek for such similar moments. For the concepts occurring in the judgments are certainly not of the same nature as the real objects which they designate, and the relations among concepts are not like the relation of things, for in the latter temporal moments always occur, and spatial ones usual do, whereas conceptual relations are non-spatial and non-temporal. In the judgment " The chair stands at the right of the table " the concept of " chair " is not placed at the right of the concept " table ".

" Thus the concept of agreement melts away in the rays of analysis in so far as it is to mean sameness or similarity, and what remains of it is simply univocal arrangement. In the latter, the relation of the true judgment to reality consists, and all those naïve theories according to which our judgments and concepts could somehow picture ' reality are fundamentally destroyed. . . . The judgment pictures the nature of the judged as little as the note pictures the tone, or as the name of the man pictures his personality." [1]

This objection, which in essentials has been repeated by many critics, who see in the theory criticized a return to the " naïve " psychological theories of truth as correspondence, can easily be answered from Wittgenstein's point of view. The minimum requirements for picturing, in Wittgenstein's sense, are first that the fact pictured and the fact used to picture it possess the same number of distinguishable parts, and second, that the structure of the first fact be identical with the structure of the second fact. Now, it may happen that the two facts possess the first requirement, but not the second. The notes of a melody, to use Schlick's example, are equal in number to the tones of the instrument or voice, yet the relation among the notes in the score and the relation among the tones of the instrument or voice are not identical, for the former relation is spatial, where the latter is temporal. Likewise, when colours are used to represent altitudes in a map, the relation among the colours may be a difference of saturation, whereas the relationship among the altitudes is that of a spatial order. A final example is the use of Mercator's projection of the latitude and longitude of the glove on a plane surface. Here the relations are in both cases spatial, but the metrical properties have been so altered that the relations differ in essential respects. Nevertheless, there is a sense in which all these pairs of facts have the same forms, and it is this sense in which Wittgenstein understands the pictorial nature of the elementary propositions. I shall attempt to explain in what this formal identity consists, and to show wherein the difficulty lies.

Wittgenstein compares the relation of the proposition and its objective to geometrical projection. It would, of course, be theoretically possible to represent every fact by a fact of the same kind. Thus " the picture can represent every reality whose form it has. The spatial picture, everything

[1] Schlick, M., *Allgemeine Erkenntnislehre*, Berlin, 1925, pp. 56–7.

spatial, the coloured picture, everything coloured, etc."[1]
Notation and spoken language is, nevertheless, arbitrarily
usually chosen for obvious reasons of utility. It is, therefore,
not possible to see immediately the inner formal connection
between the proposition and the fact. Hence it is necessary
to explain this connection by a further analysis. In
geometrical projection a figure may be projected on a surface
such that the result is visibly quite different from the
original. The laws of geometrical projection, however,
determine that certain properties remain invariant for all
possible projections of a given figure. These formal properties
which remain invariant are called the projective properties
of the original figure. The projective properties of the
original and those of all its possible projections are identical.
A geometrical science could be developed such that facts
from different sense-modalities could be used as projections
of one another. The formal geometry of such a science has,
in fact, been partially developed by Jean Nicod and Suzanne
Langer. In short, the science of geometrical projection is
by no means limited to spatial phenomena, first because the
laws of projective geometry are propositional functions which
may be satisfied by any one of several distinct groups of
entities, and second because groups of non-spatial entities
have actually been found to satisfy such laws.

The projective properties of a fact remain constant
throughout all possible projections. Hence, the logical form
of a fact may be identical with that of another fact even if
the entities and relations of the one differ from those of the
other. It is in this sense, that is in the sense of the formal
identity of projective properties, that one must understand Wittgenstein's doctrine that there must be a formal
identity between two facts if the one is to picture the other.
The criticism of Schlick does not, therefore, seem to be
justified. Moreover, his suggestion that bi-unique correspondence is the sole condition of agreement is likewise

[1] Wittgenstein, op. cit., *supra*, 2.171.

invalid. Bi-unique correspondence is a necessary, but not a sufficient, condition of agreement between propositions and fact. So far, Wittgenstein seems to be vindicated.

A difficulty remains. The proposition, as spoken or written, is a series of sounds or marks. It is, therefore, a group of facts and not a single fact, for evidently, if the connection between two sounds is a single fact, the connection between groups of sounds is a group of facts. In its significant use the proposition forms a unit. How, if facts are independent of one another, is it possible to derive one individual fact from a collection of facts ?   Wittgenstein insists that this must be done, for he says that " only facts can express a sense ; a class of names cannot ",[1] and again, that " the proposition is a fact ". It must be possible to have a fact composed of other facts, something apparently incompatible with the independence of facts. The only available explanation of this is that two distinct facts may be composed of the same objects, as for example in the case of the illusion of the reversible cube. Thus as an entity for consideration in its own right, the proposition as it stands on paper may be regarded as a series of facts (i.e. a series of marks or noises), whereas, as a symbol, the proposition is one fact. Take " Socrates loves Alcibiades ". As a factual objective in its own right, this sentence is a series of facts : " S-o-c-r-a-t-e-s l-o-v-e-s . . ." as a symbol it is not a series of facts, but one fact : " S-L-A ", i.e. a complex of three elements. But in either case it is composed of the same objects.

The essential connection between discourse and empirical reality is thus established by demonstrating the pictorial character of propositions which have empirical reference. The sense of a proposition is the method of its verification, that is to say what it represents if it is true. Sense and truth are distinct, for it is possible to understand a proposition without knowing whether it is true. The sense of

---

[1] Wittgenstein, op. cit., *supra*, 3.142.

empirical propositions is the possibility that the facts which they picture exist. This much is fairly clear.

But several problems present themselves. How do we know that all propositions are reducible to elementary propositions ? Is it possible to show that elementary propositions are exclusively concerned with picturing empirical reality ? The next step in Wittgenstein's philosophy consists in the demonstration that all propositions are reducible to elementary propositions, and that these latter are exclusively about empirical facts. This, obviously, limits discourse to the representation of empirical facts.

III

The first part of the demonstration is the proof that all propositions are truth-functions of the elementary proposition ; the second part consists in proving that the elementary propositions exist which are not truth-functions, of any other propositions. Wittgenstein describes the truth of a proposition as the agreement of its sense with reality ; disagreement of sense with reality is falsehood. Now, truth and falsity are neither properties nor relations, either of propositions or of facts. Thus, it is either redundant or nonsensical to say that " P " is true. For example, " Cæsar loves Brutus " and " It is true that Cæsar loves Brutus " say exactly the same thing. Here the addition of " It is true " is simply redundant. On the other hand, " $P = X$ is true " is nonsense, since " it is true " is not the predicate of X ; in order that P be true X must already possess a predicate. The addition of " is true ", " exists," etc., to the term X is nonsensical.[1] Truth and falsity are not properties of things, facts, names, or propositions.

Hence the words " true ", " false," " exists," " does not exist," do not stand for any entities whatsoever. A

[1] See Kant, I., *Kritik der reinen Vernunft*, Leipzig, 1924. Reclam., pp. 650–8 (A. 592–602) ; Russell, B., and Whitehard, A. N., *Principia Mathematica*, vol. i, 2nd ed., Cambridge, 1925 ; Wittgenstein, op. cit., *supra*, 4.063.4.

proposition is true when it agrees with reality, otherwise it is false. This can only be established by comparison. Now truth is not the comparison, but its result. The result simply reveals agreement or disagreement with reality, and this must be seen or shown. It cannot be expressed. This point will be developed later.

When two propositions are asserted to be true, "$p.q$," the result of the double assertion does not represent two facts and a conjunctive relation between them. Facts are such as to have no external relations whatsoever. Moreover, " and " is not the proper name of any entity. Similarly, when a proposition is negated the negation-sign does not represent any object in the world. Truth and falsity are, therefore, not objective entities. The logical constants, " and," " not," etc., are simply a part of the linguistic apparatus necessary to represent the world. This is not peculiar to Wittgenstein's theory, and I shall not proceed further with it here. It is generally recognized by logicians that symbolism contains more than the names of objects, and that these other symbols do not represent anything.[1]

The logical constants do not represent anything in the world, but are simply a part of the apparatus used in the description of the world. This will be more fully discussed later. It is stated here, without proof, to be used presently as the premise of an argument.

As I have observed, in order to prove that all propositions are truth-functions of the elementary propositions, it is necessary to prove (1) that the truth-functions do not represent anything, (2) that one proposition is a part of a larger proposition only when the larger proposition is a truth function of the smaller one, and (3) that the elementary propositions are exclusively about empirical reality.

I have indicated a few of the reasons for the first proposition. I proceed to the second. A truth-function of a set of propositions, $p, q, r \ldots$ will be represented by

[1] Wittgenstein, op. cit., *supra*, 4.0312. Hahn, Hans, " Die Bedeutung der wissenschaftlichen Weltauffassung," *Erkenntnis*, i., pp. 98–9.

$f(p, q, r \ldots)$. An example would be "p or q or r or . . ." Every truth-function is also a proposition, if $p, q, r \ldots$ are propositions. In the following manner it can be shown that all the truth-functions can be defined in terms of a single primitive operation. Let p/q be the proposition which is true whenever p and q are both false, and false when either p or q is true. Then all the truth-functions of p, q can be defined in terms of p/q. In general all the truth-functions of $p, q, r, \ldots$ can be defined as repetitions of the operation " / " on some or all of this set of propositions. For two propositions the result can easily be shown. The number of ways in which some or all members of a group of n propositions can be affirmed or denied is 2^{2^n}, for there are 2^n ways in which $p, q, r, \ldots$ can be considered as true and false, and hence 2^{2^n} sub-classes of these. The number of sub-classes of a class of n members $= 2^n$, of $2^n = 2^{2^n}$. Hence for $n = 2$, i.e. (p, q) there will be $2^{2^2} = 16$ truth-functions to be defined. These are :—

$$p/p = df \text{ not } - p$$
$$q/q = df \text{ not } - q$$
$$p/q = df \text{ not } - p \text{ and not } - q$$
$$p/q \mid p/q = df \text{ not } - (\text{not } - p \text{ and not } - q)$$
$$= p \text{ or } q$$
$$p/p/q \mid p/p/q = df \text{ not } - (p \text{ and not } - q) = p$$
$$\text{implies } q$$
$$q/q/p \mid q/q/p = df \text{ not } - (q \text{ and not } - p) = q$$
$$\text{implies } p$$
$$p/p \mid q/q = df \; p \text{ and } q$$
$$p/p \mid q/q \mid p/p \mid q/q = df \text{ not } - p \text{ or not } - q$$
$$\bar{p}/p \mid \bar{q}/q = (p \text{ implies } p) \text{ and } (q \text{ implies } q)$$

(The line over p indicates negation and thus is an abbreviation for p/p.)

$$\overline{(p/p \mid q) \mid (q/q \mid p)} = (p \text{ and not } q) \text{ or } (q \text{ and not } - p)$$
$$q/q \mid q/q = \overline{q/q} = \bar{\bar{q}} = \mid {}^0 {}^{'} q = q$$
$$p/p \mid p/p = \overline{p/p} = \bar{\bar{p}} = \mid {}^0 {}^{'} p = p$$

(I.e. *no* application if the operation is the same as two

applications on the same base which is the same as the original base considered as affirmed. The Law of Double Negation is introduced as a definition.)

$$\bar{p}/q \mid \bar{q}/p = df. \; p \text{ is equivalent to } q$$
$$q/q \mid p = df. \; q \text{ and not } -p$$
$$p/p \mid q = df. \; p \text{ and not } -q$$
$$p/p \mid q/q = df. \; (p \text{ and not } -p) \text{ and } (q \text{ and not } -q)$$

Thus all the truth-functions of p and q are successive and diverse stroke-functions. In general, if ξ is any proposition and $[\xi]$ is the class of propositions, then any truth-function of $[\xi]$ will have the form $\{\mid {}^{n}[\xi]\}$, where n represents the number of times the stroke is applied. Any proposition formed by the members of $[\xi]$ will be stroke-functions of the members of $[\xi]$. Therefore, so far as the construction of one proposition from other propositions is concerned, all propositions are constructed from other propositions out of stroke operations. Hence, all propositions are truth-functions of the propositions in which they occur. It might be the case, however, that the process of *analysis* of propositions should continue indefinitely. For example, a given proposition P might be a truth-function of p', p'', p''', etc. Each of these would in turn be truth-functions of others, and so on indefinitely. The truth-value of any compound proposition depends on the truth-values of its constituent propositions. The meaning of any compound proposition depends upon the meaning of its constituents. Now, if the process of analysis of this kind could be indefinitely continued, it would always be impossible to determine the truth or the meaning of any compound propositions. Hence there must be propositions which are not truth-functions of any lesser propositions, but out of which all compound propositions are developed. Now, since propositional compounds are truth-functions, all truth-functions will ultimately be truth-functions of the elementary propositions.

It remains to show why Wittgenstein believes that the

elementary propositions are exclusively about empirical reality. The importance of this demonstration for Positivism cannot be overlooked. If all propositions are truth-functions of the elementary propositions, and if the elementary propositions are exclusively concerned with empirical reality, then it will be impossible to say anything about the non-empirical. In other words, sentences about non-empirical things or facts will be simply nonsense, for it will be impossible to construct any legitimate proposition which could express such things or facts.

In order, then, to demonstrate the exclusively empirical content of elementary propositions, it is necessary to demonstrate the existence of logical simples. A logically simple object is an object which, according to its nature, makes any further analysis impossible. To find similar notions in the history of European thought would not be difficult and may serve to orient the reader. The " simple natures " of Descartes are such things as, relative to our understanding, are not susceptible of further reduction, and such as are the bases of all complex understanding. Some things are utterly simple, in respect of our understanding, but not necessarily simple in the ontological order.[1] These simple natures are not wholly parallel to the logically simple objects taken in Wittgenstein's sense, for the latter are regarded as simple without qualification. The monad of the Leibnizian metaphysics is an absolutely simple entity without qualification. However, since it is a non-empirical notion (being the idea of an existent substance with all its predicates) it does not quite compare with the logical simple of the present discussion. Perhaps the " simple impressions " of Hume would serve as better examples. But these are found in a discussion in which logical and psychological simplicity are not distinguished, and in which the impression is not asserted to be the ultimate basis of the real, but only of knowledge of the real. If, however, one translated Hume's

---

[1] Descartes, René, *Rules for the Direction of the Mind*, Rule XII.

" literary psychology " into the language of logic, and at the same time removed the naturalistic tendency from that system, whatever would correspond to the simple impressions, as a result of such a transformation, would be very much like the logically simple object of Wittgenstein's doctrine. But none of these comparisons is very exact.

The reasons for demonstrating the existence of simple objects as being the " ultimate furniture of the world ", to use Russell's phrase, are as follows : In order to demonstrate the exclusive concern of elementary propositions with empirical facts it is necessary to show that there is one and only one complete analysis of any proposition, that this analysis absolutely terminates in the elementary propositions, and finally that the elementary propositions are not capable of analysis save into the names which compose them. If many distinct analyses were possible, then even though a given analysis of propositions led to elementary propositions solely concerned with empirical reality, another possible analysis might very well lead to elementary propositions which were not solely concerned with empirical reality. Similarly, if there were no ultimate limit to analysis, then, although a given analysis led solely to elementary propositions of the kind in question, when carried out to any previously assigned limit, further analysis might reveal some non-empirical content in the propositions. Both of these possibilities must be excluded. The first is excluded by the fact that propositions are composed by truth-operations. The second can be excluded if the objectives of elementary propositions can be shown to be composed of logical simples.

The argument for logical simples is this. " If the world had no substance (i.e. simple objects) then whether a proposition had sense would depend on whether another proposition was true. It would then be impossible to form a picture of the world true or false." [1]

---

[1] Wittgenstein, op. cit., *supra*, prop. 2–0211–2.

... that the idea of pictures of facts begs the question (or assumes the existence of) simples.

54   LOGICAL FOUNDATIONS

As I understand it, this argument rests on two principles : first, that there is one and only one analysis of propositions about complexes, and, second, that the statement about a complex is completely analysable into a statement about its constituent parts.[1] If the argument is presented as formally as possible, this is brought out clearly. The reasoning is apagogic and must be transformed into a direct form. If the world does not consist of simple objects then : any proposition has sense implies another proposition is true ; this, in turn, implies that there are not pictures of the facts. Hence, if the world does not consist of simple objects there is no connection between discourse and reality. The argument in the direct form then is : If there are pictures of facts then some propositions have sense without being truth-functions of other propositions ; thus the existence of propositions with independent senses implies the existence of simple objects.

If, then, the world had no simples, propositions about complexes would be transformed into propositions about the constituents of the complex, and these into propositions asserting that the elements of the complexes are united in such and such ways. Inasmuch as the elements are complex, *ex hypothesi*, this process of translation continues *ad infinitum*. As propositions are pictures of facts, it would be impossible to establish any connection between propositions and reality, since the process of translation continues without end. Briefly the infinite process of analysis, or the ultimate complexity of the world, is incompatible with the pictorial nature of the propositions.

The argument allegedly demonstrates that there are simples, since it assumes that there are pictures of facts. But " pictures " in this usage means " absolutely unambiguous and direct representations ". Such pictures could exist only if there were simples. Hence, the existence of simples is implicitly assumed in the proof for simples. It

---

[1] Wittgenstein, op. cit., *supra*, prop. 2.

definitely begs the whole question. The *petitio principii* is evident from the definition of " sense of a proposition ". If propositions have " sense " in Wittgenstein's usage, then evidently the existence of simple objects upon which this sense depends is guaranteed. And, conversely, if simples exist, then correct propositions about the world will finally depend on propositions about simples. From the existence of propositions, however, we cannot infer the existence of simples, unless we either arbitrarily decide that propositions have " sense " in the restricted meaning in which Wittgenstein uses this term, or give some independent proof of the exclusive sovereignty of this meaning of " sense " by excluding the possibility of other meanings. From the existence of simples, we cannot infer that propositions exist which correctly represent the facts, since the difficulty of representing simples might be humanly insurmountable.

One might, nevertheless, attempt to argue the point in this way. If there are facts, the facts will have some structure or other. A structure without terms is inconceivable, so that the structure will be a structure of some things. A complex structure of simple things is inconceivable, and, similarly, a simple structure of complex things is inconceivable. In other words, the degree of complexity of the relations among things is relative to the degree of complexity of the things related. Simple terms are simply related and complex terms are related in a complex manner. Now, assertions are made ascribing a simple relation among things of a given kind. Hence, simple objects which are logically prior to these relations must exist if the ascription is true. This is as fallacious a proof as the former, because it assumes that there are true propositions asserting simple relations among things without questioning whether there are such propositions or such relations to be asserted.

Finally, it could simply be said that *no* conception of propositional meaning is compatible with the ultimate complexity of the world. Unless there is a final point of analysis, any analysis is foredoomed to failure. This assertion also depends upon the unjustified assumption that the sense of propositions must either be conceived as a *univocal* expression of facts, or as devoid of meaning.

It is clear, then, that the existence of simple objects cannot be demonstrated, and that all arguments attempting to demonstrate it either beg the question or have simply a verbal force.

The doctrine that the ultimate referent of significant discourse is the realm of empirical facts cannot be supported by Wittgenstein's logical atomism. There may be other ways to show the empirical content of propositions, but these do not concern the present study. Within the frame of Wittgenstein's doctrine, the existence of simple objects and atomic facts cannot be demonstrated, yet the empiricism of the doctrine depends upon the assumption that the demonstration is possible. The ideas of logical simples and the atomic facts composed of them are thus the first serious flaws in Wittgenstein's logical theory.

In the remainder of my exposition I shall, nevertheless, retain the doctrine to be taken either as an assumption or as something intuitively evident. It is interesting, however, to anticipate the consequences of the contrary hypothesis, namely that the limits of analysis are determined not by the facts themselves, but rather by the sign-language which we use to describe the facts. If the limits of analysis are determined by language, there will be an ineradicable element of arbitrariness and convention in the symbolism used to describe the world. This alternative requires some detailed explanation.

On the assumption that the world is the totality of existent atomic facts, language is composed simply of univocal and immediate pictures of these facts. The meaning of propositions is wholly determined by the empirical facts. There is no element of really essential arbitrariness in the representations of the facts. We can say neither more nor less than what is given in the empirical world, because every meaning is uniquely determined thereby.

On the contrary hypothesis, all this becomes changed. We decide what, for the purpose of a given analysis, is to be the point of departure for constructing a symbolic system. This decision immediately entails some arbitrary standard of simplicity. It is not, therefore, possible to say " this and this are determined by the facts, whereas that is determined by the unessential character of our symbolism ". Truth and falsehood, and hence meaning, will become matters determined by the facts and the symbolic system. Within such a system it will be impossible to determine to what extent the facts are responsible for the truth of the propositions, etc. Outside such a system it will also be impossible to determine the roles which the facts and the symbols play in determining truth because (1) no super-system is postulated from which to make such a judgment, and (2) comparison between two different symbolic systems would yield no answer, because a basis for such a determination would not be present in the comparison.

Absolutism and relativism in logical theory are thus opposite doctrines between which no compromise can be effected. The relativistic doctrine is to be preferred, simply on the ground that it contains no unprovable assertions. I shall return to the theory of logical relativism in my concluding chapter. The theory derives, on the one hand, from the conventionalists such as Poincaré, Le Roy, *et al.*, and on the other from the American pragmatists.

IV

If the atomic facts and the simple objects are assumed as the ultimate objectives of analysis, it follows that the ultimate referent of propositions with existential import is the realm of absolutely simple facts of experience. Language, however, contains many more elements than are comprised in the pictures of facts. There are truth-connectives, such as " and ", " implies ", etc., which have to be accounted for by a theory which reduces all meanings to the empirical content of thought. I have already dealt with the truth-connections. They are simply a part of the necessary apparatus of symbolism. The simultaneous assertion of two facts requires some sign, " and," to indicate that both are asserted. It does not follow from this that " and " stands for an entity in the objective world. If knowledge were complete there would be no false propositions, and hence no use for the negation sign. *A fortiori* there would be no use for the other logical constants. The incompleteness of knowledge requires the entertainment of propositions not known to be true, and thus the entertainment of groups of propositions not known to be true. It is, therefore, necessary to use logical constants. This presents one reason for the fact that there are more symbols in a language than objectives to which the language applies.

There are some difficulties which remain. Logical inference presents an instance of propositions which are *a priori* true. If propositions represent facts, if their truth or falsity depends upon the existence of the facts, it is clear that no proposition of logic could be *a priori* true. Yet there seem to be true propositions which do not depend on the facts for verification.

Wittgenstein's answer to this difficulty is one of his most valuable contributions to modern logical theory, and I have reserved a special chapter for it. Briefly stated, it amounts to denying that the propositions of logic express anything. They are merely formulæ which indicate the admissible transformations within a language. Given a complex proposition, the principles of logic indicate the different possible ways of expressing the same proposition or any of its constituents. For example : $p \supset q . \supset . \sim q \supset \sim p$ or $p . q . \supset . \sim (\sim p \, v \sim q)$ show how the same proposition can be differently expressed. The two parts of the principal implication express the same meaning. Similarly, $p . q . \supset . p$ shows how, given a complex proposition, we can express any one of its parts. The propositions of logic do not give expression to any fact, but rather present ways of expressing the same meaning (partially or wholly) in different ways.

Some objections still remain. It seems to be possible to express the relation between propositions and facts on the one hand, and propositions and the individuals asserting them on the other. Finally, it seems possible to express internal relations among propositions which are not formal truths of logic. Wittgenstein attempts to eliminate all of these apparent possibilities. These possibilities must be considered.

The first apparent exception to the doctrine that the ultimate referent of discourse is empirical, is the fact that some connection must exist between propositions and facts. Such a connection is not empirical. The propositions asserting this connection would then be cases of a non-empirical assertion. Wittgenstein holds that it is impossible for such a proposition really to be formulated. For him, the proposition represents what it represents, namely some empirical fact, by virtue of its logical form. The proposition asserts that things are related in a certain way by presenting the relation in which they stand if the proposition be true. By possessing a logical form the proposition reveals the form of the fact represented. It cannot represent the connection between itself and its objective, for it represents simply the form of the objective. It might be supposed that another proposition could represent the connection, but for Wittgenstein this is not possible because all that such an attempted proposition could assert is that $f = p$, i.e. that the fact and the original proposition have the same structure. The last formula is either contradictory or asserts nothing ; contradictory if f and p have different meanings, non-significant if they possess the same meaning. In general, the formal connection between propositions and facts cannot be expressed by any proposition. This connection is seen or shown by the comparison between propositions and facts, but it cannot be the subject-matter of a proposition. This may also be stated in another way. If propositions are pictures of facts, and, as being pictures of facts, possess forms identical with the structure of the facts, this community of form will be a presupposition of the possibility of symbolization. But, as being such a presupposition, the community of form cannot itself be symbolized. It can, however, be shown by exhibiting the facts whose forms are represented in the proposition, or by exhibiting the propositions whose forms mirror the structures of the facts. Inasmuch as no proposition can assert the connection between discourse and the world, the apparent exception to Wittgenstein's theory that the ultimate referent of discourse is empirical reality alone is dismissed.

It seems possible, nevertheless, to represent the connection between the proposition and the person who asserts, thinks, or believes it. This is the second alleged exception. For example : " John thinks that Mary went to town." This apparently violates the doctrine that all propositions are truth-functions of the propositions which occur in them. It seems to present a case of a proposition which cannot be reduced to elementary (empirical) propositions. This alleged case of a non-extensional proposition is eliminated by Wittgenstein's analysis.

Let A represent any person and P any proposition. Then A says (believes, thinks, asserts, etc.) P is apparently an exception to the two theses, (1) that one proposition occurs in another only as the base of a truth-operation, and (2) that all propositions are ultimately related to the empirically given facts.

The case of "A thinks P" is also interesting for another reason. Wittgenstein thinks that the meanings of signs and the sense of propositions are wholly determined by the facts to which they refer. The relation of meaning will then be an internal connection between the proposition and the fact represented by it. This relation involves only the two terms, *symbol* and *referent of symbol*, and no third term such as a person (i.e. a psychological or metaphysical subject) for whom the symbol means something. Other philosophers, who seem to see an ineradicable element of arbitrariness in symbolism, have insisted that meaning involves at least three terms, the person, the symbol, and the fact. The question is thus interesting and fundamental from three points of view. The example, " A thinks P ", seems to violate the empiricism of the Logical Positivists ; it seems to violate the so-called axiom of extensionality (that all propositions are truth-functions—extensional functions of the propositions occurring within them), and finally it seems to involve reference to a third and non-empirical element in the " meaning-relation ".

The elimination of this alleged exception proceeds along the following lines.[1] The proposition is a fact representing another fact. Hence it is possible to distinguish between the proposition, considered as a fact in its own right, and the proposition, as a meaning and thus as a vehicle of truth. Now, there is no subject in the metaphysical sense of a simple personal entity (according to Wittgenstein), so that the apparent relation of the proposition P to the subject A is really not a relation to A considered as a simple entity. Aside from this it is clear that " A says (thinks) P " is not a relation between a subject and a proposition in its symbolic use. For the proposition in its symbolic function does not occur in " A thinks P." " A thinks P " is really of the form " ' P ' says P " and this is not the relation between a subject and a proposition, but simply a co-ordination of the propositional sign with the fact for which it stands by means of the co-ordination of their objects. Thus " ' aRb ' represents the fact that a stands in a certain relation to b " means what is meant by " ' a ' is co-ordinated with a and ' b ' is co-ordinated with b ; consequently the order of ' a ', ' b ' is the same as the order of a,b ". When the proposition occurs factually, we may speak of it. It is then not a symbol, but an objective. We may say that someone utters it, or we may say that it is written in black ink. One is a fact of

[1] Cf. *Principia Mathematica*, vol. i, 2nd ed., pp. 559–666. Wittgenstein, op. cit., *supra*, 5.54.2.

here
crit. O

behaviour, the other of typography. When, however, the
proposition occurs symbolically, nothing is said about it, but,
by means of it, facts are represented. The case of " *A* thinks
P " is not a case of the occurrence of *P* as a proposition, but
simply as a fact.   The allegedly exceptional character
of " *A* thinks *P* " is thus eliminated.

Hence, " *A* thinks *P* " is no exception to the ultimately
empirical content of propositions. It is likewise no
exception to the doctrine that functions of propositions are
always truth-functions.   Finally the " meaning-relation "
is a relation between propositions and their objectives
involving no third term for whom the meaning is a meaning.

The proposition " *A* thinks *P* " is an assertion about the
behaviour of a human being on the same level as " *P* is
found in Chapter I of the Book of Genesis ". It is thus
reducible to a set of elementary (and hence empirically
grounded) propositions. *P*, in the significant use, does not
occur in " *A* thinks *P* " any more than in " *P* is found . . ."

The proposition " *A* thinks *P* " is not an intensional
function of *P* any more than " the sign *x* occurs in
$P[x$ occurs in $x\bar{R}y]$ ". Both are remarks about *P* considered
as a fact.   Therefore, all functions of *P* (in its symbolic
occurrence) are extensional functions of *P*.

In the significant use, the meaning and truth of a
proposition is wholly determined by the data which it
represents. Hence the propositional meaning requires no
supplementation by the postulation of a subject for whom
P means something. Neither more nor less can be said in
a proposition than is dictated by the facts which it represents.   Hence, the " meaning-relation " obtains solely
between proposition and fact, without introducing a person
to complete the relation.

It will be observed that all this holds only on the basis
of a doctrine which was found highly questionable. It can
be maintained that the meaning and truth of propositions
depend solely on the data only on the assumption that the
data are simple combinations of logical atoms. This has

already been called in question. If the data are not simple, or assumed to be simple, then there will be other functions of propositions than the extensional ones, and the cases of " A thinks P " or " X occurs in P " cannot be eliminated as above.

Consider, for example, the following case. We wish to explain " X is yellow " in such a way that " X is yellow " is either wholly true or wholly false. The data are not assumed to be logically simple. It will then be necessary to state how " being yellow " is determined. This would involve the axioms by means of which " being yellow " was arbitrarily determined ; for example, " yellow " lies between the two colours to which the real numbers a and b are ascribed. This axiom would be a function of " X is yellow ", but not an extensional function since " X is yellow " might be false, whereas " ' X is yellow ' is determined by Axiom N " would be true. This shows that the conclusions given above only follow from the premise that the data are logically simple, and do not follow from the contrary hypothesis.

The third difficulty which confronts the doctrine that all propositions are, in principle, empirically grounded, is that there are apparently some propositions which assert the internal connection of meanings and hence do not simply assert the existence of empirical facts. Examples of such propositions would be : (1) " The rose is red " entails " the rose is coloured " ; (2) the meaning of " P " is contained in the meaning of " P and Q " ; (3) " A is a father " entails " A has a child " ; (4) $aRb . bRc$ entails aRc.

Wittgenstein would undoubtedly admit that there are internal relations among meanings and among facts. He expressly denies, nevertheless, that these relations can be expressed by propositions. Any internal relation among facts or propositions is exhibited by the form of the facts or propositions. What is shown *in* the form of propositions cannot be expressed *by* propositions. Hence, no proposition expresses the existence of internal properties or relation.

An internal relation or property is defined as a relation or property which is not conceivable save in connection with the objects possessing it. The colour of an object must be spatial, the difference of brightness between two specific colours is necessarily what it is, etc. Propositions do not express this necessity, but reveal it in their forms. This doctrine will become clear in the next chapter. At present, it is sufficient to note that internal properties and relations are *shown* by propositional forms, but are not expressed by propositions as such.

The ways of avoiding exceptions to the empirical doctrine have been indicated. The consequences of this doctrine for philosophy and science remain to be developed. I shall outline the course of the development here, and develop it in detail in the succeeding chapters of this study.

V

If the meaning of propositions depends on the elementary propositions which are pictures of empirical facts, and if the truth of propositions finally depends upon the successful comparison of the elementary propositions with the facts, it follows that sentences which contain names or relational predicates of non-empirical entities will be simply nonsense. It will then be impossible significantly to assert anything non-empirical. Metaphysical doctrines postulating the existence of non-empirical entities will automatically be eliminated from significant discourse.

Non-elementary propositions are explicit truth-functions of the elementary propositions. Any given truth-function will be definite, and hence limited in its scope. It will therefore be impossible to assert general propositions having a possibly infinite set of instances, and thus the Cantorian idea of the real infinite becomes nonsense. This has important consequences for mathematics, for philosophy, and for science.

The mathematical infinite must be reinterpreted, so as to

avoid any assertions of infinite collections or magnitudes. Inasmuch as the proper infinite (the $\aleph_0$ of Cantor) is usually considered to be a necessary foundation for mathematical analysis (functions of a real variable, continuity, limits, and irrationals), this result involves a revision of mathematics. The infinite likewise disappears from philosophical doctrines.

The laws of natural science are usually considered to be general propositions whose scope is indefinite. For example, " all bodies fall with a constant vertical acceleration " is asserted for " all " bodies unqualifiedly. These laws will have to be reinterpreted if the scope of general propositions is limited to the elementary propositions from which they are constructed.

The doctrine that the laws of logic are tautological transformations of meaning makes it impossible to deduce anything unknown from the known. In this way deductive metaphysics, and indeed deduction in general, is eliminated.[1] Theoretical physics likewise requires much reinterpretation, since it is almost wholly concerned with deduction.

Finally, the so-called induction-problem is eliminated by the consideration that the general propositions, which inductive methods are supposed to establish, do not occur in significant discourse.

Thus a thorough revision of the usual conception of the sciences and philosophy together with logic and mathematics is entailed by the results of Wittgenstein's logical theory.

Science become a schematism by means of which singular propositions are constructed for the sake of empirical verification. In itself a scientific system cannot tell us very much about the world, for it is general and abstract, whereas the facts comprising the world are specific and empirical atoms. Science, then, is simply an organization of specific knowledge for purposes of recording and predicting specific events.

Prediction and verification are, therefore, not matters of inference. On this theory, inference *a posteriori* is never used, and can be given no justification. The theory of Probability

---

[1] i.e. deduction in the traditional sense of the term.

must likewise be changed so as to provide a place for a non-inferential use of the assessment of probability in the sciences.

Metaphysical thought is automatically rejected on the grounds that it consists of non-empirical assertions which are not capable of theoretical verification. If Wittgenstein's theory were true, it would be altogether impossible to make a non-empirical assertion. Wittgenstein and the other logical positivists must, therefore, be able to explain how metaphysical pseudo-propositions come to be expressed at all. For Wittgenstein, this occurs in one or more of the following ways :—

(1) The presentation of a propositional function, in which at least one constituent is really undetermined, in the guise of a completed proposition which contains no undetermined parts. For example : " There are at least three objects in the world." This has the form " $(\exists x, y, z) \ldots$ " because the word " object " occurs as the argument place of a variable and not as a constant. The " proposition " is incomplete, and hence is nonsense as it stands. Indeterminacy of this kind is one source of metaphysical pseudo-assertion.

(2) The attempt to say what can only be shown. Attempts to define truth, falsehood, the logical constants, numbers, in general, formal concepts, all involve this fallacy.

Not only metaphysics but much of traditional logic and mathematics would have to be eliminated in so far as the attempt is made therein to express what is essentially inexpressible.

(3) The attempt to deduce facts. All deductive metaphysics consists of a combination of this fallacy with (1) and (2). A concept is defined in such a way that consequences about reality can be drawn from it which are not ostensibly contained in the concept. St. Thomas's first three proofs for the existence of God provide examples of this. They are all deductions from implicit definitions of non-empirical (and hence theoretically unverifiable) concepts.

Philosophy, properly so-called, is therefore not a system

of general propositions. It is simply the activity of making propositions clear. Philosophical work essentially consists in the discovery of the elementary propositions on which a given proposition depends. A perfect language would thus have no need of philosophy.

These, in general, are the radical consequences of Logical Positivism in respect of other philosophies and the disciplines of logic, mathematics, and natural science. The consequences for Logical Positivism as a philosophy itself remain to be considered.

The world is not a systemic totality. What we call the world is all the atomic facts which there are. Empirical reality is limited by the totality of true elementary propositions. This is a finite, because theoretically definite, totality. The world is not systemically organized, and therefore is not a closed system. The finitude of the world of atomic facts provides no essential boundary to the world. The world is thus a finite but unbounded collection of mutually independent empirical facts. The totality of the expressible is the totality of elementary propositions. These are pictures of empirical facts. Thought is therefore limited to picturing the empirical reality. The inevitable consequence of this is solipsism. As one of Wittgenstein's critics has expressed it : " Notre travail de pensée se limite perpetuellement à reproduire, à montre le donné ; nous y sommes enfermes ".[1] An individual can only give expression to the past, present, or expected facts of his own experience. This makes it impossible to construct significant assertions about the experience of any other individual.

This radical consequence involves a further alteration of the usual view of scientific knowledge. An objective science, which is valid irrespective of the presence or absence of a particular experience or experiencing subject, has no meaning in Wittgenstein's scheme. In the first place, science, for him, is an organization of experience. In the second place,

---

[1] Feys, R., " Le raisonnement en termes de faits dans la logistique russelliene," *Revue néo-scholastique*, Louvain, 1928, 2 série, 5, pp. 157 ff.

an experiencing subject is as meaningless as the objective substratum of experience, since both are non-empirical concepts. Thus we are presented with a solipsism without a subject.

In the succeeding chapter I shall attempt to develop all of the theses presented here and I shall criticize them, so far as is possible within the limits of analytical criticism. By this I mean that I do not propose to criticize Logical Positivism on the basis of any philosophy which it specifically rejects. If there are fatal difficulties with Logical Positivism, they will be discovered by a logical analysis of this system without reference to any philosophical theories.

CHAPTER II

LOGIC AND MATHEMATICS

In the first chapter I attempted to present that part of Wittgenstein's logical theory which especially concerned philosophical questions. In this chapter I shall try to develop certain theses which are specifically related to issues of logic and mathematics.

"Logic," writes Wittgenstein, "is the investigation of all regularity. And outside logic all is accident." [1] This might also be expressed by saying that logic is the investigation of all the essential, as opposed to accidental, regularity (in so far as men speak of regularity in natural processes). But, perhaps, whatever regularity there is in nature is formal in character and so belongs to the realm of the logical.[2] In any case, the task of logic is the study of the forms of propositions and the nature of the connections of propositions. The form of the elementary proposition is wholly determined by known facts or by facts which are anticipated on the basis of what is known. The forms of propositions describing entirely new kinds of facts cannot be known and such propositions could not even be constructed. Logic is, therefore, restricted in its application to the analysis of elementary propositions already known, together with the truth-functions of elementary propositions. This means that there is no logic of induction. In a larger sense, it has another significance, as I have already tried to show.

I have already discussed the nature of the elementary proposition. Generalization is the construction of special kinds of truth-functions of elementary propositions, in

---

[1] Op. cit., *supra*, 6.3.   [2] Op. cit., *supra*, 6.3211.

particular, logical sums and products. Since the transition to these truth-functions is a natural step, I shall begin with them.

The elementary proposition consists of names in immediate combination with one another. If one or more of these names is replaced by a variable the remainder becomes what is known as a propositional function. Thus, for example, " $a R b$ " is a propositional sign. If " a " is replaced by " x ", or if the place which " a " occupies is left blank, " $( ) Rb$," we have a propositional function. If other things are related R-wise to b, the functional sign is the common mark of a class of propositions, cRb, $d R b$, $e R b$, etc. In the functional signs, therefore, there is a constant form shared by the propositions which belong to the group just mentioned. If all the constant terms are changed into variables the result is a propositional form. Thus in the above example $a R b$, replacing a, R, b by blanks, the form $( ) \{ \} [ ]$ results.

Wittgenstein calls " every part of a proposition which characterizes its sense " an expression. Whatever two propositions can have in common with one another is an expression. Thus " $a R b$" and " $c R d$ " share the expression " $( ) R [ ]$ ". The possibility of certain kinds of generalization depends upon the fact that some propositions possess the same form as others. For example, in order to say that all x's are characterized by ϕ we must be able to see that " $\phi ( )$ " is the common form of the propositions ascribing ϕ to the x's.

Generalization of this kind consists of symbolizing the constant form and the operation which creates the general assertion out of the singular (elementary) propositions which have this form. Thus " ϕa ", " ϕb," " ϕc," etc., have the form " $\phi ( )$ " in common. The assertion that the x's have ϕ is then written $(x)\phi x$. Finally, that an x has ϕ is expressed by $(\exists x)\phi x$.

In Wittgenstein's theory, all generalization is an explicit truth-function of definite elementary propositions. Such a principle differs from previous and contemporary theories in that the values of the variable are definite and therefore *limited*. Unlimited generalizations cannot be admitted under any circumstances. Although Wittgenstein does not explicitly say so, the statements of his followers and interpreters [1] involve the rejection of the actual (Cantorian) infinite.

A variable symbol is a symbol which signifies the logical form of all propositions which are values of the symbol in question. The variable symbol thus determines its values. The form remains constant, whereas the values, if there is a plurality of them, vary. In the symbolism of generality, therefore, there are three features to be distinguished. In " $(x)\phi x$ ", for example, there are mentioned : (1) the constant form of all propositions which are values of the function $\phi\hat{x}$. This form is the form " $\phi(\ )$ ". (2) The constant itself which is the " ϕ ". (3) Finally the nature of the operation which creates the truth function. Now $(x)\phi x$ is a specific function of ϕa, ϕb, ϕc, ϕd (that is, a definite number of elementary propositions). It is possible, therefore, to speak of two kinds of generality present in the symbol $(x)\phi x$. There is the accidental generality of the truth-function. That a, b, c, d happen to possess ϕ is not logically determined, for it might happen that $\phi a . \phi b . \phi c$ but $\sim \phi d$. Then there is the essential generality of the form of the function itself. If I know what kind of an object a is I know that it might possess ϕ. Likewise, if I know what kind of a property ϕ is, I know how it may occur in facts, i.e. I know that it *may* be a characteristic of a. For example, knowing a spatial object involves knowing that it can be red in colour.

This leads to the conception of two kinds of generality which do not coincide but mutually presuppose each other. In order to know that b can be coloured I must have previously encountered b in one or more facts in which this

---

[1] Kaufmann, Felix, *Das Unendliche in der Mathematik*, Wien, 1930 ; Waismann, F., " Logische Analyse des Wahrscheinlichkeitsbegriffs," *Erkenntnis*, Bd. i.

was the case. In order to know that ϕ can be the colour of something or other, I must have previously encountered ϕ in that situation. The possibility, therefore, that ϕ can occur in each of a set of facts does not entail ϕ's occurrence in all of them, but in at least one. The actuality that ϕ is the colour of all of a set of facts involves the possibility that ϕ can occur in more than one fact.

There are therefore two interpretations of generality. " All " in " All numbers are generated from O by the addition of unity " and " All men are mortal ", do not possess the same meaning. Likewise, " all triangles are closed figures bounded by three straight lines " and " all triangles are less than four square miles in area " are not the same kind of generality. The difference, according to Wittgenstein, lies in the essential character of the former and the accidental character of the latter. These examples serve to present the difference between logic and mathematics as essentially general disciplines and natural science as an accidentally general one.

The validity of logic and mathematics depends on the presence of some kind of essential generality in the concepts and propositions of these disciplines. The precise determination of the nature of this generality must be rendered as clearly as possible to the reader. Wittgenstein himself does not give a sufficient discussion of this subject for several reasons. In the first place, essential generality cannot be discussed but must be shown. Once it is pointed out, the observer is supposed to grasp it just as children, having been repeatedly presented with groups of two and three, are supposed to grasp the essence of five. In the second place, it is difficult to separate the two kinds of generality present in a single symbol. I shall, therefore, have to depend on some of Wittgenstein's commentators and followers for the explanation.

The doctrine that the *a priori* can be given in experience is not new with Wittgenstein. It is to be found in Husserl, Kant, and even in Leibniz and Aristotle. The doctrine of all of these thinkers is associated with metaphysical theories which find no place in the present connection.

In Wittgenstein's theory the *a priori* can be grasped in a single experience. It has no sources other than experience and it consists in the recognition of certain formal properties of the facts presented in experience. Essential generality can thus be grasped in the experience of certain facts. Some instances may serve to prepare the way for detailed discussion.

There is the recognition of sameness throughout a set of facts in which all but one object varies. If ga, fa, ϕa . . . are given it can be *seen* that all these facts possess an invariant element, the object a. Again if ϕa, ϕb ϕc are given it can be seen that all possess the character ϕ. The presence of the same quality (object, etc.) through a series of different facts is an instance of essential generality. This may be more accurately expressed by saying : There is an essential invariance present in certain facts, all of which vary in every conceivable respect in constituency.

Other examples : If the symbol " 4 " is replaced by " IIII " and the symbol " 3 " by " III ", it is shown by direct inspection that the meaning of " 3 " is contained in that of " 4 ". This exhibits the presence of an internal relation between the meanings of two symbols. If B is between A and C, and C between B and D, then it can be seen that C is between A and D. This is another instance of internal relations. Finally, from $P_1 \equiv P.Q$ and $P_2 \equiv Q$, it is seen that P_2 follows from P_1. All these cases are instances of internal relations among meanings.

It is observed that, although the examples are features of certain experiences or meanings, experience can neither destroy nor create them. This is why we say that the propositions of logic and mathematics are neither refutable nor establishable by any experience. It is but a seeming paradox that the logical features of facts and propositions are exhibited in experience but yet are neither established nor refuted by any possible experience.

With these general remarks we may return to consider the nature of truth-functions. All molecular, i.e. all non-elementary propositions can be constructed from the elementary propositions by setting out the combinations of the truth-possibilities of the elementary propositions, and the affirming or denying some or all of them in all possible ways.

For two elementary propositions there are $2^2 = 4$ combinations of their truth-possibilities. Thus :—

P	Q
T	T
F	T
T	F
F	F

It is easy to see that the possible ways of affirming or denying some or all of these truth-combinations is $2^{2^2} = 16$. Thus :—

P	Q	1 $p \supset p$	2 $\bar{p} \lor \bar{q}$	3 $p \supset q$	4 $q \supset p$	5 $p \lor q$	6 $\overline{(p \equiv q)}$	7 $\bar{p}$	8 $\bar{q}$	9 q	10 p	11 $p \equiv q$	12 $\bar{p} \cdot \bar{q}$	13 $\bar{q} \cdot p$	14 $\bar{p} \cdot q$	15 $p \cdot q$	16 $\overline{(p \cdot q)}$
T	T	T	F	T	T	T	F	F	F	T	T	T	F	F	F	T	F
F	T	T	T	T	F	T	T	T	F	T	F	F	F	T	F	F	F
T	F	T	T	F	T	T	T	F	T	F	T	F	F	F	T	F	F
F	F	T	T	T	T	F	F	T	T	F	F	T	T	F	F	F	F

Each of these columns, 1–16, is a truth-function of P, Q. In general, it can be said that every proposition which is a truth-function of $(P, Q, R, S \ldots)$ is an expression of agreement or disagreement with the truth-possibilities of the elementary propositions. Any function involving (P, Q) is thus represented :—

$$f(P,Q) = (T/F) \, P.Qv(T/F) \, P. \sim Qv \, (T/F) \sim P.Qv \, (T/F)$$
$$\sim P. \sim Q$$

(where (T/F) means " either true or false ", the " or " being exclusive). This expresses the rule by which, given any set of elementary propositions, all other propositions can be created. Wittgenstein expresses this somewhat differently. It will be recalled that all truth-operations can be expressed in terms of the " stroke ", symbolized by " / ", and means " neither . . . nor . . ." Let :—

> $P = $ any elementary proposition.
> $\bar{P} = $ *the* elementary propositions, i.e. the class of elementary propositions.
> $\xi = $ any proposition whatever.
> $\bar{\xi} = $ the propositions (all propositions).
> $N(\bar{\xi}) = $ the negation of every member of (ξ).

$$N'N(\bar{\xi}) = N^2(\bar{\xi}).$$

Then the general form of truth-function (that is, *any* truth-function) will be $\{\bar{P}, \bar{\xi}, N(\xi)\}$. This means that any proposition can be created from the set of elementary propositions by negating them all, then by taking any subset and negating them, etc. For example, if (P,Q,R) are the total values of $(\bar{P})$, any truth-function of $\bar{P}$ will be :—

> $N^n \, (P, Q, R)$. In particular,
> $N^1 \, (P, Q, R) \; = \sim P. \sim Q. \sim R$ and
> $N^2 \, (P,Q,R) \quad = PvQvR.$

If the function " total affirmation " is to be produced, the following procedure is adopted.

$$N^1 \, (P, Q, R) = \sim P. \sim Q. \sim R \; ;$$

a sub-set of $(\bar{P})$ is $[P]$, another is $[Q]$, another is $[R]$. Let these be, in turn, the values of $(\bar{\xi})$ in the general form, $\{P, \bar{\xi}, N(\bar{\xi})\}$. This will yield NP, NQ, NR respectively. The set $(\bar{\xi}) = [\sim P, \sim Q, \sim R]$ may now be formed. The operation N on the new set, i.e. $N^1(\xi) = N^1[\sim P, \sim Q, \sim R]$ yields $P.Q.R$. In this way any proposition can be built up from the elementary proposition by means of the " stroke ". $\{\bar{P}, \bar{\xi}, N(\bar{\xi})\}$ is thus the general rule for constructing propositions. It incidentally brings out the relationship between a set of propositions (or, in some cases, a given proposition) and a proposition created out of this set by means of a truth operation. The transition from one proposition to another is represented by the formula :—

$$\bar{\eta}'\{\bar{\xi}, N'(\bar{\xi})\} = \{\bar{\eta}, \bar{\xi}, N'(\bar{\xi})\}$$

where η is the set of propositions (or the proposition) upon which the operation N is performed. The bases of such an operation are contained in the result. For example :—

$$[P, Q], N(P, Q) = \sim P . \sim q.$$

All this formalism brings out two principal ideas. In the first place all truth-functions of the elementary propositions are the result of one kind of operation on the elementary proposition. Inasmuch as this operation can be given by a single general rule, the forms of any truth-function can be anticipated. There is something essentially regular here which belongs to pure logic.[1] It is the exhibition of a form common to all truth-functions, or a rule by which each special truth-function can be constructed. It is possible, therefore, to anticipate every possible truth-function *a priori*. It is, incidentally, shown also that the non-elementary propositions depend explicitly on the elementary propositions in every respect. In the second place it is shown by this development that a general invariant form exists. These results are fundamental for logic and mathematics as will presently be seen.

The two kinds of generality are the accidental and the essential. That all propositions are truth-functions of the elementary propositions is a case of an essential regularity which, showing itself in any single case of truth-function, does not depend upon the empirical verification of single instances for its existence. That all propositions include mention of space, on the other hand, depends upon an empirical investigation for the establishment of its truth. The word " all " accordingly has two distinct meanings which are not to be confused. The first meaning is what the

[1] And it also shows, incidentally, that the logical constants do not describe anything, for otherwise we would be able to anticipate the forms of all facts of a certain kind.

older logicians called an intensional meaning, and what Wittgenstein calls an internal meaning. The second is extensional. The former can neither be refuted nor established by empirical tests. The latter is always subject to establishment or refutation by empirical investigations.

Logic and mathematics are supposed to belong to the realm of the essential. Wittgenstein's two principal theses are, therefore, that logic and mathematics can neither be established nor refuted by empirical tests, and that they are concerned with meanings and the relationship of meanings. Logic and mathematics say nothing about the empirical world, but present the essential rules for transforming the expression of a given meaning into other expressions by exhibiting the essential internal properties of meanings and their essential internal relationships. It follows as a corollary from this fact that if we knew everything, or if what we knew was clearly organized, we would have no need for logic and mathematics, inasmuch as we would see the internal properties of our meanings and we would have no need to transform them into other clearer meanings. Calculation in logic and mathematics is necessary only because it is not humanly possible to grasp all the complicated relationships of meanings at one time.

I turn now to Wittgenstein's specific views on mathematics and logic, and shall consider logic first.

It will be noted in the matrix of truth-functions that there are three distinguishable cases or kinds. There is the case in which all the combinations of the truth-possibilities are affirmed. This is the case:—

P	Q	$(P$ or not $- P)$ and $(Q$ or not $- Q)$
T	T	T
F	T	T
T	F	T
F	F	T

Then there is the case in which all these truth-possibilities are denied. This is :—

P	Q	(P and not − P) and (Q and not − Q)
T	T	F
F	T	F
T	F	F
F	F	F

Finally, in addition to these extreme cases, there is the class of cases in which some of the possibilities are affirmed and others are denied. An example of this is :—

P	Q	P implies Q
T	T	T
F	T	T
T	F	F
F	F	T

The truth of a truth-function depends upon the truth of the bases. In the case of " P implies Q ", if the base P is true and the base Q is false, then the function " P implies Q " is false. However, in the case of " P or not − P, and Q or not − Q ", the bases may vary in all possible ways in respect of truth and falsehood without violating the truth of the function, since the function affirms all the possible variations of the truth-values of the bases. Similarly, in the case of " P and not − P, and Q and not − Q ", any variations of the truth-values of the bases P, Q will not make the function true, since it denies all these cases. The first extreme case allows every truth-combination of the elementary propositions, whereas the second excludes every truth-combination. The former is true under all circumstances, the latter under none. Only the class of cases in which some combinations are affirmed and others denied, exclude some and include others of the truth-combinations, hence only these cases can be true under certain circumstances and false under others.

Wittgenstein calls the first extreme a tautological function, the second a contradictory function, and the intermediate cases significant or real propositions. The schematism of the three cases can be represented as follows :—

Taut. $(P,Q) = df.$ $P.Q$v$P.\sim Q$v$\sim P.Q$v$\sim P.\sim Q.$
Cont. $(P,Q) = df.$ $\sim (P.Q)$v$\sim (P.\sim Q)$v$\sim (\sim P.Q)$v$\sim (\sim P.\sim Q).$

Real $(P, Q) = df.$ any affirmation of *at least one* and denial of *at least one* of the combinations.

The denial of a tautology yields a contradiction, and the denial of a contradiction yields a tautology. Thus, if it is denied that P is either false or true it is affirmed that P is neither false nor true. The relationship expresses what philosophers meant by saying that the denial of a truth of reason involved a contradiction. The denial of a real proposition yields another real proposition. This is what is intended by Hume's idea that the denial of a proposition about matters of fact yields another proposition which is " ever so conformable to reality ". In the matrix on page 74, there are eight pairs of contradictories :—

1 denies 16
2 denies 15
3 denies 14
4 denies 13
5 denies 12
6 denies 11
7 denies 10
8 denies 9

The denial of the truth of reason (1), yields a contradiction

(16) ; the denial of a matter of fact yields another of fact (2–8, 15–9). Since contradictions result only from denying tautologies (i.e. logical truths or truths of reason), the denial of a real proposition cannot produce a contradiction. This is what philosophers meant by saying that the contrary of every matter of fact can be denied without contradiction.

Philosophy has frequently asked why truths of logic could be unconditionally true, and yet why they expressed no facts about the world. Wittgenstein has satisfactorily answered this question. Truths of logic are unconditionally true because of a formal property possessed by all such truths. It does not especially matter what meaning is given to truth and falsity. It is only necessary to assume that every elementary proposition has at least one and at most one of these truth-values. Then the truth-function which agrees with all the truth-combinations, the tautology, cannot be falsified by any variation of the truth-values of the elementary propositions. The formal property of certain combinations of symbols, which is called tautologicality, is solely responsible for the unconditional truth of the truths of logic. It is a property of certain symbols and has nothing to do with what is symbolized. It is, therefore, absolutely true and yet says nothing about the world.

The results of this explanation of logical principles for philosophy are of great importance. If logic can say nothing about the world, a deductive metaphysics is quite impossible. The elimination of *deductive metaphysics*, already accomplished to a large extent by Hume and Kant, is completed by this demonstration.

The nature of logic can further be clarified by considering some usual cases. The following example will serve to illustrate some important aspects of logic. Take " $P.QvR.\supset QvR$ ". This is a formal tautology for :—

P	Q	R	P	QvR	$P.QvR$	$P.QvR. \supset .QvR$
T	T	T	T	T	T	T
T	T	F	T	T	T	T
T	F	T	T	T	T	T
T	F	F	T	F	F	T
F	T	T	F	T	F	T
F	T	F	F	T	F	T
F	F	T	F	T	F	T
F	F	F	F	F	F	T

I.e., since $(P.QvR) \supset (QvR)$ could only be false if the antecedent were T and the consequent F, and since this cannot be produced by *any* manipulation, the proposition is unconditionally true.

There are three aspects of this tautology which are revealed by analysis. (1) It is unconditionally true, (2) the meaning of the consequent is contained within the meaning of the antecedent, and (3) the consequent says less than the antecedent. In general, it is a characteristic of all formal reasoning that the meaning of the consequent is the same, wholly or in part, as that of the antecedent. Formal reasoning is, therefore, the expression of the same idea in different ways. It is nothing but a manipulation of symbols. It says nothing about what is symbolized and, therefore, says nothing about the world.

It does show the internal relatedness of one given meaning to another, and its essential significance is brought out by this circumstance. For a part of the meaning of language is shown by the fact that two different arrangements of symbols can express the same meaning.

This is Wittgenstein's philosophy of logic. When it is

applied specifically to the problems which have vexed logicians for a great number of years, its importance as a discovery will be evident. I shall attempt to show only so much of this as is necessary to illustrate the general elimination of metaphysical questions from logic.

One of the great problems in logic has been " How many primitive (i.e. undefined) ideas and propositions are necessary to express and demonstrate all possible truths of logic ? " With the aid of Sheffer's work, Wittgenstein has shown that one operation and one general rule are sufficient to express every possible truth-function of any given number of propositions. One primitive idea, i.e. " P/Q ", and one rule, i.e. $\{\bar{P}, \bar{\xi}, N(\bar{\xi})\}$ (where " $/$ " $=$ " N ") are sufficient to express every proposition whatever and, *a fortiori*, every proposition of pure logic (since there are fewer logical propositions than propositions altogether). The second part of the question concerning the number of propositions necessary and sufficient to prove all the possible logical truths there are can now be easily answered.

In the first place, says Wittgenstein, " proof in logic is only a mechanical expedient to facilitate the recognition of tautology where the reasoning is complicated." [1] The 'deduction of a set of properties from the logical axioms is therefore not the primary question. The primary question is " How can the tautology be recognized ? " and Wittgenstein has shown that this can easily be done by the matrix-method. The second question is " How many logical truths about n propositions are there ? " and Dr. Paul Weiss [2] in a remarkable development of the matrix-method has shown how this can be determined. The demonstration is so instructive that it ought to be included here. For n elementary propositions there are 2^n possible truth-combinations and 2^{2^n} possible ways of affirming and denying the combinations. For $n = 2$, we have $2^2 = 4$ truth-combinations and $2^{2^2} = 16$ truth-functions. Among these there is exactly one tautology.

[1] Wittgenstein, op. cit., *supra*, prop. 6.1262.
[2] " Two-valued Logic : Another Approach," *Erkenntnis*, Bd. ii.

If we combine each of these 16 with one another, as ante-cedent and consequent, there are $2^{2^{2^2}} = 256$ truth-functions which result. How many tautologies are among this group of 256 ? It is clear that there will be 3^{2^n}. For let any one of the antecedent truth-functions be represented by x_k (k here varies from 1 to 16) and any one of the consequent functions by y_k. (It is clear that if the value of k is the same for x and y, $x = y$.) Now we have the matrix—:

Xk	Yk	$Xk \supset Yk$
T	T	T
F	T	T
T	F	F
F	F	T

The case of tautological implication excludes $Xk = T$ and $Yk = F$. For $Xk = T$, Yk must be $= T$. Whereas for $Xk = F$, $Yk = F$ or T. There are then only three com-binations of 2^n elements admitted. This is 3^{2^n}. In general, given any number n of elements, the total number of tautologies involving them is 3^{2^n}.

*　　　　*　　　　*　　　　*

The construction of all tautologies with n constituents is thus given by a mechanical procedure. The completeness of a set of axioms can be established mechanically by the method outlined above. There is just one point where a further improvement of the matrix method seems desirable. Weisberg [1] has shown that the minimum number of propositional variables necessary in a system of axioms sufficient to generate all the theorems of mathematical logic is three. If the matrix method is equivalent to the deduction of theorems from axioms it should show some

[1] Cf. *Monatshefte für Math. u. Physik*, Leipzig, 1931, xxxviii, Bd. 1. Heft, p. 24.

reason why three propositional variables are necessary for the construction of a system of theorems. If this improvement is not made there will always remain some suspicion that logical proof contains something more than the mere revealing of tautologies.

The present state of the matter is this: All truths of logic are tautologies. Proof in logic consists in reducing complex tautologies where the reasoning is not clear to simple tautologies. The mechanics of proving all theorems of logic nevertheless require certain specific conditions placed on the structure of the axioms. A lacuna exists here which must be filled if the logical omnipotence of the matrix-method is to be proved.

The philosophical importance of the discovery that logic consists of tautologies is very great. Modern thinkers had long been divided on the question concerning the nature of logical truth. Empiricism and rationalism gave opposing answers to the question and both answers were evidently unsatisfactory. We can put the question somewhat differently. How, if logical propositions assert nothing about the facts, can they be significant at all?

Wittgenstein's answer to this question is, I believe, definitive. Logical propositions are used for the transformation of one proposition into another which has the same meaning as the former but which has a different form. They are significant because they reveal the community of meaning underlying different propositional forms. Nevertheless, they give expression to no facts and hence do not express anything. These two circumstances are not incompatible. Logic applies to the world only in the sense that it reveals the forms of the propositions which are used to describe the world, that is, logic shows that different expressions convey the same sense.

Another means of explaining how the propositions of logic (1) express no " sense " (i.e. express no possible state of affairs), and yet (2) are nevertheless not " senseless " is this: an operation is what must happen to a proposition with a given form in order to produce another proposition with another form. Thus, given "$p v q$", denial produces "$\sim p . \sim q$". Now some operations on a given proposition yield the same proposition or part of the same proposition in a different form. Thus, given "$p \supset q$" we can produce "$\sim q \supset \sim p$", which is the same as "$p \supset q$" differently expressed. There are certain operations, therefore, which do not alter the sense of the proposition on which they are performed. The base of such an operation is, as a consequence, equivalent to its result.

An operation which does not alter the sense of its base expresses no fact about the world. It is purely symbolic transformation. It conveys no "sense". It is not senseless, however, since it shows the various ways of expressing the same sense. A rule of symbolism is thus significant for the descriptive apparatus through which facts are pictured, although, since it is a rule of *symbolism*, it says nothing about what is symbolized.

I shall only suggest the philosophical bearing of Wittgenstein's discovery. It puts an end to all deductive metaphysics. Whatever else may be said of Logical Positivism, it seems to me to be a clear conclusion that this thesis is demonstrated, namely, that whatever can be established by purely logical methods has the sole value of revealing the interconnection of meanings, and so has nothing to say about the world, i.e. no proposition of pure logic has existential import. Metaphysics which attempts to demonstrate any fact about the world is, therefore, condemned to frustration.   "interpretation about" vs. "fact of"

Another important result of Wittgenstein's analysis of logic is his theory of definition. As long as definitions were phrased in Aristotelian terms it seemed possible to draw conclusions from definitions, and thus conclusions which had more than a verbal force. The Aristotelian definition consisted in giving the proximate genus and the specific difference of the thing defined, as e.g. "man" = *df.* "rational animal". This depended on the Aristotelian assumption of substances. Wittgenstein's theory of definitions (in agreement with that of most modern mathematicians), dispensing with this assumption, makes it impossible to draw any conclusions from definitions which have more than a verbal force. For Wittgenstein, a definition is a rule of translation either within a language or from one language to another.[1] In either case, it is clear that the definition itself is simply an " expedient in presentation ". It asserts nothing about the meanings of the signs defined or the signs by which it is defined, for the defined sign signifies something only by way of the signs by which it is defined. It is finally necessary to understand the meanings of some signs by a method of elucidation which presupposes the possibility of understanding the signs without the use of nominal definitions at all. All definition, properly so-called, is purely nominal and nominal definitions assert nothing. Deduction from definition is therefore impossible.

I wish to consider Wittgenstein's theory of logic in somewhat greater detail. Propositions belonging to logic have, as I said, been variously characterized by the great historical philosophers. The most naïve characterization is the one which assigns all propositions which are intuitively or demonstrably certain to the realm of pure logic. This view is wholly mistaken on at least three counts. (1) Some propositions are " intuitively certain " which do not belong to logic. This shows that the criterion of certainty is psychological rather than logical and hence cannot serve us in a logical capacity. (2) Some propositions which are not intuitively certain belong to logic. For example, even those who understand the " stroke " notation (" P/Q " = " not $- p$ or not $- Q$ ") could not decide that Nicod's axiom, i.e. $(p/q/r) \mid (t/t/t) \mid (s/q \mid [p/s/p/s])$ was a logical axiom merely on the ground of intuitive certainty. (3) The criterion of certainty leaves the interconnection of axioms and their consequences entirely obscure. Descartes was never able

---

[1] Op. cit., *supra*, prop. 3.261, 3.343, 4.241.2.

successfully to combine the criterion of certainty with that of demonstrability.

Some empirical philosophers of the nineteenth century, especially John Stuart Mill, were inclined to deny the existence of logic altogether as a set of unconditionally valid propositions. That all truth was derivable from experience meant that no *a priori* logical principles were significant. This view contains an atom of truth, but only an atom. Logical truths are not existential in import, or, in Wittgenstein's phraseology, they assert nothing. This, however, is not to deny their value and validity. Empiricism, in its more extreme form, has been inclined to reject logic altogether. This, it is clear, is a mistake.

The Critical Philosophy of Kant realized the distinction between analytic and non-analytic propositions, and between *a priori* and *a posteriori* truths. It failed to realize that all *a priori* truth was analytical and almost succeeded in re-introducing a spurious method of deduction into philosophy. Kant certainly believed that the synthetic *a priori* judgment was a valid mode of inference which could convey information about the world.

According to Wittgenstein's analysis, all the former views were mistaken. The analytic truths, the tautologies, presuppose the existence of elementary propositions ; these are, of course, empirically determined as to meaning and truth ; rules for the manipulation of these elementary propositions in certain definite ways yield analytic propositions. The analytic propositions say nothing about the word because they include every possible variation of the truth-values of the proposition occurring within them. They are not, however, senseless, as some of the empiricists supposed.

Not all necessary truths are tautologies. The expressible truths are tautological, as I have said. But there are other unavoidable necessities which belong to mathematics rather than to logic, but, because they have a wider application than mathematics in the ordinary sense, I shall discuss them here. They are all concerned with the internal connection of meanings.

If, for example, certain propositional forms are presented, the internal relations among them are revealed by a correct notation. Three important cases are the following :—

(1) $P \supset Q . P \supset R . \supset . P \supset Q . R$

(2) $a < b . b < c$ entails $a < c$

(3) $\phi_1 T_1 S_1 . \phi_2 T_1 S_1$

(where $T = $ a moment of time, $S_1 = $ a point or area of space, $\phi_1 = $ some given colour, $\phi_2 = $ some other colour) is an impossible combination of signs.

(1) Is a tautology and its tautologicality can be expressed by the matrix-method. The circumstance that the sense of $P \supset Q . R$ is contained in the sense of $P \supset Q . P \supset R$ can only be seen when the sense of either $P \supset Q . R$ or $P \supset Q . P \supset R$ is known. It cannot be expressed because if meaning cannot be expressed, then, *a fortiori*, interconnection of meaning cannot.

(2) If we know that a signifies some number (1111 . . .) and b a number (111111 . . .) and c a number (1111111 . . .), we already know that the first is less than the second, the second less than the third, the first less than the third. The fact that, e.g. " 1111 " contains " 111 " is shown by the arrangement of the symbols. This cannot be expressed but can be shown by a clear notation.

(3) That a spot cannot be coloured by two different colours at the same time seems to be a formal contradiction, since $\phi_1 S_1 T_1 . \sim \phi_1 S_1 T_1$ is a contradiction and $\phi_2 S_1 T_1$ would seem to be a possible case of $\sim \phi_1 S_1 T_1$. We cannot infer this, however, so that it is not a formal contradiction. $\phi_1 S_1 T_1$ and $\phi_2 S_1 T_1$ formally exclude one another. This, according to Wittgenstein, cannot be expressed but can only be shown by the form of the proposition. We can see that a one-valued function cannot take two values, that a function of two arguments cannot have more than two values of its arguments at one time, etc., but we cannot

express this because we can only *present* propositional functions but can never talk about them (except in the unimportant way, e.g. as facts of acoustics or typography).

The existence of internal relations among meanings presents necessities which are not formal tautologies, and which, therefore, do not belong to the domain of logic. One especially important branch of such internal relations is presented by mathematics.

* * * *

Wittgenstein's theory of mathematics thus depends on two principal theses. First, mathematics cannot be derived from logic, and second, mathematics consists of showing the internal relatedness of meanings (though not in the tautological sense).

The first thesis rests on the doctrine (which I briefly discussed in the preceding chapter and must now expand) that there are two distinct kinds of generality, accidental and essential.

The generality of propositions (such as " every x is ϕ ", " There is an x which is ϕ ") depends entirely on the accidental course of events. As such, " $(x)\ \phi x$ " is a truth-function of ϕa, ϕb, ϕc, etc., where $a, b, c \ldots$ are all the values of the function $\phi \hat{x}$. In order to write such a function it must be presupposed that $a, b, c \ldots$ are all known. This, then, is an accidental generality. It follows at once that numbers cannot be defined as classes of similar classes without losing the absolute generality which is characteristic of mathematics. If we said, for example, that 2 is the class of all couples, i.e. that " $2 = df.\ \hat{a}\{(\exists x,y)x \neq y . a = \iota'x \smile \iota'y\}$ " is a correct definition,[1] we should render the notion of " twoness " dependent on the empirical existence of the classes containing two members. A universe is conceivable in which things are arrangeable only in triads, and in such a universe " two-ness " would have no meaning according to the definition. Again, if similarity of relations is defined

---

[1] *Principia Mathematica*, 54.02

as it is in *Principia Mathematica*, where it is made to depend on the existence of a correlator, the concept would have no meaning in a universe in which there were no ordinal correlators.

Finally, for another example of the "extreme realism" of *Principia Mathematica* : if the multiplicative axiom (which states that there is a multiplicative class for every class of existent classes) depends on the existence of a selector (a relation which selects one member of each existent class in the class of existent classes), a universe would be conceivable in which no selectors existed ; in such a universe the multiplicative axiom would be false.

Now mathematical truths cannot be made to rest on the accidental course of events (unless, of course, we wish to sacrifice whole sections of mathematics). Another way of putting this is that mathematics should contain no existence-theorems which can be interpreted in the sense of *factual* existence. The *Principia Mathematica* (as well as other similar works) contains at least four such doubtful theorems (the existence of at least one class, the axiom of reducibility, the multiplicative axiom, and the axiom of infinity), and thus cannot be regarded as logically unobjectionable.

There are two ways of avoiding this difficulty. One involves the introduction of extensional functions which are arbitrarily defined for the purpose of avoiding the afore-mentioned difficulties. There is no apparent objection on purely mathematical grounds to this procedure. It is not suitable for a philosophical foundation of mathematics because the new functions are unexplained in terms of the primitive ideas of the system. The other method consists of rejecting the whole attempt to establish mathematics on logic. This is Wittgenstein's procedure.

Mathematics, therefore, must depend on the second kind of generality which is what Wittgenstein calls the *essential* generality. This does not depend on the course of events in any way. That $2 + 2 = 4$, that the numbers are the posterity of zero in respect of the relation "immediate predecessor ", etc., can be neither established nor refuted by the factual nature of the world. These formulæ depend solely on the internal relations among concepts and among the symbols which represent them. Mathematics cannot be asserted. It must be shown. I shall try to show why Wittgenstein believes this to be so. First, however, I shall proceed with Wittgenstein's critique of Russell's method of deriving mathematics from logic.

According to Wittgenstein, Russell is guilty of two principal fallacies : First the confusion of essential and accidental generality, and second the fallacy of arguing in a circle. A class is the extension of a propositional function and a propositional function is a kind of (predicative) adjective which (1) shows the common mark of several facts and (2) requires completion in order to convey a sense.[1]

That is, a function determines a range of values, each of which renders it a complete proposition, and it is the common mark of all propositions thus produced. Now it is clear that this description of a propositional function is circular. If it is defined as the common mark of a class of propositions it presupposes the existence of the class which it generates. On the other hand, if it is something incomplete *ex hypothesi*, it cannot presuppose the class in question. The only way out of the muddle is to retain the two characteristics of the function, viz. the fact that it is a general form and the fact that it is something incomplete, while. keeping these characteristics quite distinct so that they do not depend on one another in this vicious fashion. In other words, the essential generality of the function (1), and the incompleteness of the function (2) which is the basis for its accidental application to the facts which simply happen to exist, must be kept distinct.

Russell did not do this. For example, consider the definition of *two*. *Two* is the class of all couples, i.e. a specific instance of a class of similar classes. Now, in defining

---

[1] This is essentially Frege's view. (1) is the Zusammengehörigkeit, and (2) the Erganzungsbedürftigkeit of the function.

a given number as the class of similar classes, we presuppose a basis for the one-one correspondence by which we ascertain the similarity in question. This basis, however, can only be in the common characteristic which the classes share. The definition of the number two (and *a fortiori* the definition of numbers in general) is viciously circular.[1]

Similar remarks apply equally well to the definition of " similarity of relations ", and the " ancestral relation ", and, in an interesting way, to " identity ". I shall consider the first two cases later. " Identity " is defined in *Principia Mathematica* as follows :—

$$(1) \quad x = y = df. \quad (\phi) \; \phi!x \equiv \phi!y, \text{ i.e.,}$$

x is identical with $y = df$, every predicative property (and hence, by the axiom of reducibility, every property) of x is a predicative property of y and conversely). This involves a definition of identity of properties. We should then have to define (2) $\phi = \psi \; . \; = df. \; (x)\phi x \equiv \psi x$. Now, although (1) and (2) are independent, the possibility of $\phi x \equiv \phi y$, or of $\phi x \equiv \psi x$ involves the implicit assumption that " ϕ " is the same " ϕ " in " ϕy " and " ϕx ", and, likewise, that "x " in " ϕx " is the same " x " as " x " in " ψx ". Therefore, identity of qualities is presupposed in the definition of identity of individuals, whereas identity of individuals is presupposed in identity of qualities. The definition of either kind of identity presupposes the other. Identity, *qua* identity, cannot therefore be defined without circularity.

Wittgenstein avoids all of these difficulties simply by not attempting to define numbers, identity, and other mathematical concepts. The formal concepts of mathematics are, and must be, presented by exhibiting variables, i.e. by showing the forms of the objects which fall under the concept. They cannot, in any case, be *defined*.

I shall now give Wittgenstein's reason for believing that mathematical concepts must be shown. The internal

---

[1] This is purely expository. In my opinion, the objections are all invalid. But to explain this here would involve an unnecessary digression. See, however, Chapter X.

properties of a proposition are those properties which alone are essential to its sense. It is these properties which relate the propositional picture to its objective fact. Propositions show the logical form of reality by depicting the atomic facts. This " showing " is accomplished via the fact that the proposition possesses this logical form (which constitutes the internal feature of the proposition). Now this form cannot be expressed in definition or description by any proposition, for it is logically prior both to the proposition which possesses it and to any other proposition. The logical priority consists in the fact that the logical forms which picture realities constitute the presupposition of all representation (picturing, expressing), and so cannot be represented in their turn without circularity.

Therefore, on the theory that propositions in the last analysis are pictures of facts, it is impossible to represent the logical form of a proposition in any way. If, for example, we tried to represent what a given proposition had in common with its objective, i.e. if we tried to describe the logical form of the proposition, we would find ourselves representing this logical form over again. The form would have been neither described nor defined, but simply exhibited. Now " showing " is certainly neither defining nor describing ; the logical form would not have been defined or described.

It is thus possible only to exhibit the logical form of propositions and all attempts to formulate the rules of logical grammar finally come down to exhibiting the form which, for reasons just given, cannot be described. Logical grammar, then, consists essentially in pointing out the structures of propositions by exhibiting logical prototypes, that is, by indicating the forms which several propositions have in common. Logical grammar does this. It is quite clear that the *important* rules of logical grammar cannot be formulated but must be shown by clearly exhibiting logical forms.[1]

That a proposition possesses a formal property can neither

[1] Wittgenstein, op. cit., *supra*, prop. 2.172, 2.173, 2.174, 4.041, 4.1212, 4.123, 4.1274.

be asserted nor denied, because a formal property cannot be described. It is therefore not a part of any science to deal with formal concepts. In this sense mathematics is not a branch of knowledge.

I am now prepared to expound the positive side of Wittgenstein's doctrine of mathematics. It must be remembered that, inasmuch as formal concepts cannot be described, the theory of mathematics does not consist of assertions, but simply of elucidation, i.e. a method of showing what cannot be said. An elucidation is, strictly speaking, a kind of important nonsense, important because it is valuable in helping us to understand mathematics, nonsense because it attempts to assert what can only be shown. Nevertheless, it is very difficult to avoid such important nonsense. It is harmless as long as it is realized that an elucidation does not really express anything.

The common characteristic of a class of propositions which have no constituents in common is what is called a logical prototype or a formal concept. In significant discourse the formal concepts are presented when the objects which fall under them are presented. For example, take the series of propositions :—

$$aRb$$
$$(\exists x)\ aRx.xRb$$
$$(\exists x,y)\ aRx.xRy.yRb$$

This shows what is meant by the statement that b is a successor to a. We cannot define this relationship but we can give the formal concept of the " term of a formal series ". This is done by giving the first term, any arbitrary term, and the operation of producing the successor of the arbitrary term. Thus, in the case above, $\{a, x, x R y\}$ is the general term of the series. Every proposition of the above series has the common character represented in the variable formula $\{a, x, x R y\}$. This variable is called the *general term of a formal series*.[1] Such a series is always

[1] Wittgenstein, op. cit., *supra*, prop. 4.1292, 5.2522.

ordered by an internal relation among its terms and hence must be shown by exhibiting the general form. This form, however, is already presented when the series or any part of the series is presented. The objects which fall under the formal concept contain or possess the formal concept. It is, therefore, simply an expedient of elucidation to set forth these variables by themselves.

There is, therefore, a difference between formal concepts and " proper " concepts.[1] A proper concept is given by a function. Thus " ϕx " = " x is red " is a proper concept, whereas $\{a,\ x,\ \Omega\ 'x\}$ is a formal concept. In *Principia Mathematica* and most of the other logical systems, formal concepts and functions were treated as being on the same level. In this way the asymmetry of a relation was treated as a property of the relation just as the redness of a spot is a property of the spot. According to Wittgenstein's analysis this is the fallacy of confusing the essential and the accidental properties of facts and of the propositions which represent them. Formal concepts are always presented by variables.

This is the foundation of Wittgenstein's theory of mathematics. Mathematics deals with formal concepts such as number, successor, and the like. Wittgenstein proposes to develop the entirety of mathematical propositions out of operations on formal concepts.

Numbers are defined as exponents of operations. In the first chapter we saw that the general form of truth-functions is the formula $\{\overline{P},\ \overline{\xi},\ N(\overline{\xi})\}$ which shows that " every proposition is the result of successive application of the operation $N\ (\overline{\xi})$ (= negation of every value of $(\overline{\xi})$) to the elementary propositions. If this operation [2] is repeated twice it has the form $N^2(\overline{\xi})$. A specific number is the expression of the specific repetition of operations of this kind. *Number in general* is the general concept of the repetition of operations.

Following this idea, specific numbers are defined thus :—

[1] Wittgenstein, op. cit., *supra*, 4.126.
[2] Wittgenstein, op. cit., *supra*, prop. 6.001.

$$x = df. \ \Omega^{0}{}^{\prime}x$$
$$\Omega^{\prime}x = df. \ \Omega^{1}{}^{\prime}x$$
$$\Omega^{\prime}\Omega^{\prime}x = df. \ \Omega^{1+1}{}^{\prime}x = \Omega^{2}{}^{\prime}x$$

In general, $\Omega^{\prime}\Omega^{r}{}^{\prime}x = df. \ \Omega^{r+1}{}^{\prime}x$. Thus, *zero* is the number which indicates that *no* operations on a term have been performed, *one* is the number that indicates that an operation has been performed but not repeated and, in general, $r + 1$ is the number which indicates that an operation has been performed on a term on which r operations have been performed. These definitions can be transformed into a simpler notation as follows :—

$$0 + 1 = df. \ 1$$
$$0 + 1 + 1 = df. \ 2$$
$$0 + 1 + 1 + 1 = df. \ 3$$

The general form of number is, therefore, $\{0, x, x + 1\}$. This is also the term of the series of numbers.

An important consequence for mathematics as well as philosophy results from this theory of number. Their consequence will be clearer if Wittgenstein's theory of number is contrasted with that of Russell in order to see significance. For Russell (following Frege and Cantor), a number is a class of similar classes. In order that a given number may exist it is therefore necessary that there actually be a class with at least as many members as the number in question requires. Now the inductive cardinal numbers form a class. This class of all inductive cardinals is denoted by $\aleph_0$. In order that $\aleph_0$ have any significance it is necessary that an actually infinite class of individuals exist. Mathematics will be self-contradictory unless this is true. This is a genuine difficulty, because we always, in practice, perform operations of only finite number inasmuch as our operations are explicit and hence definite. Thus, although only finitely many operations are performed, we must, according to Russell, assume the hypothesis of an infinite number of operations which, in fact, never exists. But if this first infinity does not exist the higher infinite cardinals do not exist. There is thus an air of hocus-pocus about the whole development of transfinite arithmetic which must somehow be corrected.

The difficulty does not occur in Wittgenstein's theory of mathematics. The mathematical infinite is the indication that no essential limitation characterizes the number-process because the structure of this process is given by the general term $(0, \xi, \xi + 1)$, in which, ostensibly, no limitation to the successive application of the operation " $+ 1$ " occurs. The infinite is thus only a regular rule by which a logical procedure can be carried on without limitation.

The importance of this theory for philosophy is immediately evident. Finitude and infinitude are characteristics of essentially different species of operations. There is no genuine or proper infinite in the Cantorian sense. Although the real world is finite and the description of that world limited to the finite number of propositions about it, the world is infinite in the sense that it possesses no essential limitation. There are also some specific applications of this conception of infinity to the theory of probability and induction.

I return to mathematics. Mathematics consists of calculating with equations. Equations require the idea of identity. Now, according to Wittgenstein, identity is not a primitive relation among things. The use of the symbol of identity in mathematics requires an explanation which removes all ontological significance from it.

Identity is not a relation among things. If " a " and " b " are two names, then " $a = b$ " is contradictory if the names are names of distinct individuals. On the other hand, " $a = a$ " does not express anything about the entity called " a ". Likewise, it expresses nothing about the name " a ". The only correct use of the symbol of identity is when it occurs between two symbols and expresses the identity of *meaning* of these symbols. Here, again, identity of meaning cannot actually be expressed, for in order to understand the meaning of an expression it is necessary to understand whatever essentially expresses sense in the expression. If the meanings of two expressions are known it is superfluous to add that these meanings are the same or different. Whatever is superfluous in a sign-language is meaningless. Strictly speaking, therefore, the sign of identity is meaningless. It has one legitimate use. If there are redundancies in a language so that the same meaning can be expressed legitimately in different ways, the sign of identity can be used to bring together the different ways of expressing the same sense. This would be superfluous in the case of a perfect language in which identity of meaning would be expressed by identity of symbols and not by a sign of identity.

Mathematics employs the sign of identity to show that different number-expressions have the same meaning. Equations are thus simply the symbolic rules which express the " substitutibility " of one expression for another.[1]

Mathematical proof consists essentially in reducing two expressions of different form to expressions of the same form. Thus, in the proof that $2 + 2 = 4$, the procedure consists simply of showing, by substituting equivalent expressions, that the symbol $2 + 2$ and the symbol 4 are reducible, by definition, to the same symbol. For example, $2 + 2 = 4$ is proved as follows :—

$$
\begin{aligned}
2 + 2 &= \Omega^{2'} \Omega^{2'} x \\
&= (\Omega' \Omega)' (\Omega' \Omega)' x \\
&= \Omega' \Omega' \Omega' \Omega' x \\
&= \Omega^{1 + 1 + 1 + 1} {}' x \\
&= 4
\end{aligned}
$$

This follows from the definition of number given above.

The number is something which characterizes a propositional form and, in order to see that two expressions are numerically equal, it is only necessary to see that, under admissible substitutions, they possess the same form. It is necessary, in other words, to exhibit number by exhibiting form, and to exhibit identity of number by exhibiting

---

[1] Wittgenstein, op. cit., *supra*, prop. 6.2323, 6.24.

identity of form. This is done in mathematical proof by applying the definitions.

This theory of mathematics can easily find a place for all elementary arithmetic and algebra. Inequalities might, at first glance, seem to provide especial difficulties. However, it seems clear enough that they could be treated in the following way :—

$$x < y = df. \quad x + z = y$$
$$x > y = df. \quad x = y + z$$

Similarly, ratios could be defined as follows :—

$$\frac{m}{n} \quad df. \quad mx = ny$$

A series of ratios would then be defined as a double series of integers. The limit of a series is a little more complicated. Felix Kaufmann, who has carried out this part of Wittgenstein's programme, gives the following definition :—

$\frac{r}{s}$ is the limit of $\frac{P_1}{Q_1}, \frac{P_2}{Q_2}, \frac{P_3}{Q_3}, \ldots \frac{P_n}{Q_n} = df. \, (k)(\exists z):(n)n > z:$ $(\exists n)m,z :$

$$Q_n r > k \mid Q_n r - P_n S \mid$$

That is to say : " Given two series of natural numbers :

$P_1, P_2, \ldots P^n, \ldots, Q_1, Q_2, \ldots Q^n, \ldots : \frac{r}{s}$ is said to be the limit-value of $\frac{P_1}{Q_1}, \frac{P_2}{Q_2}, \ldots \frac{Pn}{Qn}, \ldots$ if, for every natural number k, a natural number z can be found such that, for every n greater than z, $Q_n r > k \mid Q_n r - P_n s \mid$ obtains." [1]

It is not necessary to give the somewhat lengthy series of definitions leading to the construction of irrational numbers. The procedure is the same throughout. All number concepts are defined in terms of the natural integers.

*　　*　　*　　*

If this programme is finally successful it will be possible to develop the whole of mathematics (in so far as it involves number) from the natural numbers, which are determined

---

[1] Kaufmann, Felix, *Das Unendliche*, op. cit., *supra*, p. 117.

by the general form of number and by the definition of specific numbers given above.

It is not within the scope of this essay to criticize the present theory of mathematics, first because it would require a digression irrelevant to the main issue, and, second, because the theory has not been developed in sufficient detail to enable the critic to see whether it can deal with some of the more problematic aspects of mathematics. For the present purpose it is necessary simply to understand that " number " is not a proper concept, i.e. it is not a predicate of things. It is merely a feature of certain symbols which describe the facts, and as such belongs to the realm of symbols rather than to the realm of facts.

I shall briefly summarize the ideas in this chapter. Logic consists of tautologies and mathematics of equations. A tautology is a truth-function which is true irrespective of the variations of truth-values of its constituent propositions. It says nothing about the world because it includes all possibilities of truth and falsehood of its constituents and hence is true irrespective of the existence or non-existence of facts to which these constituents refer. It cannot be empirically verified and hence is without sense (*sinnlos*). It is not senseless (*unsinnig*) for it shows the logical relation among different symbolic complexes which say the same thing. The value of tautologies is their application as transformation-rules of symbolism.

Mathematics consists of equations of numerical expressions. A number is a feature of a propositional form. Since all forms must be shown (exhibited) numerical features must *a fortiori* be shown. Numbers, therefore, cannot be defined as functions or classes but must be presented by a variable expression which is the common mark of a class of propositions which share the form of which the number in question is an essential feature. Numerical equality involves the sign of identity. The only legitimate use of this sign is as an indication that two expressions are reducible to one and the same expression.

Logic and Mathematics show the essentially regular characteristics of a sign-language. The propositions of logic and the equations of mathematics would, therefore, be unnecessary to a being who was able to grasp the sense of each symbol in an enormously complicated language. This shows that logic and mathematics express no facts about the world.

The principal fallacy of the old logic was the confusion of essential and accidental generality. The essential generality of logic and mathematics (which can only be shown) is again an internal characteristic of certain symbols, whereas the accidental generality of ordinary general propositions is an explicit truth-function of propositions about the facts. This difference makes it possible to treat infinity as the concept of " the successive application of an operation to its own result " rather than as the concept of a really infinite totality. Failure to recognize the difference introduces many pseudo-problems, of which the problem of the continuum in mathematics [1] and the induction problem in science are outstanding examples.

SUMMARY OF PART I

I shall repeat only those logical principles which are fundamental to the chapters which follow.

The proposition is a picture of the facts which it represents. If the fact exists the proposition is true ; otherwise it is false. *The sense of a proposition is the method of its verification.*[2] It is possible to understand a proposition without knowing whether or not it is true because it is possible to know how it could be verified without actually performing the operation necessary for that verification. This is what chiefly distinguishes sense from truth. False propositions have sense as well as true ones ; this would be impossible without a difference between meaning and truth.

[1] i.e. whether the number of real numbers is comparable to any member of the series of transfinite cardinals.

[2] This definition of " sense " is exactly equivalent to " the possibility of the fact pictured " for Logical Positivists.

physically possible vs. 'picturable' ? e.g. Pegasus

There are, however, certain elements of a sign-language which do not represent facts and it is necessary to find a place for them. These are truth-functions and formal concepts.

Truth-functions of propositions are combinations of elementary propositions by means of logical constants. Since all the constants are reducible to conjunction (" . ") and negation (" ∼ "), it is sufficient to show that these signs are used as an adjunct to representation but represent nothing themselves. The truth-functions are a part of the descriptive apparatus of symbolism, but they do not, by themselves, symbolize anything

The structural identity between a proposition and its objective cannot be named, described, or defined. It is a presupposition of the possibility of symbolism and cannot be symbolized in its turn. It can only be shown by seeing that the proposition is really a picture of what it symbolizes. Any characteristic of the structure of propositions and facts must remain inexpressible since structure is itself inexpressible and can only be shown.

The internal essential relations among propositions can be presented only by variables, i.e. by presenting the general forms of these propositions. The knowledge that a variable gives the form of a class of propositions can only be obtained when we understand each of the propositions whose common characteristic is given by the variable. In the last analysis, the understanding of logic, natural science, and mathematics depends on the understanding of the most fundamental propositions, the elementary propositions.

The elementary propositions are univocal representations of the ultimately simple facts. Since the facts are data of experience, it follows that the verification of all propositions reduces finally to the verification of elementary propositions. This verification is immediate, direct, and univocal.

The idea of the logical syntax of a language must be explained (1) in terms of the relation of complex symbols to the simplest possible symbols, and (2) in terms of the relation between a symbol and its objective.

(1) The truth-functions of all kinds are definable in terms of the idea of mutual rejection. A general form of truth-function shows how to develop all truth-functions from the elementary propositions and how to reduce all propositions to elementary ones. This is also accomplished by definitions.

Thus by means of rules of construction, definition, and tautologies, it is possible to determine the meaning of any complex proposition by reducing it to elementary propositions.

(2) The relation of symbol and objective is inexpressible.) Therefore the only way in which an explanation could take place is by way of demonstrative elucidations. These elucidations must contain the undefined symbols. The symbols must be understood before the elucidation is understood. An elucidation is, strictly speaking, nonsense, because it attempts to express what cannot be expressed. It is useful and important, but it does not express anything, and is theoretically superfluous.

There are three principles which I shall assume as known throughout the succeeding parts : (1) the immediate and univocal verification of elementary propositions.

(2) The nature of the inexpressible feature of propositions.

(3) The distinction between essential and accidental generality.

Almost everything that follows depends on these doctrines.

PART II

THEORY OF SCIENTIFIC METHOD

In this part of my essay I shall be concerned with the Positivistic account of natural science. It will be necessary to develop many ideas which do not have a direct bearing on my principal theme. For the sake of completeness this is unavoidable. The ultimate tenet of the Logical Positivists is that the only significant propositions are those of the sciences. As a result, it is pre-eminently necessary to understand clearly what these thinkers conceive science to be. Moreover, since assertions of probability are not empirical in content, it will be necessary to show how they can be given meaning within the limits set by Positivism.

I shall, therefore, concern myself with the three most important matters pertaining to scientific method, probability, induction, and law. Under the last named head I shall consider the nature of experimentation, or the establishment of natural laws. The theory of probability, because of its close connection with logic, and also because it is supposed to be the basis of rational induction, will be given attention first. Then I shall consider the solution of the problem of induction and the consequent speculation about the nature of scientific law.

CHAPTER III

PROBABILITY

The theory of probability is important in the philosophy of the Positivists for several reasons. In the first and perhaps least important place, the Positivists demand that a complete logical theory shall be able to explain all concepts (propositions) which are not directly about *reality* in terms of concepts (propositions) which are about *reality* and about the relations among such concepts. It is necessary, therefore, to give an account of the concept of probability, which means that probability is not to be considered as a primitive idea. Secondly it is necessary to explain probability and its application in such a way as to avoid a purely descriptive theory of science. Thirdly, it is necessary to have such a theory of probability as would avoid all realistic interpretations of natural law.

It must be explained at the outset that there is no one theory unanimously held by all the members of the present positivistic school. There are, in fact, three principal theories current among them, of which only one will be developed in any detail in this essay. There is the revised version of the frequency-theory of R. von Mises. This runs counter to the main doctrines of the school for many reasons; in particular, because it leads to a descriptive theory of science, and because it contains one serious mathematical error. There is also the theory of Hans Reichenbach, which consists of a kind of logical calculus. In this theory truth and falsity are abandoned as absolute concepts, and are the limiting cases of a continuous series of probability-values. This theory likewise conflicts with the fundamental tenet held by most of the members of the school, namely that the truth or falsity of a proposition is an absolutely determinate matter, and that there is no middle ground. Finally, there is the theory that probability is a branch of pure logic. This, in one form or another, is held by Wittgenstein, Carnap,[1] and Waismann, and is unquestionably the one most consonant with the general body of doctrine which characterizes Logical Positivism. Hence, although this theory does not have the unanimous assent of the group, I shall devote more attention to it than to the theories of Reichenbach and von Mises.

The requirements of any theory of probability seem to be as follows : Such a theory must explain the concept and the operations with it, so as to account for its use in the sciences. It must, at the same time, be logically consistent, and, in general, free from any objections which might be raised on logical grounds. The last, but by no means least, requirement is that it must provide a satisfactory basis for the so-called logic of induction.

It is a consequence of the general theory of science which will be presented that the last requirement, i.e. that inductive logic must be satisfactorily founded upon probability, results from a confusion about the nature of scientific method. As will be seen, the major part of science consists of records of individual experimental results and formulæ. There are comparatively few general propositions in the advanced sciences, as, e.g., chemistry and physics, and likewise comparatively few in the less advanced sciences, e.g. biology, for that part which is most definitely determined consists of formulæ of a quantitative or qualitative sort. This is not to say that there are no instances of induction in the sciences as induction is ordinarily conceived, but rather that the number of such instances decreases as a science progresses.[2] As a consequence, the

---

[1] Carnap, perhaps, would now say that the logical theory explains *one* use of the concept of probability.

[2] On this point see Hans Cornelius, " Zur Kritik der wissenschaftlichen Grundbegriffe," *Erkenntnis*, Bd. 11, p. 210 : " Obviously, if we wish to regard the task of induction as consisting of inferring the occurrence of events in the future from the occurrence of a number of cases of similar events in the past, then Russell and Husserl are correct. Such induction always yields only more or less—in general quite a mediocre—probability. And the famous case of the thousand white swans, which yields no guarantee

problem of induction is not what it is ordinarily conceived to be. Ordinarily, the problem of induction is conceived to be : How can problematic inferences of the truth of general propositions be justified from an incomplete number of their instances ? Or, better : How are inferences about the unknown to be justified ? This is, obviously, a misstatement of the problem, (1) if scientific procedure is not inferential in the sense in question, (2) if general propositions can only be established as true when the total number of their instances is known to be true, (3) if science, generally speaking, is not concerned with the truth of general universal propositions. If the positivist theory is correct, all of these conditions hold, and hence the problem must be restated. For the present, then, it is sufficient to know that the theory of probability to be delineated omits any consideration of the logical problem of induction. The theories which have been discussed in the Viennese Circle correspond roughly to the usual grouping of probability-theories, and something more must be said about those theories which have been rejected as being out of the main current of positivistic thought.

There is, to begin with, the logical theory of Hans Reichenbach. It is based upon the consideration that whenever a series of measurements is performed, each member of the series differs somewhat from the other. Following the customary interpretation, this disparity is attributed to errors of observation, or, better, to variations of observation. The doctrine proceeds now as follows : no assertion can be regarded as unconditionally true or false, because of the variation of observation, etc. On the contrary, one can only assign to a given assertion a probability lying between " falsehood " and " truth ", which are limiting

that all swans are white, is only a further example of such unjustified and unjustifiable induction ; a kind of induction which has no place in the exact sciences and can have none. But there are thousands of examples of general propositions which are obtained by induction and which are indisputably correct . . ." Again, p. 212 : " Induction is nothing other than the formulation of experiences in exact concepts and in the general existential judgments expressed with the aid of these concepts."

values. In order to have a propositional calculus which can be profitably employed in science, a many-valued system must be constructed in which each proposition is merely probable. More exactly, the relation in which one proposition stands to another, e.g. implication, will be one of probability. Thus, given a system of laws hypothetically assumed, a proposition P implies a proposition Q to a certain degree of probability. Thus, if $x \epsilon P$, $y \epsilon Q$ then instead of $x_i \epsilon P \supset y_i \epsilon Q$ we have $x_i \epsilon P \supset_m y_i \epsilon Q$, which must be read " implies to the degree m ". The calculus proceeds along the usual lines. It is important to see that probability here, as in Keynes' theory (but for other reasons, of course), is necessarily a primitive notion. It is also clear that the ground upon which the concept of probability is made fundamental is the denial of the absoluteness of truth and falsity and that this denial is based upon the variations in the several results of measurement.

If these variations are allegedly due to errors of observation, truth and falsity are surreptitiously assumed, for the idea of one error implies the existence of a fixed truth which has escaped attention. If the variations are really ultimate, it seems as arbitrary to assign probability-numbers to the propositions describing them as to assign the ordinary truth-values, because the upper and lower limits of probability are 1 and 0 respectively. These limits require some interpretation and are usually regarded as " the true " and " the false ". At all events, they are fixed limits. If the variations of the data are ultimate, it is difficult to understand how any probability-number can be assigned to a given proposition. Moreover, the substitution of probability for truth and falsehood seems to depend on a play upon words. If one says " ' the weather is summer-like ' is true to a degree p ", one might just as well, on the same data and methods of measurement, have said " ' the weather is summer-like to a degree p ' is true ". This method of introducing the concept of probability appears, therefore, to be highly unsatisfactory.

The frequency-theory of R. von Mises [1] has somewhat greater plausibility. In it, probability is regarded as the limit which a series of statistical frequencies approaches when the number of frequencies increases without limit. This theory purports to be purely empirical. It will have nothing to do with the so-called probability *a priori*. On the other hand, it limits statements of probability to what seems to be a very small class of cases by means of definitions and other requirements.

In this theory probability can be mentioned only when there is a collective (*Kollectiv*), i.e. when there is " a mass phenomenon, a repeating process, or, in general, a series of observations satisfying certain requirements, which series one thinks of as being extended without limit ". [2] The conditions which the collective must satisfy are : (1) " the relative frequencies of the character (under consideration) must possess a definite limiting-value, (2) the limit must remain invariant if a part of the elements is arbitrarily selected from the total." [3] This second condition is called the " principle of irregularity ". It is now possible to speak of the probability of the occurrence of a definite character within a collective under consideration as the limiting value of the relative frequency of the occurrence of the character, when the number of elements is imagined to be increased without limit.

The only way in which to derive such values in concrete cases is, of course, by means of a statistical investigation. It is clear, on this theory, that probability-values cannot be calculated with the method of pure mathematics, or of other sciences. [4]

Many objections to this theory occur to one at once. The theory is obviously unfit to take care of many instances of *bona fide* probability and hence is limited, it would seem, to

[1] R. von Mises, *Wahrscheinlichkeit, Statistik, und Wahrheit*, Wien, 1928. See also the criticism by Benjamin Ginzburg, *Philosophical Review*, May, 1934, pp. 7–14.

[2] von Mises, op cit., pp. 11–13.   [3] von Mises, op. cit., p. 29.

[4] von Mises, op. cit., p. 180.

purely descriptive formulations. The mention of a limiting value, which is not a descriptive concept, but a mathematical one, does not save the theory from this limitation. The prediction of a celestial event of a kind which had never occurred before would be out of the question without introducing a whole set of arbitrary assumptions from the sciences, which is forbidden by the requirements of the theory.[1] The idea of a set of equi-probable cases so determined because of some common property which they possess would simply be non-interpretable within von Mises's theory. And these two exceptions are sufficient to condemn the theory on the ground of its narrowness. For there are evidently two kinds of probability in the sciences. One is ordinary statistical probability which the frequency-theory deals with fairly well. The other is the probability of an event based on some knowledge derived from the sciences. An example of this sort is the probability that a certain number will turn up when a die is thrown. The statistical theory treats both kinds in the same way, whereas it is evident that one can say with conviction that the probability of throwing a six with a die whose faces are of *equal* areas, which are *exact* squares, whose centre of gravity *is* the intersection of the diagonals, etc., is 1/6. This conviction is based upon considerations other than statistics, and it is clear that the scientific use of probability includes cases similar to that of the die. When, for example, an astronomer states that certain intra-stellar phenomena are probable on data obtained from the exterior of the star, he reasons somewhat in this manner : if some of the conditions satisfying certain laws of terrestrial phenomena are known to exist on the exterior of a star, then it is probable to such and such a degree that the consequence of these conditions obtaining on the earth will also obtain within the interior of the star. While some of the data in the example may well be statistical, it is quite clear that other parts of the data are not. In particular, the appeal to laws, i.e. to

[1] von Mises, op. cit., p. 180.

formulæ *almost perfectly realized*, is not to anything statistical in the proper sense of the word.

A *more serious objection* to the statistical theory has been raised by Waismann [1] on purely logical grounds. This is the mathematical error to which I referred. Probability is defined as the fixed limit which the relative frequency approaches as the number of instances increases without limit. The notion of infinity introduced at this point is questionable. For it is clear that in the mathematical use the term (excepting, of course, the highly doubtful theory of alephs and omegas) is not applicable to an empirical series. Waismann writes, " only series of a definite extension are presented in a statistical observation. Now, in order to obtain its concept of probability, the statistical theory goes beyond this fact and imagines, e.g. that the series of die-throws is infinite, that is applies the concept of the mathematical number-sequence to this series. Now one thing is clear ; the infinite is always the law which generates a sequence and nothing more. Indeed, it is a consideration completely familiar to every mathematician that operation with infinite series is nothing other than an operation with the laws which generate the series. We resort to this law alone if we speak of the convergence of a sequence, and not to the factual arrangement of the terms of which we can survey only a finite number. Briefly, a mathematical series is something essentially regular, the properties of which we completely survey. In comparison, nothing is so evident about a statistical series as its irregularity, and this demonstrates at once that it is not a mathematical concept. Hence, whoever requires of a convergent series of numbers that it be constructed without a rule—and this is the essential point—demands the obviously impossible, for neither the mathematical nor the empirical series could satisfy such a condition. On the contrary, it must be clearly stated that a statistical series does not possess the properties of a

[1] " Logische Analyse des Wahrscheinlichkeitsbegriffs," *Erkenntnis,* Bd. 1, pp. 231-2.

mathematical sequence, and that we cannot transfer the property of the accidental and unpredictable from the empirical forms to the mathematical ones without destroying the *a priori* and necessary characteristic which is the property of mathematics. If the irregularity-principle of von Mises is formulated (so as to hold for the case) that every sub-series, however chosen, approaches the same limiting-value as the total series, then the principle, literally interpreted, is certainly false. For among the sub-series there certainly exist some which approach another limiting-value or do not converge. The only way to meet all these difficulties is to see: that the irregularity-principle cannot be formulated; that it is senseless to exhibit a mathematical series and subsequently to explain that such a series obeys no law of formation; finally that, in an exact language, the non-existence of regularities is expressed by the fact that laws are not formed and not by the statement of an axiom of irregularity." [1]

The logical and empirical objections to the frequency-theory of von Mises render it an unsatisfactory basis for the calculus and application of probability. It is also objectionable on the ground of the general tenets of Positivism. For the statistical theory cannot, unless it is used only descriptively, avoid metaphysical assumptions. The ideal limit toward which a statistical series is supposed to converge must have being in some realm or other. If we suppose that its existence is to be found in the purely mathematical system, we have violated the conditions of the theory [2] and have at the same time implicitly assumed that mathematical existence and empirical existence are somehow comparable. For we assume that the factual observations and calculations approach an ideal mathematical limit. This Platonism is quite inconsistent with an empirical philosophy. On the other hand, if we

[1] And conversely, that the existence of regularity is expressed by the formulation of laws and not by a law of causality. Cf. Wittgenstein, op. cit., *supra*, t. 36.361.
[2] von Mises, op. cit., *supra*, p. 180

suppose that the mathematical limit actually has a factual manifestation which we can only roughly approximate, we must assume the existence of some noumenal realm beyond the reach of direct observation. This, too, is intolerable in a positivistic theory of nature.

The only theory consonant with Positivism is one in which probability is a *point of departure*, rather than an ideal limit to which the factual connection of things approximates. This can be explained briefly now, but must wait for a detailed exposition in its proper place. The ordinary statistical conception of probability represents it as a limit similar to the limiting concepts of geometry. If geometry can be applied to the world by the use of ideal limiting concepts, why cannot probability theory employ the same devices? If empirical surfaces can be replaced by geometrical surfaces whose proportions are entirely regular and in conformity with certain known laws; if laws of nature can be formulated in algebraic equations and hence further laws deduced, then why is it not possible to use the mathematical concepts of limit-values in the theory of probability? Just as the natural law or the geometrical connections are the limits which the observed facts approximate but never reach because of errors of observation, so the concept of the limit of a frequency is an ideal entity toward which the observed frequencies approach with ever increasing exactitude, as our measurements and observations become more exact and greater in number.

The argument, although very old and familiar, will not stand under a close scrutiny. It is well known that many systems of geometry and of mechanics exist, any of which can be used in the description of nature. It is not inconceivable that two wholly distinct geometrical systems or systems of mechanics could be used, with equal success, for the description of natural phenomena. We know how frequently it has been the case that two distinct systems, for which transformation-formulæ exist, have been used in the description of nature and in the formulation of its laws.[1] Which of two such systems is the real system to which the factual connections actually correspond ? It is clear that we cannot say, and this shows at once that the explanation of idealization just outlined is of doubtful validity. As Waismann (who owes this to Wittgenstein) has said : " The usual conception is this : e.g. if we measure the ratio of circumference and diameter of a number of circles, we obtain numerical values, which are inexact, but which become more exact as we approximate finer methods of observation. We then say : ' The number π is the ideal limit to which the results of measurements approach with unlimited, increasing exactitude.' Is this correct ? We hesitate at the word ' exact '. When do we call a measurement exact ? For example, if in spite of the greatest care the measurement of a circle yields another value for this ratio, we never say : ' The propositions of geometry are false ; experience teaches that π is not the same value for all circles,' but we say : ' We have deceived ourselves, our measuring rod has been deformed, the figure was not a circle, and so on.' That is to say, we hold the number π constant, irrespective of the measurement, and regard it as the criterion of correct measurement of circles. The number π is the measuring rod with which we determine the quality of the observation. Hence it is just the converse of the usual conception. The number π is not the ideal limit-value which we learn to know more exactly by means of factual measurements, but it is the previously given measurement rod by which we judge the degree of exactitude of a measurement. The propositions of geometry are a system of rules applied to factual measurements by which we determine, e.g., whether a given line is straight, whether a given body is a sphere, etc. . . . These rules are the syntax of the concepts with which we describe the factual spatial connections. . . . Idealization does *not* mean that the factual measurements are refined

[1] See Nicod, J., " Geometry of the Sensible World," in *Foundations of Geometry and Induction*, New York, 1930, pt. i, ch. 2.

in thought without limit. It means, rather, that the observations are described by concepts of a previously given syntax (and with a syntax which is capable of unlimited exactitude). One does not approximate the ideal, one rather proceeds from it." [1]

It will be seen later how these considerations apply to the description of nature in natural laws as such. At present it is important only to see that the theory of probability must offer an ideal set of concepts and operations from which to proceed in the determination of regularities in nature. Probability is, then, the method of determining whether or not laws exist.

The theory which is the most satisfactory for Positivism is the work of Wittgenstein and Waismann, but has further roots in the work of von Kries. [2] It begins with the consideration that probability expresses a relationship between two propositions, that is that one proposition is probable to such and such a degree on the data supplied by some other proposition. In order to determine in what the relationship consists the matrix method developed in an earlier chapter must be considered. Given two propositions, p, q, there is the following matrix :—

p	q
T	T
T	F
F	T
F	F

Following Wittgenstein, the truth-possibilities which verify the proposition will be called its truth-grounds. Then if Tp is the number of truth-grounds of p, and Tpq those common to p and q, the probability of q given p is Tpq/Tp. Thus, in the case where p and q are elementary and hence

[1] Compare Wittgenstein, op. cit., *supra*, 6.341. " Mechanics determine a form of description by saying ' All propositions in the description of the world must be obtained in a given manner from a number of given propositions—the mechanical axioms '."

[2] J. von Kries, *Die Principien der Wahrscheinlichkeitsrechnung*, Freiburg, 1886.

independent propositions, the probability of q given p is :—
$$Tpq/Tp = 1/2.^1$$

This schematism, although undoubtedly logically correct, is, nevertheless, too abstract to yield a usable theory of probability. It is necessary, therefore, to turn to Waismann's improvement of the theory.

We begin with the notion of a Spielraum (field). A proposition is said to determine a Spielraum if it describes a situation as being true or false. The situation is the Spielraum.[2] Thus, " The die falls with the 6-face up " is a proposition which determines a Spielraum. Two propositions may determine the same Spielraum (hereafter to be called field) in which case they are formally identical. The field of one proposition may include the field of another, or it may overlap that of another, or it may wholly exclude that of another. These relations may be thought of as topological ; i.e. as Euler-diagrams. The three cases would then be illustrated as :—

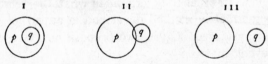

I. If one field p encloses another q (i.e. if all truth-grounds of p are also truth-grounds of q), then the proposition describing p entails that describing q, or it may be said q follows from p.

II. If one field p partially overlaps another q (if some of the truth-grounds of p are also truth-grounds of q), then the proposition p gives a certain probability to the proposition q.

---

[1] $Tp = Tq$ because any two elementary propositions are logically independent of one another, and hence independent for probability.

[2] Cf. Wittgenstein, op. cit., *supra*, prop. 4.463. " The truth-conditions determine the range, which is left to the facts by the proposition." Thus, if p means aRb and if q means ϕa, then the Spielraum of $Pv\sim q$, i.e. of $aRbv\sim\phi a$ allows a total variation

$$p.q$$
$$p.\sim q$$
$$\sim p.\sim q \text{ but excludes } \sim p.q;$$

i.e. all these variations lie within the range (Spielraum) determined by $pv\sim q$. $\sim p.q$, however, lies outside that range.

III. If one field p lies wholly outside another field q (if no truth-grounds of p are truth-grounds of q), then p contradicts q.[1]

We have three relationships among fields and hence among the propositions describing the fields, namely *inclusion*, *overlapping*, and *exclusion*, hence *entailment*, *probability*, and *contradiction*.

The concept of the measure of a field may now be introduced. Let p be a field or a proposition describing the field. Then $\mu(p)$ is the measure of the field p. The measure (p) must fulfil the following requirements :—

1. $\mu(p)$ is a real positive number.
2. If p is contradictory, $\mu(p) = 0$, and if p is tautological, $\mu(p) = 1$.
3. If p and q are incompatible, then $\mu(p\lor q) = \mu(p) + \mu(q)$.

A propositional measure is not completely determined by these conditions, since measure-numbers can be generated by the use of different systems of measurement. The probability of q given p is then defined by the ratio :—

$$\text{Prob. } q \text{ given } p = \frac{df. \; \mu(p.q)}{\mu(p)}$$

In terms of topological analogy, the probability of q given p is the ratio of the magnitude of the field common to p and q and the magnitude of the field of p.

It is easy to see that the entire calculus of probabilities as given, e.g., by Keynes, follows from this definition. Thus—

$$\text{Prob. } p \text{ given } p = 1$$
$$\text{Prob. } p \text{ given not-}p = 0$$

---

[1] The only case in which two fields are exclusive is the case in which $p = r.a$ and $q = s.\sim a$. If p and q have no internal parts in common (e.g. if $p = a.b.c.d$ and $q = e.f.g.h$), or if p and q are two elementary propositions, then p and q have at least one truth-ground in common. Hence, their fields overlap to that extent. For the field is the variation left to the facts by the proposition. Hence, two elementary propositions do not exclude the possibility that both may be simultaneously true. Therefore, the only case of exclusive fields is $p = r.a$, $q = s.\sim a$. Q.E.D. It should perhaps be added that if $p = fx$ and $q = gx$, i.e. $p = $ "x is red" and $q = $ "x is blue", then $p.q$ is impossible, because p and q are mutually exclusive, but in a different way from $a.\sim a$. Wittgenstein has treated of this possibility in *Proc. Arist. Soc.*, 1931.

$$\text{Prob. } p \text{ given } (pvq) = \frac{\mu(\,(p)\,.\,(pvq)\,)}{\mu(pvq)} = \frac{2}{3}$$
$$(\text{where } \mu(p) = \mu(q)\,)$$

If a group of propositions $P_1, P_2 \ldots P_n$ is now taken, which, it may be said, constitute all the relevant knowledge concerning the occurrence of q, then—

$$\text{Prob. } q \text{ given } P_1 \ldots, \text{ i.e. } \pi P_n = \frac{\mu(\,(q)\,.\quad(\pi P_n)\,)}{\mu(\pi P_n)} \quad {}^{1}$$

Again, there are three distinguishable cases, namely probability of q given $\pi P_n = 1$, probability of q given $\pi P_n = 0$, probability of q given $\pi P_n = x/y$ (some real positive number such that $0 < x/y < 1$). In the first case, all the conditions under which q occurs are known. In the second case none of the conditions under which q occurs is known, i.e. nothing of the sum of the knowledge is relevant to the occurrence of q. More strictly, if the conditions under which q does not occur are known, and if these conditions are πP_n, then the probability of q given $\pi P_n = 0$. If probability of q given $P_{n-1}.P_n =$ the probability of q given P_{n-1}, then P_n is irrelevant to q and so on.[2]

The third case is the one which is usually regarded as that of probability.[3] As Waismann says : " Probability begins at the point where we know something about the conditions under which an event occurs, but where this knowledge is not sufficient to construct propositions with certainty." [4] In this instance we say that a determined and definite part of the conditions under which an event has occurred have been fulfilled. Thus, to return to a former example, if the nature and number of elements and radiations, etc., in the

---

[1] πP_n means " the logical product, $P_1.P_2.P_3$ ". Thus πP_n is all the knowledge relevant to the occurrence of q.

[2] See Keynes, *Treatise on Probability*, p. 55.

[3] Although the three cases are all, strictly speaking, within the definition and must be considered in practice for (1) there may have been an error in considering the conditions exhaustive, and (2) there must be some means within the theory of probability to distinguish between the probability of an event theoretically known as certain on the basis of an identical law and the probability of an event excluded by such a law.

[4] Waismann, op. cit., *supra*, p. 237.

exterior of the sun are known, and if the laws governing the behaviour of such things on the earth are known, and if no evidence is at hand which would render the argument by analogy from terrestrial to solar conditions invalid, then the astronomer reasons that the condition C on the interior is probable on the total data, πP_n, known to him, or that some of the circumstances under which C occurs have been fulfilled. Or, to take a simpler example, if, other things being equal, the centre of gravity of a die is known to be shifted from the geometrical centre, then the probability of a 6 turning up is $<$ or $>$ $1/6$. Here some of the conditions under which a 6 turns up (or does not turn up) are known.

It must be clearly understood that an event itself is neither probable nor improbable, for the event will occur or not, *tertium non datur*. Probability is not expressed by a proposition, but is a connection between propositions. The probability-proposition, says Wittgenstein, is an extract from other propositions. It may easily be seen, on this view, how this is so. The knowledge we have consists of propositions known or believed to be true. The statement of probability is a proposition about the relationships of propositions known to those believed on the basis of what is known.

It is equally clear that the theory presented here is not a subjective theory since it makes no reference, not even an implicit one, to any subjective phenomena as such. " It merely expresses the logical relation between two propositions." Those who support subjective theories usually consider the probability-number as an assessment of the degree of rational belief attaching to a given assertion. This degree of belief has no place in the present theory. The only point at which one can conceivably regard this theory as subjective is where it asserts that probability is a relation between known propositions and those merely entertained. It is clear, however, that this is a misnomer, for the probability is the numerical relation itself and not any essentially subjective phenomenon. This theory does not tell us the degree in which we believe, nor that in which we ought rationally to believe. The assessment of probability is the statement of a relationship *a priori* or *a posteriori* between a given kind of proposition and that kind of proposition usually associated with it. This (as is evident) is not subjective in the sense in which a theory of probability is commonly said to be subjective.

Probability thus turns out to be a numerical relationship. The calculus of probabilities accordingly becomes a branch of pure logic. From the definition

$$q \text{ Probable on } p = \frac{\mu(q)\mu(p)}{\mu(p)}$$

all the axioms and theorems follow.

For example, the probability of avb given h is $a + b/h = a/h + b/h - ab/h$, which when translated into the definition, becomes :—

$$\frac{\mu(a + b)\mu(h)}{\mu(h)} = \frac{\mu(a)\mu(h)}{\mu(h)} + \frac{\mu(b)\mu(h)}{\mu(h)} - \frac{\mu(ab)\mu(h)}{\mu(h)}$$

which can be verified by a little reflection.[1]

The test of any theory of probability is whether it can be applied significantly to empirical data and *whether it has a solution for the paradoxes*. The first question will be considered later. At the present time the logical consistency of the theory must be considered, for a necessary condition (but not a sufficient condition) of consistency is the elimination of paradoxes. The necessary and sufficient conditions of consistency of the theory of probability are (1) avoidance of paradoxes and (2) deduction from purely logical or arithmetical theorems. The first is equivalent to the possibility of a constant application to actual concrete cases. (Concrete in this usage does not exclude geometrical examples.)

One of the best known paradoxes is that of Bertrand.[2]

---

[1] The proof that probability is a branch of logic is given briefly in Th. Radakovic, " Die Axiome der Elementargeometrie u. der Aussagenkalkül," *Monatsheft ef. Math. u. Phys.*, 1929.

[2] See J. M. Keynes, op. cit., *supra*, pp. 47–8.

What is the probability that a chord drawn in a circle at random will be less than the side of an inscribed equilateral triangle ? We can make several assumptions. First, let one end be fixed and the direction chosen at random. The probability will be 2/3, because the circle at any fixed point will be divided into three equal parts by the vertex of the inscribed equilateral at that point. Then assume that the end and direction is chosen at random ; the probability is 1/2. Finally, assume that the midpoint of the chord is chosen at random. This point must be farther from the centre than half the radius if the chord is less than the side of the inscribed figure. Here is the probability of 3/4 because the area of the circle beyond 1/2 the radius is 3/4 of the total area.

The paradox is obviously that, from different assumptions, we get different probabilities for the same occurrence. Waismann [1] thinks that the paradox can be resolved in the following way : " . . . a class of chords cannot be measured without further assumptions. The several solutions of the problem correspond to just as many specializations of the metric. Our conception (of probability) suggests this result as the natural one, indeed, from the beginning to the expected consequences, it removes the appearance of paradox from those facts."

The metric is the system of measurement of fields which is employed. We begin with a metric and calculate the *a priori* probabilities on the basis chosen. If the experiment is then performed by allowing a rod to fall upon a circle, the posterior probabilities will be either (1) one of the results expected from one of the possible metrics chosen, or (2) another probability. In the former case the metric whose prior probabilities are realized in the posterior probabilities will be considered as the correct one. In the latter something else must be taken into account, such as, e.g., physical factors. From the logical point of view, this seems to be

[1] Op. cit., *supra*, p. 241.

satisfactory. Most of the paradoxes of geometrical and other abstract probabilities are of a kind similar to the one cited.

The use of the calculus of probabilities presents another problem. Two distinct cases arise. On the one hand there are mere relative frequencies of events, the mechanism of which is unknown. Vital statistics provide many examples of this case. In this instance it is easily seen that the probability and relative frequency coincide completely, since *no* laws, conditions, etc., are known on the basis of which a metric might be formed. On the other hand, there is a whole class of cases provided by games of chance. Here certain conditions are known such that prior probabilities can be formulated. For example, it is known that the equality of area on the surface of a die, together with the geometrically central position of the centre of gravity, renders the cases equally probable. In a word, there is thus formed a metric derived from experience and spatial measurements, etc., such that equi-probable cases can be designated on the basis of which prior probabilities are calculable. In the instance in question the calculus can be applied, and the statement made that all the circumstances known, including the natural laws hypothetically assumed, give to the occurrence of one of the events no more probability than to the occurrence of the others.[1]

The formation of prior probabilities is not made, of course, on an arbitrary basis. Without a dependable system of measurement and without a system of laws already formulated, it is impossible to assign prior probabilities. It might be said at this point that we must depend upon statistical frequencies in the last analysis after all, and that, as a consequence, we have not really avoided using the same foundations as the statistical theory. In the sense that recurrences in experience must be depended on for knowledge of regularity in nature, the charge is well founded. It is not, however, as potent as it sounds. For the point of divergence from the statistical theory is the same as before.

---

[1] Wittgenstein, op. cit., *supra*, 5.154.

While the assignment of prior probabilities depends upon experience, some of which is statistical, the meaning of probability remains the same. It is a point of departure for further investigation of nature. Once it is established that experience and laws yield a metric with which to assign prior and equal probabilities, the calculus may be applied with confidence. Then, if the experimental results agree with the calculated probabilities, it may be said that the results of experiment are independent of the circumstances unknown to us. In case the experimental results do not agree with the calculation, it is said that the results of experiment are not independent of the unknown facts. The use of the calculus is not so much to anticipate the natural phenomena as to discover the existence of unknown circumstances on which the phenomena are dependent. It is well to remark that dependence and independence have a technical significance. Thus, if the probability of a_1, given a_2, and the data h, equals the probability of a_1, given h; and if the probability of a_2, given a_1, and the data h equals the probability of a_2, given h, then the probability of a_2, given h, and a_1, given h, are independent. That is, if $a_1/a_2h = a_2/h$ and $a_1/a_1h = a_2h$, then a_1/h and a_2h are independent.[1]

The calculus and concept of probability is a system of terms and rules by means of which the relations among propositions are assessed. Just as a system of geometry does not actually describe the spatial connection of objects, but rather is a set of rules according to which these relations are interpreted, so this calculus does not describe the facts, but rather yields a set of rules by means of which the connections of facts are to be judged. Just as that geometry is chosen which yields the simplest description of nature, i.e. the one which has the fewest deviations, so the metric of probability is chosen for the same reason.

When the *a priori* probabilities are realized in subsequent experimentation, that is when the *a priori* and the *a posteriori* probabilities substantially agree, we say that the distribution

[1] J. M. Keynes, op. cit., *supra*, p. 138.

of events is a matter of " chance ". Otherwise we search for " laws ". Neither " chance " nor " laws " are objective in the sense that they are part of the structure of nature as such. But chance or law are not subjective in the sense that chance is a mere gauge of our ignorance and law the gauge of our knowledge. The point is that laws are the formulæ which yield the least irregularities in the description of nature. In this sense they are neither subjective or objective as these words are ordinarily conceived. Likewise, " chance " is the expression of the fact that we have formulated no laws. There are no " objective " chances in the sense that processes do not follow some routine. It is rather that this routine is unknown to us, or that the routine yields a distribution corresponding to what can be calculated in prior probabilities. The degree of probability determines whether we should speak of chance or law.

This is the theory which is most satisfactorily adapted to the needs of Logical Positivism. It is, as has been shown, a logical theory, for the concept and the rules by means of which it is employed are theorems of pure logic and arithmetic. It is, moreover, free from inconsistencies of a purely logical nature. Probability does not remain a primitive idea, but is derived from the fundamental notion of the truth and falsehood of propositions and from the notion of number. In agreement with Keynes and other writers, Wittgenstein and Waismann think of probability as a logical relation among the propositions of our knowledge. The principal advance of this theory over others is that it states explicitly what this relation is. The fundamental sign a/h in Keynes's system is a primitive idea which satisfies the axioms conceived as functions of it. The definition, by means of the concept of a metric, of this sign by $\frac{\mu(a.h)}{\mu(h)}$ that is, the ratio of the measure of ground h and consequent a to the measure of the ground h alone, renders the concept no longer a primitive idea, but a derivative of purely logical primitives. This, undoubtedly, is an advance.

The application of this concept is possible in a greater number of instances than is the case with the statistical theory, and recommends itself on this ground. For the statistical theory, it is quite impossible to assess the prior probabilities of such cases as those of which examples have been given, without the introduction of special axioms or without inconsistency. The present theory has no difficulties of this sort. It is, however, limited to cases to which the application of a metric is possible. And this, it seems to me, is a serious objection.

This limitation prevents the use of probabilities in all kinds of non-quantitative cases. Such cases occur very frequently in the sciences of anthropology and psychology. For example, take the complicated set of inferences which constitute *The Golden Bough*. This book is admittedly based upon probabilities. Concerning its inferential structure, Sir James Frazer writes : " . . . if we can show that a barbarous custom, like that of the priesthood of Nemi, has existed elsewhere ; if we can detect the motives which led to its institution ; if we can prove that these motives have operated widely, perhaps universally, in human society, producing in varied circumstances a variety of institutions specifically different, but generically alike ; if we can show lastly that these very motives, with some of their derivative institutions, were actually at work in classical antiquity, then we may fairly infer that at the remoter age the same motives gave birth to the priesthood of Nemi. Such an inference, in default of direct evidence as to how the priesthood did actually arise, can never amount to demonstration. But it will be more or less probable according to the degree of completeness with which it fulfils the conditions I have indicated." [1] This example of the use of probabilities in scientific work illustrates a legitimate case of probable inference. With some reflection it will become evident that the use of a metric is quite impossible here. A quantitative metric directly applied is, of course,

[1] Sir James Frazer, *The Golden Bough*, abridged edition, New York, 1922.

out of the question. The indirect application of such a metric would involve the determination that certain instances were of equal, lesser, or greater magnitude than others. Such a quantification can be made only by an arbitrary convention or by the explicit introduction of axioms as to the nature of an instance, say, of magical practice. Neither method is at all satisfactory, and both are really inconsistent with the nature of measurement. As a consequence, this kind of probability is ruled out. But it is the sort most frequently employed in the less advanced sciences in which quantitative measurement has not yet found a place. Is it to be said, then, that the use of probable inference in these sciences is illegitimate ? If so, that is tantamount to saying that they can never advance to a more exact state of knowledge, for it is well known that such sciences depend upon probable knowledge more than the exact branches of knowledge. However, if the possibility that such sciences can advance is admitted, then a theory of probability which disallows the use of a non-quantitative assessment of the relative value of data, which cannot be quantitatively appraised, must be regarded as inadequate.

An even more serious difficulty arises in any application of the theory under consideration. It is well known that the probability of an event may remain substantially the same, irrespective of the number of instances under consideration. Thus, there is the probability that a die will fall showing the 6-face 1/6 of the time. This may be assessed *a priori* by the determination of equi-probable cases using the metric. *A posteriori*, however, the probabilities may be 1/6 for ten throws or for ten thousand throws, yet the assessment based upon the latter is more fully trusted than the one based upon the former. This theory gives no reason for trusting the one rather than the other, although it is clear that it is one of the tasks of the theory of probability to present criteria of its correct employment.[1] It may be

[1] See also E. Zilsel's remarks in *Erkenntnis*, Bd. 1, p. 263, on a similar point.

objected that this is the problem of induction rather than that of probability. To this the rejoinder is obvious. The attempt to separate the two problems is futile and misguided. As a consequence, the theory as it is presented is undoubtedly correct, from the standpoint of logical rigor. It is simply a branch of the theory of probability, and not the entire theory itself.

Waismann's answer to this objection seems to be singularly weak. He says : " It is clear to us that the probability-calculus can teach nothing about whether this relationship will likewise hold in the future. We do not know that, and if we assume it, it is a conjecture based on induction, just like every other conjecture. To investigate the justification of a conjecture can never be the task of the probability-calculus." [1]   But this is only true on the assumption that the entire theory of probability coincides with the probability calculus, an assumption which will be found to be unjustified.

For the problem is simply this : The probability of an event can be increased by the number of its previous instances,[2] as well as by the completeness of knowledge of the conditions under which it occurs, and some branch of the theory is required to tell how the former can be so. The theory of the metric does not apply to the number of instances at all, but only to the conditions of which the event in question is the consequent. Hence, it is an incomplete theory. This is a more serious defect than is evident on first view, for the relation between the calculated and the observed values of a probability is one of the principal concerns of the theory of probable inference. Waismann's theory has very little that is satisfactory to say about it.

[1] Op. cit., *supra*, p. 241, note.
[2] Jean Nicod, *The Logical Problem of Induction*, p. 281.

CHAPTER IV

INDUCTION

Perhaps the future development of positivistic thought in Europe and America will present solutions of the difficulties involved in the theories of probability current in the Circle. It is not, it seems to me, too much to expect a wholly satisfactory theory of this subject within the limits of the principal doctrines of the school.

I cannot believe that similar success will attend the solution of the induction problem. Here the difficulties are so great as to involve a surrender, or at least a profound alteration, of doctrines fundamental to the school. This is because the solution offered by the Logical Positivists depends on an analysis of general propositions which in turn depends on the doctrine of elementary propositions. This doctrine was not demonstrated.

The usual formulation and treatment of induction should be brought before the reader in order that he may see, by contrast, the full significance of the positivistic doctrines concerning it. I shall begin, therefore, with a brief review of the subject.

It should first be noticed that certain solutions of the problem of induction are wholly out of the question for Positivism. The idea of necessary connection or causation has already been eliminated by the logical theories of Wittgenstein. The facts are independent of one another. The existence of one fact does not involve the existence of any other. Hence necessary connection is out of the question. Likewise, there is no postulate of empirical thought which guarantees a regularity among events, because there is no absolute principle of invariance in the form of empirical thought. This eliminates the Kantian method of treating the problem. Finally, the world is not a *system*, but only a set of facts. This eliminates the Hegelian method. There remain only (1) the logical method of Keynes, and (2) the possibility of eliminating the induction problem by analysis.

Induction has been described in one of the classic treatments of the subject as the process of discovering and proving general propositions.[1] What this means obviously depends upon the way in which a general proposition is conceived. That is, there would be important differences in theories of induction, depending upon the interpretation given to the general proposition. For example, the conception of the general proposition as a sum or product of individual propositions should yield a different inductive theory from the conception of it as a denial of the negatives of these. Thus, if $(x) . \phi x = df. \sim (\exists x) \sim \phi x$ and if $(\exists x) \phi x = df. \sim (x) \sim \phi x$, then $(x) \phi x$ would be true if it were known that there was no case of $\sim \phi x$. From this it could not be inferred that $(\exists x) \phi x$ for it is clear that $\sim (\exists x) \sim \phi x$ and $\sim (\exists x) \sim \phi x$ can both be true on this theory. Such a theory would have to treat every inductive generalization of the form $(x) \phi x$ as requiring $(\exists x) \phi x$ as a true premise in order to consider the induction to be initially possible. I shall not pause over these details.

If induction is considered as being the establishment of general propositions of existential import, then it is essential to know what kinds of such propositions are usually involved in induction.

This résumé will be limited to those kinds usually discussed in the traditional treatment of the subject. They are : " If x is a ϕ then x is also an f for every x," and " If x is a ϕ then x is an f for at least one x ". When these are the results of induction they are usually described respectively as reasonings " from these cases to all cases of the kind in question " and " from these cases to at least one case of the kind in question ". Perhaps the best treatment of the problem of induction has been done by John Maynard Keynes. He summarizes the older theories and offers his

[1] Mill, J. S., *System of Logic*, London, 1843, Bk. III, ch. i, sec. 2.

own solution which is generally regarded as the most important given at the present time. I shall give a résumé of his account. This will serve to orient the reader as well as could briefly be done. Following Keynes [1] I shall call that character which a number of individuals have in common the positive analogy and express it in accordance with custom as $(x)\phi x \begin{subarray}{l} x = a_n \\ x = a_r \end{subarray}$; that character ϕ' which is to be possessed by at least one individual and not to be possessed by at least one other individual is called the negative analogy and is expressed by $(\exists x)\phi' x . (\exists x) \sim \phi' x \begin{subarray}{l} x = a_s \quad x = a_t \\ x = a_r \quad x = a_r \end{subarray}$. ϕ and ϕ' can represent indifferently an individual character or a set of such characters. Then $(x)\phi x \supset fx$ and $(\exists x)\phi x \supset fx$ will represent the two kinds of inductive generalization mentioned above.

There are several cases which arise in the discussion of induction but the discussion, without any great loss of generality, may be restricted to two of them, the perfect analogy and the general case of imperfect analogy, Suppose, then, that there is a generalization of the form $\phi x \supset_x fx$, e.g. "all men are mortal", or "all reflected light is polarized".

Let it be supposed further that the knowledge of the examined instances of the generalization is complete. It is known, then, that nothing is true of all the examined instances which is not included in the generalization; that is, it is known that all the known instances of ϕ are instances of f and that $\sim (\exists \psi)\phi x . \psi x \supset_x fx$, or that $\sim (\exists \psi)\phi x \supset_x fx . \psi x$. We have here what is known as a perfect analogy. Keynes then states that any perfect analogy is a valid basis of a generalization if there is a principle which eliminates spatio-temporal differences as unessential. This principle is what Keynes calls the uniformity of nature.

Perfect analogies rarely occur. The more usual case is the one with the following characteristics: We know that $\phi x \supset fx$ holds for the examined instances $x_1 \ldots x_n$; our knowledge of the examined instances is incomplete, that is,

[1] Keynes, J. M., *Treatise on Probability*, pp. 223 ff.

there may be other analogies as yet undiscovered; there are analogies known to be true of some of the examined instances and not known to be false of any. If ψ represents these last-mentioned analogies, then we say that $\phi x \supset_x fx$ is probable, given $(x) \begin{matrix} x = a_n \\ \phi x . \phi_1 \, x \supset fx \\ x = a_1 \end{matrix}$, and $(\exists x) \begin{matrix} x = a_s \\ \phi' x . \\ x = a_r \end{matrix} (\exists x) \begin{matrix} x = a_s \\ \sim \phi' x \\ x = a_r \end{matrix}$ and $(x) \begin{matrix} x = a_s \\ \psi x. \\ x = a_r \end{matrix}$

There is, then, a known positive analogy ϕ_1 for all the examined instances not taken into account by the generalization, a known negative analogy, and some sub-analogies true of some of the instances and not known to be false of any. We increase the probability of such an induction by reducing the superfluous resemblances ϕ_1 (which reduces the possibility of a plurality of causes), by increasing the differences ϕ' among the instances (which reduces the possibility that there are analogies common to all the instances which have been overlooked), and by reducing the sub-analogies (which tends to reduce the possibility that the known positive analogy is less than the total positive analogy).

As is obvious, this is done by increasing the number of instances and by increasing our information concerning the known instances. The mere number of instances is never important *per se*, but only in so far as this increase reveals a decrease of the superfluous positive analogy, and an increase in the negative analogy. The principle of increasing the negative analogy is almost evident, according to Keynes, because of the fact that a single additional instance, if it greatly reduces the superfluous positive analogy, yields more insight to the generalization than a great number of instances which have little or no effect in reducing the superfluous positive analogy.[1] The principle which supports such an

[1] I suppose that this means (1) if nature always presented the same kind of events or (2) if nature never presented the same kind of events, laws could not be discovered because (1) we could not begin to single out one uniformity rather than another, or (2) we could never find any uniformities. Therefore, mere repetition cannot increase the probability of an induction.

induction is known as the Limitation of Independent Variety. The independent variety of a system consists of the ultimate terms when these ultimate terms are independent. The principle states that the number of independently varying characteristics of any system of facts is finite. If, then, the number of independently varying characteristics is limited, there is a possibility of increasing the probability of an induction beyond a mediocre limit.

Keynes thinks that the principle of limitation can be supported by inductive evidence without circularity. This condition is most important of all for, if the principle of limitation enables us to increase the probability of induction, we must possess some reason prior to this principle for entertaining it. The principle must either be *a priori* or *empirically grounded* or *arbitrary*. It is almost certainly not *a priori*. It cannot be arbitrary because the only system admitting of arbitrary assumptions are postulational ones and nature is not among these. The principle must therefore be based upon empirical evidence.

The data of the imperfect analogies are as above :—

Proposition of generalization : $\phi x \supset_x fx$. It is known that for n cases : $\phi x . \phi_1 x \supset fx$, i.e. a property of x denoted by ϕ and another property of x denoted by ϕ_1 involves the property f for n examined cases. It is known that $(\exists x) . \phi'x . (\exists x) \sim \phi'x$, i.e. some property ϕ' of x is possessed by at least one x and not possessed by at least one x. Finally, there are properties ψ known to be possessed by some x's, and not known to be false of any, i.e. $(x)\psi x$. Now the number of

$$x = an\text{-}m$$
$$x = a_1$$

independent and different properties of the x's is supposed to be finite. Let their number be ξ. Then as the number of ψ and ϕ_1 decreases, and the number of ϕ' increases, and if there are no negative instances of $\phi x \supset fx$, the probability of $\phi x \supset_x fx$ approaches certainty, for the number of all different and independent properties of $x \leq \xi$. The number of ways ϕ' in which x's differ approaches $\xi - Nc'(\psi . \phi_1 . \phi . f)$

and the number of ways $\phi_1\psi$ in which x's are similar approaches $0 + Nc'(\phi.f)$. In the limit, the x's are alike only in the common characteristics ϕ and f. Therefore $\phi x \supset_x fx$ would be true.

The critics of Keynes, notably Nicod,[1] have shown to general satisfaction that the hypotheses of Uniformity, Determinism, and Limitation will not suffice to increase the probability of an induction above a mediocre limit and that the probability of these hypotheses cannot be validly increased by empirical evidence. If Keynes's account of induction is regarded as a fairly definitive account, the whole logic of induction seems to totter on its foundation as a result of criticism. The present state of the matter seems to be that the only successful method of induction is simple enumeration and that even this method will not increase the probability of an induction beyond limit. The reasons for the failure of Keynes's methods may be briefly indicated here. The finitude of the independent variety of the system under consideration is a necessary but not a sufficient condition for increasing the probability of a generalization beyond a mediocre limit. Unless the number of independent variations of x's is known, it is never possible to eliminate the ways in which x's are alike which are not included in the generalization. Similarly, it is not possible to increase the differences beyond a mediocre limit. Such increase could only be established by experiment and enumeration of observed cases. It is then a *petitio principii* to invoke the principle of limitation in any particular case of generalization. Keynes tries to avoid this by establishing a probability of the principle of limitation on other grounds than the generalization under consideration. But then the increased probability of the *other* generalization on which the principle depends for its probability will have to be justified by the principle. Since there is a finite number of generalizations, the argument becomes circular.

---

[1] Nicod, Jean, *The Foundation of Geometry and Induction*, London, 1929.

Furthermore, the possibility of negative instances can be reduced only by taking account of the number of x's themselves. Keynes' principles do not limit the number of x's. Even though the negative analogy is increased without limit and the positive analogy approaches 0, the possibility of $\phi x . \sim fx$ is still present.

In general the plurality of causes and the possibility of negative instances cannot be avoided by Keynes' method. The deductive procedure used by Keynes fails to provide sufficient conditions for increasing the probability of induction beyond a mediocre limit.

These considerations leave the induction problem where it was in the time of Hume. The advances in the theory of probability have entailed corresponding advances in inductive method. The problem, however, of how the likelihood of generalizations not known to be true is validly increased, remains unsolved.

The fact that no one has been able to give a satisfactory account of induction, not to speak of a solution of the problem set by it, has led the Positivists to regard the traditional statement of the problem as meaningless. Their arguments are simple but forceful. The chief problem is, of course, how to validate inductions from " these to all " or from " these to any ". In the atomic logic discussed in earlier parts of this essay, this problem cannot be stated. In that logic, as we discovered, there are only two meanings of " all " or generality. There is the accidental generality as it occurs in empirical propositions which consists of an explicit, and therefore finite, conjunction or alternation of elementary propositions. And there is the essential generality exemplified by mathematical or logical structures ; the latter is irrelevant here. Now, if general propositions are finite logical sums and products, there is no induction problem in which they are involved because it is quite clear that we are not concerned with such limited assertions in science and practice. Thus " all swans are white " may mean " this and this and this swan are white " or it may mean " it is the nature of a swan to be white ".[1] In the former case we cannot write " all " unless we have some way to determine what, when, and where beings answering to the description of " swan " are. In such a case no problem arises, because we have made an arbitrary determination. In the latter case we have an intensional judgment and cannot appeal to experience to give us a criterion of its correctness.

In general, for Positivists, induction is not the establishment of universal enumerative propositions because science is not concerned with them. It is also not concerned with non-enumerative general propositions because, for the Positivists, these do not have existential import. Likewise, and for similar considerations, it is not the establishment of existential propositions. If we know, e.g., that $(\exists x)\phi x$ we require no induction to establish it. If we do not know it we cannot entertain it as a hypothesis, at least not in this form. Such a judgment, if empirical, must be an explicit function of ϕa, ϕb, ϕc, etc., and if it is that function we already know something about its empirical possibility, i.e. that it has occurred. Hence induction is not concerned with the existential judgment. Only one possibility remains, namely that induction is concerned with singular propositions which are to be verified in the future.

The correct statement of the process of induction for Logical Positivism is : " Induction is the process of formulating singular propositions from specified propositional functions and the subsequent verification of these propositions." [2] There is no problem of induction left since there is nothing logically questionable in the process as it was just described. The kinds of propositional functions chosen will be the simplest available. " Simplest available " means " whatever formalism will enable us to describe with the greatest economy and to predict with the greatest ease ".

---

[1] The cases are : (1) (x) x is a swan $\supset x$ is white. (2) swan $= \hat{x}(\phi x)$ where ϕ is complex and means (ϕ_1, ϕ_2, ϕ_3). Then ϕx entails ϕ_1, i.e. $\phi =$ swan, $\phi_2 =$ white.

[2] Blumberg, A., *Monist*, October, 1932.

Now we can see that Keynes' principles of induction are undoubtedly the correct ones, although the use to which he puts them are, from the Positivist point of view, senseless. We tend to increase the negative analogy and decrease the superfluous positive analogy in order to achieve a maximum of simplicity in our formalism.[1] We seek to formulate the simplest law which will describe our experience. This attempt to find the simplest law will lead naturally to the rejection of superfluous analogies, because we can easily see that superfluous analogies produce an unnecessary complication in our formalism. Likewise we seek as many variations as possible in the events described by the law so as to be careful to avoid using more laws than required as an absolute minimum. Keynes's methods are the correct methods, but they are not *logical methods* of deriving conclusions. Rather, they are operations enabling us to formulate functions of the simplest form consistent with adequate description and successful prediction.

For the Positivist, then, induction presents no problem because it is not a logical process but rather a psychological one. Perhaps, in order to describe induction without an appeal to what is as vague as psychology and its terminology, it should be said that induction is a kind of activity which consists in the search for the simplest arrangement of experience. As such there is obviously no logical problem. There is, however, a problem which arises when we attempt to render the nature of inductive activity more explicit by formulating it in a rule of behaviour. It is necessary to anticipate a little in order to see this.

In the previous chapter it was found that it is illegitimate to assert a principle of irregularity in cases for which no law exists. In such cases we " show " the non-existence of law, i.e. regularity, by not formulating any law. Similarly, when

---

[1] Simplicity means several things. In the case of laws of a quantitative (algebraic) form, it means : Fx is simpler than fx, if Fx contains a smaller number of parameters and is of a lower degree than fx. In the case of qualitative formulæ it means : $\phi\hat{x} \supset f\hat{x}$ is simpler than $\psi\hat{x} \supset f\hat{x}$ if $\phi = \phi_1 . \phi_2$ and $\psi = \psi_1 . \psi_2 . \psi_3$.

there is a regularity, we express this by formulating laws rather than by asserting a principle of regularity or of causality.[1] To formulate a rule of action in the case of induction would seem to be just as illegitimate as to formulate a principle of causality. Let me explain more carefully.

Feigl, for example, suggests that induction should be regarded as a prescriptive principle similar to the rule of substitution and inference in the logical calculus instead of a descriptive principle. From this point of view he formulates the principle of induction as follows : " Seek to achieve a maximum of order by logical operations upon elementary propositions. Generalize this order (whatever its form be : causal, statistical, or other) with a minimum or arbitrariness, that is, according to the principle of simplicity." [2] Thus the principle is neither a proposition nor a propositional function, but a rule of operation upon the proposition.

It is difficult, then, to see what status this rule might occupy in discourse. In some theories of knowledge there is a place for both prescriptive and descriptive principles. Thus, in W. E. Johnson's logical theory we have the distinction between epistemic and constitutive conditions which, although not completely parallel to the former pair of terms, serves to illustrate our point. *In the epistemology of positivism there are neither prescriptive principles nor epistemic conditions, for propositions alone constitute the content of knowledge.* Accordingly, there is no room for a *principle* of induction in a theory of knowledge which has no place for prescriptive rules of any kind.

[1] Wittgenstein, op. cit., 6.36.361. " If there were a law of causality it might run ' There are natural laws '. But that clearly cannot be said ; it shows itself." Compare Jeffreys, H., *Scientific Inference*, Cambridge, 1931, p. 211. " The principle of causality now becomes the aggregate of all scientific laws, whether known or awaiting discovery. To accept it implies a hope that we may some day know all laws. . . . As a working rule it may be valuable for its psychological effect, but there is so far no definite reason for believing it true, and science can get on quite well without it."

[2] Feigl, H., " The Logical Character of the Principle of Induction," *Philosophy of Science*, vol. i, No. 1, 1934, p. 28.

That this is a serious difficulty will be seen from the reflection that, although there is a perfectly legitimate solution for the so-called problem of induction within the Positivistic principles—a solution, indeed, required by these principles—there is no means whatsoever for the verbal expression of the results which have been attained. When the solution has been obtained and when we cannot express the positive aspect of the result at all, we justly suppose that something is amiss in the theory which is found to be in this impasse.

It must be said, of course, that the critique of former theories stands even though the difficulty remains. But in order to surmount the difficulty we require an expansion and revision of the theory of discourse so as to yield a place for prescriptive principles. When we do this the whole structure of discourse must be altered. Since such an alteration entails, among other things, an abandonment of the principle that all significant assertions are reducible to elementary propositions, the critique of induction which rests upon such a principle fails to be convincing. This reopens the entire problem of induction.

I shall summarize the results of the foregoing discussion. Induction has been described as the discovery and establishment of general propositions. Keynes (and other recent writers) supposed that such propositions are usually of the kinds " ϕx implies fx for every instance of x " and " ϕx implies fx for some instance of x ". He then believed that, given a situation in which an instance was known but incompletely examined, and given that a further positive analogy ϕ_1 exists for all known instances and, lastly, that there is a known negative analogy ϕ' and some sub-analogies ψ, the method of increasing the probability of such an induction so that it approached the condition of a perfect analogy, would be to increase the negative analogy and to decrease the superfluous positive analogy and the sub-analogies by increasing the number of instances or by increasing the knowledge of the instances known. Some general principles of nature were required in order to validate such a method, in particular, the Uniformity of Nature and the Limitation of Independent Variety.

Criticism of these methods, which are as old as Mill and even Bacon, comes from three principal sources. First, Nicod showed that, on the assumptions, the elimination of superfluous positive analogies must remain incomplete and that the probability of the generalization would necessarily remain mediocre. He also showed that even the mere enumeration of instances (induction by confirmation) would not exceed any limits. Secondly, the principles of Uniformity and Limitation were shown to be neither *a priori* nor merely arbitrary but inductive. Nicod again showed that their inductive strength was not sufficiently great to support particular inductions made with Keynes' methods. Thirdly, the question arose whether there are any significant general propositions outside the finite sums and products (which, so far as induction is concerned, are not in question). It was decided that such general propositions as were supposed to be the objects of inductive inquiry did not exist.[1] The problem of induction had been wrongly stated. So much for the negative results.

Induction for the Logical Positivists is the process of discovering the simplest arrangement of experience, i.e. the process of formulating the simplest laws which will verify our singular assertions (expectations). Since general propositions are not the proper object of inductive inquiry, induction is concerned with singular propositions. The positive

---

[1] A further consequence of this is that the principles of Uniformity and Limitation are pseudo-propositions. It cannot be said, for instance, that there are only finitely many objects in the world or that there are only finitely many groups of independently varying phenomena. The term "object" is meaninglessly employed in a proposition without a further specification as to the precise kind of object involved. Cf. Wittgenstein, op. cit., 4.1272. "Whenever the word 'object' (thing, entity, etc.) is rightly used it is expressed in logical symbolism by the variable name. For example, in the proposition 'there are two objects which . . .' 'object' is expressed by $(\exists x, y) \ldots$' Whenever it is used otherwise, i.e. as a proper concept word, there arise senseless pseudo-propositions. So one cannot say 'There are objects' as one says 'There are books' . . . And it is senseless to speak of the *number of all objects*."

result is, then, that induction is the prediction and subsequent verification of singular propositions which are formulated within a scheme or law. The law is not a proposition but a sort of propositional function or model on the basis of which propositions are formulated. The principle of induction is a prescriptive injunction to choose those laws which enable us to predict successfully with the greatest ease and to describe with the maximum of simplicity.

It was found that this result was demanded by the failure of the logical theories of induction as well as by the principles of the positivistic logical doctrine.

But it was also found in the course of our criticism that there was no easy way to formulate the principle of induction within the limits of that logic because there was no room for prescriptive principles there.

This difficulty is particularly serious in that it rendered the whole doctrine suspect, and, in so far as it was suspect, the critique of former theories was vitiated to a large extent. The problem of induction, then, still awaits a satisfactory solution.

Perhaps the fact should also be mentioned that no explanation is forthcoming why we trust laws which have been confirmed a greater number of times and why we anticipate events often repeated in the past with a greater degree of expectancy than those laws and events which have been confirmed and repeated infrequently. It will be seen that the absence of explanation lies in the nature of the positivistic theory of logic and induction. There is no place for epistemic conditions in the logic and the inductive theory is not a logical theory. Without these we cannot hope to explain the logical or psychological ground of expectation. It is and must remain a complete mystery on the Positivistic principles.

Chapter V

THE NATURE OF NATURAL LAWS

The purpose of this chapter is to describe that part of the doctrine of Logical Positivism which concerns the laws of science. This theory of scientific concepts and laws and systems corresponds roughly to the theories of nineteenth century Positivism, although there are important divergencies. It must also be recognized that the statements of the contemporary Positivists are by no means in complete agreement. Briefly stated, the contemporary Positivistic theory of natural law is : Laws in science are not general empirical propositions capable of verification. They are schemata or models from which singular propositions can be constructed. We can verify the singular propositions derived from laws, but it is meaningless to speak of the verification of laws themselves because they are not propositions. It is also, in an important sense, meaningless to speak of the meaning of laws, because laws are not propositions and cannot be verified, and therefore cannot " mean " any fact. Laws have meaning only in the sense that they are abstracts from which meaningful statements can be constructed. This is the view which is generally entertained by the Positivists of the Viennese Circle and related groups.

The rejection of the usual view that natural laws are general propositions is required, as I have shown, for several quite different reasons. On the usual view there is no solution for the logical problem of induction. This view, moreover, requires us to assert propositions which cannot be given a definite meaning in terms of singular propositions. Thus it has been thought that $(x)\ \phi x$ asserts a general fact just as ϕa asserts an individual fact. If this were tenable there might be some reason for the belief that laws were general propositions, that is, expressions of general facts. But such a view makes it impossible to understand how individual instances follow logically from general propositions ; that is, the view that there are general facts and individual facts makes it inconceivable how there could ever be any relation between the two. Another reason is that general propositions are logical sums and products with an indefinite (perhaps infinite) number of summands or factors. But such sums and products could never be written out, therefore the expression of the general proposition is always an incomplete expression. The completion of the expression involves the specification of all the values which the argument x can assume, and this can only be done when these values are explicit and finite. The only tenable interpretation of general propositions, therefore, is that they are finite logical sums and products i.e. finite and explicit truth-functions of a specified set of elementary propositions. But this renders the view that laws are general propositions untenable, for general propositions are mere descriptive summaries of the past, whereas laws are used to predict the future. Since laws cannot be general propositions, they must be propositional functions.

Another consideration makes this conclusion even stronger. Theories of the general proposition, in particular the universal proposition, can be divided into the following groups :

A. Extensional theories.

1. The universal proposition is an explicit, and therefore finite, extensional function of elementary propositions.

2. The universal proposition is an implicit extensional function of elementary propositions. The factors may therefore be finite or infinite in number but, in any case, will be indefinite.

3. The universal proposition is an explicit extensional function with a definite number of factors which may be infinite.

B. Intentional theories.

1. The general proposition is an intensional function of elementary propositions.

The mathematical nature of infinity eliminates A 2 and A 3. The infinite is not an actual number, but the structure of the number process. A 2 is likewise out of the question for other logical reasons. An implicit extensional function is a contradiction in terms. A 3 is out of the question for the same reason. An explicit extensional function with infinitely many terms is self-contradictory. B 1 fails because intensional functions which express truths about empirical nature do not exist. This leaves A 1 as the sole alternative. Laws, therefore, do not coincide with general assertions.

Laws, however, appear to be general propositions and we must be able to explain why this is so. First the instances which confirm a law constitute a general proposition. If $\phi \hat{x} \supset \psi \hat{x}$ and if further n instances of the law have been verified, then, although the law remains a variable function, $\phi \times_{x=az}^{x=an} \supset \psi x$ is a general proposition. Laws are mistaken for general propositions, then, because it is assumed that the quantification of the function has been omitted for the purpose of brevity. For example, Jeffries says that Laplace's equation means " For every point p outside matter, with co-ordinates (x, y, z), if V is the gravitational potential, then $\frac{\delta^2 V}{\delta x^2} + \frac{\delta^2 V}{\delta y^2} + \frac{\delta^2 V}{\delta z^2} = 0$ obtains " [1] This cannot be the case if Wittgenstein's theory of general propositions is correct, because not all the values of the arguments can be specified. Nevertheless, the mistake is easy to make.

Laws, then, are propositional functions. Instead of using the function $\phi \hat{x} \supset \psi \hat{x}$ for the purpose of generalization, it is treated as a pure variable and singular propositions are formed from it. Blumberg explains this very clearly in his article in the *Monist*, for October, 1932. " Laws in the

[1] Jeffries, H., *Scientific Inference*, Cambridge, 1931, p. 48.

descriptive sciences," he writes, " are not propositions but models—usually quantitative in form—for building propositions. A law or hypothesis, therefore, is confirmed, not verified. A law is said to be useful in so far as it enables us to predict, i.e. in so far as the propositions constructed upon it as a model turn out to be true ". A law is not a description of what is known but a method of formulating propositions for the sake of experiment. Schlick makes the same point in somewhat different terms, but it is instructive to compare what he says with what has already been quoted. " Natural laws do not have the character of propositions which are true or false but rather set forth instructions for the formation of such propositions. . . . Natural laws are not ' general implications ', because they cannot be verified for all cases ; they are rather directions, rules of behaviour, for the investigator to find his way about in reality, to anticipate certain events. . . . We should not forget that observations and experiment are acts by means of which we enter into direct connection with nature. The relations between reality and ourselves frequently stand in sentences which have the grammatical form of assertions but whose essential sense consists of the fact that they are directions for possible acts." [1] Blumberg and Schlick would, I suppose, regard " instructions " (*Anweisungen*) and " models " as being two aspects of the same thing. The law is a structure used to create propositions. Its only significance consists of its character as an instrument.

This view seems to be a sort of pragmatism applied to science, but there exist important differences between Pragmatism and Positivism which must be pointed out at once to avoid any confusion. Instrumentalism in the positivistic philosophy is applied solely to scientific laws and to prescriptive rules, such as rules of operation in mathematical disciplines and scientific procedure. A thoroughgoing pragmatism such as that of Dewey or

[1] Schlick, M., " Die Kausalität in der gegenwärtigen Physik," *Die Naturwissenschaften*, 1931, p. 151.

Bridgman regards all thought (propositions) as instrumental in character. For the positivists, laws are said to be useful only in so far as they give rise to true propositions. For instrumentalism, laws as well as all other intellectual instruments are said to be true only in so far as they are practically successful.[1] The positivistic explanation of law is obviously designed to " save " the concept of truth. The pragmatic account of law is designed to absorb law into the general instrumentalism of pragmatic theory. It is easily seen that the two points of view do not really coincide in any respect, although both Pragmatists and Positivists have noted the strong resemblances which do, in fact, exist between the schools.

I now turn to the details of the theory of natural law. A law is a kind of propositional function from which singular propositions are created for the purpose of subsequent verification. For example, take $\phi\hat{x} \supset \psi\hat{x}$. (This is what Ramsey called a variable hypothetical.) Assume that this means " The llama is a woolly beast ".[2] It does not mean " All llamas are woolly beasts " which is written " $(x)\phi x \supset \psi x$ ". Nor does it mean that " some individual llama is a woolly beast ", which is written " $\psi(\iota x)(\phi x)$ ". In other words it is neither a universal nor a singular assertion, or rather it is not an assertion at all. The correct verbal rendering of " The llama is a woolly beast " is " being a llama implies being a woolly beast ", which asserts nothing but only presents a scheme from which assertions can be made and subsequently verified. The question is, what kind of assertions can be made from such a scheme. From the foregoing it seems that universal and particular propositions are ruled out. Therefore, although $\phi\hat{x} \supset \psi\hat{x}$ is not a singular proposition, the singular proposition $\phi(\iota x)(fx) \supset \psi x$ may be formed from it by the designation of the further property f,

[1] This is by no means an adequate representation of instrumentalism as a system. Here we are only interested in indicating differences in the two points of view.

[2] I am following here some examples and discussions from John Wisdom's " Logical Constructions," *Mind*, 1931–3, but for a purpose quite different from any that he, perhaps, would sanction.

or the singular proposition $\phi a \supset \psi a$ may be used (where a is the name of some individual). This proposition may be verified positively or negatively by an experiment (the conditions for such an experiment being " Finding a mammal in the South American Andes $(=f)$ which possesses a set of properties $(=\phi)$ collectively called ' being a llama ' and observing whether it possesses the further property $(=\psi)$ called ' being woolly ')." This law will be retained as long as llamas turn out to be woolly beasts ; as long as such remains the case the law is said to be useful or correct. This shows how laws can be explained in a non-metaphysical manner. There is no induction problem involved in such a consideration because laws are used rather than believed and because there can be no question of verifying a law. Only the singular proposition formed from the law is capable of verification. The law itself is said to be " confirmed " or to be " the correct formula ".

If this explanation is applied to the quantitative laws of physics certain problems arise which must be taken into account. For example, " Bodies fall with a constant vertical acceleration toward the earth," is a law. This means " being a body implies falling toward the earth with a constant vertical acceleration ". The same considerations hold as in the case of " the llama is a woolly beast ". This is a propositional function from which singular propositions can be derived by giving empirical values to the co-ordinates of a body, etc.

Almost all laws of physics have the forms $f(x) = y$, $f(x, y) = z$, etc., i.e. the form of equations in which some variable is a function of some other variable. For example, if $x =$ the displacement of a body on an inclined plane, $t =$ the time, then there is a function $5x = t^2$. This is a propositional function which yields a correspondence between values of z and values of t. It shows a possible relationship between two propositional functions such that when the value of one function is determined a corresponding value of the other is determined. The functionality is plural in the sense that it is a fixed relation between two propositional functions. The law in question might be written " displacement of a body z being $5x$, implies time of displacement is t^2 ", the equational form being a convenience. We may assume that $5x = t^2$ has the form of an identity. It is not, however, a logical identity in the same sense as $5 \cdot 20 = 10^2$, for if x is observed to be 19 and t is 10, then $5x = t^2$ in this case is not satisfied. The relation between the temporal and spatial interval is invariant and remains an equation only as long as the observed magnitudes have certain values. The law fails to be confirmed if, given a value of one of the variables, the calculated value of the other is not equal to the subsequently observed value. This law is retained only as long as the observed values are exactly or approximately equal to the calculated values. This description of a physical quantitative law satisfies the general explanation of law which Blumberg and Schlick have given. $5x = t^2$ is a model or directional formula from which singular propositions can be constructed for the purpose of experimentation. The law is satisfied and confirmed when such singular propositions as are constructed from it turn out to be true.

Let us now consider the problems which arise especially in connection with quantitative laws.[1]

Quantitative laws are usually differential equations. The functionality expressed by them is absolutely exact, i.e. for a given value of one of the variables, the other variable is absolutely determined in value. This is what is meant by the invariant nature of law. The known data from which the law is derived (by abstraction) as well as the unknown facts to which it is applied, are inexact. Measurement of spatial intervals, for example, yields slightly different results for successively applied measuring instruments. The same obtains to the measurement of time. The inexactitude of the data seems incompatible with the

---

[1] And *mutatis mutandis* for many qualitative laws, e.g. the one about llamas.

exactitude of the law. " The co-ordinates which determine acceleration can only be taken from observation ; they are observed magnitudes and hence subject to errors, they are never exactly given but only within certain limits with a definite probability. Therefore the law does not have a precise sense but is subject to the limitation of a range of variation (*Spielraum*)." [1]

Again, all laws are derived from empirical data. These data are inexact in two ways among others. First, there is rarely, if ever, an exact correspondence between the numerical values for the exact observations. Instead of a double series of values, such as—

t	0	5	10	15	20	25	30
x	0	5	20	45	80	125	180

it is more frequently the case that we would have something like—

t	0	5	10	15	20	25	30
x	0	5	19	44	81	124	

Secondly, the exactitude of the measurements is restricted. The instruments are so calibrated as to give readings to the fifth of a second and a hundredth of a centimeter. Closer measurements are not usually possible (excepting quite indirectly with complex instruments and more complex theories about these instruments).[2] The physical law derived from the variant sequences obtained by instruments whose calibration is somewhat gross is, nevertheless, a function which would hold only if there were an invariance in the sequence and if the measurements were exact within any degree of approximation.

The general problem, then, is to discover how invariant laws are derived from variant data and how such laws are applied to individual cases in whose determination measurements are frequently too gross to fall within an exact application of the law. This is a problem for Positivism

---

[1] Pannekoek, A., " Das Wesen der Naturgesetzes," *Erkenntnis*, Bd. iii, pp. 389–400.
[2] This example is from Jeffries, loc. cit., *supra*.

because (1) it explains the confirmation and utility of laws in terms of the prediction of consequences, and (2) because laws are usually exact functions.

The problem is to explain how a calculated value which varies somewhat from a subsequently observed value can be said to be a true consequence of a law. Suppose that $5x = t^2$ is the law and that for $t = 15$, $x = 45$, but that $x = 45 \pm 1$ is observed. How can this be regarded as a true proposition about displacement, formulated by using the law. A true consequence would seem to be 45 exactly for $t = 15$. How can $x = 45 \pm 1$ be a true proposition if $x = 45$ is the prediction ? Moreover, how can an invariant law be derived from variant relationships between the values observed prior to the formulation of a law ? The inexactitude of nature seems incompatible with the exactitude of law. It should be remembered that the problem is not " how can a law be true in general if it is slightly false in almost every instance ? " This is an insoluble problem in the first place, and in the second place it cannot arise for the positivist because laws are not propositions which are true or false but propositional functions which yield propositions. The problem is (1) how can an invariance of various parts of events be derived from variant relations among these parts?, and (2) how can an observed value which differs slightly from a calculated value be regarded as a confirmation of the law from which the calculation is made ?

The general answer of the Positivist is that invariant laws are derived from observed variant relations by taking that particular invariant functional relation among the observations from which the deviations are less than the deviation from any other invariant functional relationship designed to describe the same data. Laws, in a general and indefinite way, may be said to describe the data from which they are derived, but they do not describe these data exactly. They are the closest invariant description of the data. They are also the closest simple description of the data. Invariant and simple formulæ are chosen because they constitute the only method of describing all the data according to a simple plan and the only way of predicting. The law itself is not a description and it is not a prediction. However, descriptions and predictions result from it. Descriptions result when the closest numerical value is given to the independent variable in the law which will yield a unique determination for the dependent variable closest to its observed value. Predictions arise in the same way, save for the fact that we do not know whether the calculated value will be approximately equal to the value subsequently observed. As long as the two roughly coincide we retain the law.[1] The calculated value may be regarded as a true prediction if the observed value does not deviate from it by more than a pre-assigned limit.

This answers the questions proposed above. A law is an invariant derived from variant relations among the parts of events quantitatively measured. The differences are so slight from a descriptive point of view that the law may be said to be the most exact invariant scheme for describing data, admittedly variant. It is also the most exact invariant scheme for predicting the relations among data which are admittedly variant. Invariant and simple schemes of law are used because they present the only means of describing a set of data according to one method and of predicting the same set. Thus $5x = t^2$ produces an exact description of the first series of observations and the simplest description in invariant form of the second set. This law also makes it possible to predict more accurately than a law which would describe the data exactly.

Wittgenstein explains this aspect of law in a very instructive illustration. " Imagine," he says, " a white surface with irregular black spots. We now say : ' Whatever kind of pictures these make I can always get as near as I like to its description if I cover the surface with a sufficiently fine square network and now say of every square that it is

---

[1] Of course, it is usually determined by the step of the instrument used in measurement to what extent the calculated and observed values may deviate without necessitating an abandonment of the law.

white or black. In this way I shall have brought the description to a unified form. This form is arbitrary because I could have applied with equal success a net with a triangular or hexagonal mesh. It can happen that the description would have been simpler with the aid of a triangular mesh ; that is to say, we might have described the surface more accurately with a triangular and coarser than with the fine square mesh (or vice versa), and so on. To the different networks correspond different systems of describing the world." . . . ' That a picture like that instanced above can be described by a network of a given form asserts nothing about the picture. For this obtains of every picture of this kind. But the fact that it can be completely described by a definite network of definite fineness does characterize the picture. Likewise nothing is asserted about the world by the fact that it can be described by Newtonian mechanics ; but something is asserted by the fact that it can be described in the particular way in which it is described. The fact, too, that the world can be described more simply by one system than by another says something about the world. Mechanics is an attempt to construct all true propositions required in the description of the world according to a single plan." [1] This metaphor expresses the Positivistic theory very clearly. The irregular spots correspond to the facts of the world, the network to the law of system of laws. The abstract form of laws and systems says nothing about the world because there are other possible laws and systems which can be used as the material for description (e.g. Newtonian mechanics and Einsteinian mechanics ; Euclidean and non-Euclidean geometry). The fact that any one system can be used in the complete description of the world says nothing about the world because it might just as well be completely described by another system. That the world can be described by system A says nothing about it. That, however, it is completely described

---

[1] *Tractatus*, 6.341.2.3.

by a given system A of definite quantitative values does say something about the world ; namely it is a complete and actual description of the world and not merely a possible description.

That one system can describe the world more simply than another likewise says something about the world, namely that the structure of the events of the world is such as to be adaptable to a simpler description than we had, perhaps, previously imagined. This simplicity, when it exists, may be called genuine simplicity in contradistinction to the simplicity-postulate of Occam's Razor, which is a rule of symbolism.

The principal difference between a set of laws and a system of laws is that the latter is a unified deductive set of propositional functions called axioms and theorems, all of which are in the same language and bear some connection to one another, whereas the former consists of different laws for the different departments of nature without any connection obtaining among the members of the set. Some systems of law are more completely systematized than others and to that extent are simpler formulations. The system of mechanics in which gravitation and inertia fall under the same principle is simpler than that in which the two phenomena fall under different principles. The greater unity of a system constitutes a mark of greater simplicity. A set of physical laws is likewise more complicated than a system of physical laws.

The deductive aspect of a system of laws is the tautological connection between the axioms and consequences. Neither the axioms nor the consequences are tautologies for, if they were, there would be no possibility of applying them to the world. Only the connection between axioms and consequences is tautological. When a science advances to the state in which it is possible to present all or most of the laws in a system, this indicates that the material used in the description of the events constituting the subject-matter of the science can be completely expressed in the same language. If all true propositions about some kind of events can be constructed from the laws systematically organized, then we say that that part of the world can be put into a system. It may be the case that propositions not predictable (constructible) from known laws can, nevertheless, be formulated in the same terminology as those propositions which can and are, in fact, predictable (constructible) from the laws.

*   *   *   *

A brief summary of the Positivistic explanation of the nature of law will be in place here. The motivation for the Positivistic theory of law is threefold : (1) the avoidance of any metaphysical assumption in the concept of law and nature, (2) the avoidance of a purely descriptive theory of science, (3) a satisfactory treatment of induction. These three points require individual consideration.

(1) The usual explanation of law is that laws are general or existential assertions directly about the facts or the events of the world. In the case of quantitative laws an especial difficulty arises in this view. The laws do not usually fit the data exactly. The idea of errors must be understood in order to take account of a discrepancy between the values of empirical magnitudes as calculated and the values as observed. The assumption must be made that there are real (true) values. Adjustments must be made in a law so that the calculated values and the observed values differ by as little as we please. The difference between the true and the observed values is called error. The difference between the observed and the adopted values is called the residual. Finally the difference between the true and the adopted values is called the error of the adopted values. However much this procedure is to be recommended on the purely technical grounds of the so-called theory of errors, it seems clear that there is no logical justification for the procedure. Laws are conceived as being true general assertions about facts. There is not an exact agreement

but only an approximate one between the prediction and the observations. It must be assumed that the law, if true, agrees exactly with the true values and that discrepancies are to be imputed to observation itself. The wholly unjustifiable theory of unobservable " true " values is responsible for this assumption. This seems to cast grave reflections upon the original assumption that laws are general assertions about nature. The Positivist attempts to avoid the necessity of such assumptions by denying that laws are assertions.[1]

(2) He is strengthened in this attempt by powerful arguments from the logical aspect of the question. Laws are used for the purpose of prediction, whereas general assertions, if true, can only report what is known. Moreover, the general assertion can only be a function of individual assertions and these must be limited in number and quite specific in kind. Laws and general assertions cannot coincide. Laws are not enumerative in any sense of the word, for the precise character of the instances satisfying a law cannot be discovered by an examination of the law. Logical considerations alone lead to the rejection of the doctrine that laws are of the nature of general (enumerative) empirical propositions. Another consideration proves 'that laws are not general propositions. Science is both descriptive and predictive. General assertions are, at most, descriptive. If laws constitute the structure of a science they cannot be limited to a purely descriptive function. Moreover, they cannot at the same time describe and predict. They must partake of a nature somewhat different from general propositions, although they must, at the same time, provide the materials for description as well as for prediction.

(3) Finally, and this was discovered in a previous chapter, the doctrine that laws coincide with general empirical assertions raises an insoluble problem about induction set by this doctrine. Inductive method must be justified and

---

[1] See Jeffreys, H., *Scientific Inference*, Cambridge, 1931, ch. v; and Ritchie. A. D. *Scientific Method*, London, 1923, p. 132.

this can only be done by the elimination of any logical problem of induction. The only way seemingly open to the Positivist is to reject the traditional explanation of law. The doctrine outlined is substituted for the traditional one. Laws are schemata or models from which singular propositions are constructed for the purpose of experiment, that is, for the purpose of subsequent verification. They must partake of the nature of propositional functions.

The simplest law from which true propositions can be constructed is selected on heuristic, logical, and empirical grounds, that is " the simplest law which can be made to harmonize with our experience " allows for prediction with the greatest ease and accuracy, contains no unnecessary and hence meaningless terms, and reveals the degree of simplicity to be found in the factual connections. These three aspects of simplicity do not coincide. The economical simplicity of law eliminates any meaningless terminology in the symbolism. The empirical simplicity is a gauge of the simplicity of the objects with which the law is concerned.

Laws thus provide the material for the description of known and surmised facts. They are invariant formulæ from which the factual connections deviate as little as possible (or, in the case of some qualitative laws, not at all). Their principal value is practical, in that they enable the scientist to predict. This is why they need not fit the data exactly.

Laws are regular invariant formulæ applied to variant connections and derived from variant data. This would present an insoluble problem if they were general assertions capable of truth and falsehood. But because they are not propositions there is a facile solution to the problem. Laws are formulæ of the nature of propositional functions. When a set of data is given, there are three possibilities : (1) There may, in rare cases, be an invariant relation obtaining among the data, e.g. very accurate determinations of the direction and acceleration of falling bodies. (2) There may be an almost invariant relation obtaining among the data, e.g. the relation of time and displacement of bodies rolling down an inclined plane or " llamas are woolly beasts ". " Almost invariant " means that we can, by a process of abstraction, discern what precise relation would hold if the observational data were very slightly adjusted. (3) There may be no discernible relationship among the data or, at most, a statistical correlation (among the data), e.g. temperamental maladjustments of people whose names end in patronymics, or relation between height and colour of grain in corn. In the first case the law is formed by abstracting the common form from the data and no problem exists since an invariant law is derived from invariant real connections among known data. The third case presents no problem because laws cannot be formulated. The second case presents the problem : with what justification do we effect a conceptual alteration of the data so as to formulate an exact law ? Economy alone, at the expense of fidelity to the factual, is not a sufficient justification. The simplicity of the most exact formula, if it has merely heuristic value, is not sufficient. The justification is, of course, first, that only an invariant function or formula will allow for the description of all data of a certain kind according to a single scheme, and second, only an invariant function or formula will allow for the prediction of the unknown with precision. In brief, there is no simple method of generating exact or nearly exact descriptions of the data from a variant involved formula, but there is a simple method of generating almost exact descriptions and predictions of the data from a simple invariant formula. The necessity of a simple uniform method of description and prediction, as well as the heuristic value of simplicity, constitutes the justification of abstraction in the case of natural laws. Abstraction does not entail falsification or fictionalization in this instance because (1) the law is not intended to be a true representation of facts but a method of making representations approximating as close as we please to the data. In fact, laws are instruments of investigation as experiments are instruments of investigation. Both provide the necessary means of representing the facts.

There is an additional value in the use of formulæ with regular and uniform properties. Such formulæ make deduction possible because, given a set of formulæ, we know *a priori* all their consequences. Many variations and transformations in the method of expression are, therefore, given in a scheme of laws in geometry and mechanics. This allows for the extension of laws over a wide area of different kinds of phenomena.

The methods of prediction, measurement, description, calculation, etc., all have one thing in common. This is the invariant schematism all of whose properties are given *a priori* by means of which the factual occurrences are measured in respect of their regularity. Laws, geometrical systems, measuring devices, are kept constant either by controlled experiments, or by postulates, or by invariant functional expressions, etc., and investigations are made in order to discover whether the invariance in these schemes or devices is duplicated in reality, and to what degree of exactitude this duplication is realized.

*   *   *   *

The obvious and powerful advantages of this and similar explanations of natural law have been noted by writers who have nothing in common with Positivism. It cannot be denied that many of the most perplexing problems of scientific method find in it a simple and powerful solution. This solution seems to be of purely theoretical significance, that is, it appears to be simply elucidatory, the procedure of the sciences remaining unaltered in practice. In a general sense this is true. But in at least one branch of method alterations of a practical character may be expected. This is the theory of errors.

I am not competent to judge whether the Positivistic

explanation of natural law will affect the type of theory used in describing microscopic phenomena, but the essays of Werner Heisenberg seem to indicate that his innovations were initiated by considerations of a kind similar to those which have occupied my attention here.[1] However, on the whole, the doctrine in question is of purely philosophical import, determined by considerations pre-eminently logical.

I found that the theory of probability as a branch of logic failed of complete generality. A further difficulty in it would seem to be the significance of a probability-proposition within the scheme of pure logic. The proposition asserting that p is probable to some degree on the data q is not an elementary proposition. On the other hand, it is an assessment of the numerical value of certain conditions (short of the total) under which an event occurred. It is difficult to see where an enumeration of facts or propositions would find a place in the scheme of elementary propositions and truth-functions of elementary propositions. Although we have a satisfactory theory of probability, the expression of probability within positivistic logic eludes us. Likewise in the consideration of the problem and nature of induction I found that the solution of the induction problem and the statement of the character of inductive activity were highly plausible. However, no satisfactory expression of the principle of induction could be given within the logical scheme of positivism. The solution, having been discovered, could not be expressed.

A similar difficulty exists in the present case. If the logical doctrines of Wittgenstein and others entertaining similar views are correct, there are only the following classes of propositions :—

(1) Elementary propositions and truth-functions of elementary propositions.

---

[1] Of course the need for a new method was created by the practical failure of the Bohr theory to account for certain observed effects. I have in mind only the direction and character of the innovation.

(2) Tautologies and contradictions.

Other kinds of seeming propositions, such as : (1) Modal, (2) Intensional, (3) Prescriptive, (e.g. operational rules, general methodological principles, etc.), (4) Essential (e.g. statements about internal relations, identity of essences, etc.), formulations are ruled out as being non-significant. There are two kinds of nonsense which must be carefully distinguished. There is the nonsensical assertion resulting from an attempt to say what cannot be said but must be shown or exhibited. This is only nonsense when the attempt is made to express it in symbolism. Then there is the nonsensical assertion consisting of a combination of signs which have no determinate meaning (no specific and empirically verifiable content). The elimination of the first consists in the demonstration (1) that the sentences do not express what they are intended to express, and (2) that we can understand the world without such vain attempts at expressing the inexpressible by " seeing " what cannot be put into symbols. The elimination of the second consists in the demonstration that some symbols or parts of symbols do not have a fixed and verifiable significance. In the case of the first kind of nonsense, it is shown, e.g., that modal propositions can be reduced to non-modal forms or dispensed with altogether. " Possibility, impossibility, and necessity are not expressed by a proposition, but by the fact that an expression is a genuine proposition, a tautology, or a contradiction." To take another example, that which intensional propositions assert can either be reduced to extensional definitions or contain only what can be shown. Thus that " all swans are white " means " the set of characters constituting ' being a swan ' includes the character ' being white ' " ; or that " all red things are coloured ", can be seen in any assertion of the form " is red ", colour being the sign of a formal concept not separable from its exemplifications. In the case of absolute nonsense, for example, " Cæsar is a prime number," " adjectives love analysis," etc., it can easily be demonstrated either that the combination of words is logically (syntactically) inadmissible, or it can be demonstrated that the individual words have no determinate significance. In any case, the sentence can be shown to be theoretically unverifiable. Prescriptive principles are not so easily dealt with because they seem to be significant ; yet it is clearly impossible to verify a command. At best we can only obey one. However, there is no place in the logical scheme for commands.

Laws present an altogether unusual case. They are propositional functions and therefore incomplete expressions. If completed, these expressions might be meaningful ; therefore they cannot be eliminated on the grounds of non-significance. However, they are never completed in the sense required and so are not capable of theoretical verification. They occupy a place in the interstices of completed and incompleted meaning and cannot be said either to mean anything or not to mean anything. It is, of course, easy to retort that laws are structures from which meanings can be derived and that they present no difficulty within the scheme of scientific language, but some place must be found for them, and this can only be accomplished by an enlargement of the schematism of discourse. This is impossible unless we are prepared to grant that there are meanings not capable of verification *per se*, i.e. unless we admit that there are sentences whose test of significance is not that of verifiability. The Positivist is not prepared to do this.

This, then, is the first logical difficulty which I encounter in the Positivistic theory of science. The logical doctrines of the Positivist set limits to significant discourse which exclude many important and meaningful statements. Prescriptive principles, rules of language, and laws of science are excluded from the realm of significant assertions. Again, it will be said that these are things which can be shown and not said. That this is not a sufficient reply will be obvious to anyone who can see that it is impossible to make any clear distinction between what can be shown and

not said, i.e. between what is important nonsense, and what
is complete nonsense.

The logical significance of laws is brought into question
by the foregoing considerations. But there are other and
equally important reasons for doubting the success of the
Positivistic theory.

It is necessary, in scientific procedure, to make a
distinction between causal and non-causal laws on the one
hand, and chance on the other. A causal law is a law of a
certain invariant form. A non-causal law is usually of the
statistical form. Chance is the absence of law. The
Positivist now says that causal and statistical laws exhibit
a regularity in the world and that equally divided
probabilities or statistical frequencies which have no trends
show irregularity, i.e. are chance distributions.

How can the existence of a law exhibit a regularity in the
course of events ? The law itself says nothing about the
world, being incomplete and not capable of verification.
Therefore, successful prediction from a law alone can
determine anything about the world. Indeed, a function
will not be called a law unless this success in prediction is
realized. Thus Schlick says : " For the physicist as
investigator of reality the only thing of importance, the
only determining test, that which is the sole essential, is
that the equations derived from certain data also hold good
for new data. Only if this is the case does he regard his
formula as a natural law. In other words, the true criterion of
regularity, the essential characteristic of causality, is the
realization of predictions [' realization of predictions '
being synonymous with ' confirmation of a formula for
data to which it has not been applied either in past or
future ']. . . . The corroboration of predictions is therefore
the only criterion of causality. Reality speaks to us only
in this way ; the construction of laws and formulæ *per se*
is purely the work of man." [1]

[1] Die Kausalität in der gegenwärtigen Physik," *Naturwissenschaften* 13,
February, 1931.

The existence of formulæ from which successful predictions have been made shows the existence of regularity. This regularity is statistical or causal according as the laws have the statistical or causal form.[1]

This seems to be satisfactory, but is it really so ? The physicist regards a formula as a law if (1) the number of predictions from it is very great, or (2) the deviation from the law (the difference between predicted and observed values) is very small, or (3) conditions (1) and (2) both obtain. This is because he wants to be reasonably sure that the success of prediction is not due to chance agreement.

There is no mention of these further criteria of causality in the Positivistic account and this for a good reason. Use can be made of such criteria as the number of successful predictions or the smallness of deviation only when a method of rational induction is admitted. The possibility of this has been eliminated by the Positivistic treatment of induction.

The result of this consideration is very interesting. The Positivist can still speak of the utility of laws. A law is useful and retained as long as it continues to produce successful predictions. It is no longer possible to regard successful prediction as an indication of anything about the course of events in the world. In other words, it is not possible, as Schlick maintains, to suppose that the existence of formulæ (functions) from which successful predictions have been made exhibits regularity in the world. It is not difficult to see why this is the case.

A function from which a very small number of successful predictions have been made would not necessarily exhibit regularity because the predictions, however successful they may have been, might have been due to chance.[2] That is, the success of the predictions does not necessarily indicate anything about the type of regularity in the actual course

[1] Laws of mechanics are of the causal form ; that of entropy, of the statistical form.

[2] I cannot precisely define the word " chance " in this usage, but the sense is clear.

of events nor even that any causal regularity exists, first, because any arrangement of events can be exactly described by a sufficiently complex formula, and second because a small number of predictions might be due to the accidental agreement of prediction and subsequent observation. If there are no canons by means of which to determine the number of successes required to eliminate the possibility of chance agreement, there is no way of knowing that a formula really describes the course of events and really applies to data to which it has not hitherto been applied. The mere existence of laws, in Schlick's sense, exhibits nothing about the world.

Suppose, however, that the number of successful predictions has been very great. There remains the necessity of another canon to determine the magnitude of deviations which are to be allowed without entailing the abandonment of the formula. For if there are deviations (and these exist in most cases) we cannot know what type of regularity exists unless we have some way to limit the admissible magnitude of the deviations.

The Positivist cannot, in strict logic, speak of the existence of regularity or causality in the world as being a consequence of the existence of successful formulæ. We can, of course, speak of the existence of laws of the causal form and laws of the non-causal form, but this, it is evident, says nothing about the events but only about the schematism by means of which the events are described. At times Wittgenstein seems content with saying just this when he writes : " The law of causality is not a law but the form of a law. ' Law of causality ' is a class-name. And as in mechanics there are, e.g. minimum laws, such as that of least action, so in physics there are causal laws, laws of the causality form." [1] But presumably the fact that causal laws are successfully used shows something about the world. As I believe I have shown, this is not the case without further qualifications, such as the number of successful

[1] Op. cit., 6.32.321.

predictions and the order of magnitude of deviations required to eliminate chance agreement.

That the Positivist will not admit the necessity of these qualifications is evident for the obvious reason that he has eliminated the possibility of a rationale of induction, without which " great numbers " cannot be given a place.

Let us take a similar instance in the theory of probability. If we have obtained what we consider to be a satisfactory metric, then we can, in many cases, designate prior and equal probabilities to each of a possible set of events. As long as the posterior probabilities continue to agree with prior probabilities we say that all conditions relevant to the occurrence of the several events are taken into account in the metric, i.e., that the occurrence of the events is independent of the unknown circumstances. If, however, there are runs favouring the occurrence of one event rather than another when we have the prior probabilities calculated as equal, we say that not all the relevant events have been taken into account in the metric, i.e. that the occurrence of the events is not independent of the circumstances unknown to us. These runs must be " long " before we doubt the correctness of the prior assessment of probability, for it is known that short runs favouring one event frequently occur. Hence the conclusion that the prior probabilities either have or have not been correctly assessed must depend upon a very great number of trials. We cannot say that we shall continue to regard the prior probability as correct as long as nothing to the contrary occurs, because we require a great number of experiments to determine whether the posterior probability really agrees with the prior assessment, since a chance agreement is not out of the question in a small number of experiments. The difficulty here is similar to the one in the case of prediction from formula.

It is clear, then, that the Positivistic theories of law do not take into account all the principles necessary for making assertions about the connection of law and reality. The doctrine that laws are propositional functions rather than general assertions was introduced (1) to eliminate the problem of induction, and (2) because laws cannot be regarded, from the standpoint of Wittgenstein's logic, as general assertions. The result is that (1) admitting the success of the elimination of the traditional problem of induction, the induction problem reappears in a new form, (2) the nature of law remains ambiguous even in the guise of a propositional function.

There is one last difficulty with the doctrine that a law is a propositional function. This difficulty becomes particularly acute in the consideration of certain epistemological problems.[1] It can be regarded as a purely scientific problem. There are two uses of laws in science which are, one might say, radically distinct. One is the use of a law as a structural model from which singular propositions are constructed for the purpose of subsequent experimental testing. This is the Positivistic conception and, with some of the required alterations indicated above, may be a satisfactory account of law in this usage. Then there is the use of a law as the premise to an argument as, e.g., in the statement of the grounds of a probability-assertion. Thus it is often said : " If such and such laws obtain and if such and such data are at hand, then event E is probable to such and such a degree." Here laws are mentioned as premises to arguments, i.e. as general hypothetical propositions which may be categorically asserted in the cases in which we have reason to believe that they have, in fact, been fulfilled. But whether categorically asserted or hypothetically entertained, laws as premises to probable or necessary inferences play an altogether different role from that in which they are used as models. A law as a premise to an argument must be regarded as a completed proposition and not merely as a preliminary to a proposition. Since it is abundantly clear that such a usage of law is frequent in scientific assertions,

---

[1] In particular, the doctrine entertained by Carnap, Russell, *et al.*, that objects and events are logical constructions of sense-data. (Carnap calls them " Elementarerlebnisse ".) Of this, more later. I refer, of course, to Carnap's earlier doctrines.

it is also clear that a complete theory will have to explain it. Positivism, as I have shown, cannot do this.

In later sections treating of epistemology, I must consider the doctrine that a physical object is a law of certain phenomena [1] rather than a permanent substratum. Law here is a propositional function of which any given phenomenon of the kind in question is a value of the function. However, difficulties arise as in the example of probability. A physical thing, say a table, which has been destroyed, cannot be regarded as a law of certain phenomena (acoustic, tactual, visual, etc.) because the function has been completely and finally satisfied. A table, having been destroyed, is a finite, completed series of empirical facts, whereas a table which we have reason to believe still exists is a law about certain occurrences. A physical thing which is known to exist in the present observable environment is frequently employed while our attention is concentrated elsewhere. It is frequently used as the basis of an argument, e.g. " If the chairs have not been moved up to the table, I shall stumble over them in the dark." In any of these instances the thing is not a law (function) of certain phenomena, but is assumed to be a presently existing thing. Here, again, are two uses of law which have nothing in common save the form of discursive expression.

In general, then, whenever law is used as the premise to an argument, it is used as a hypothetical or categorical assertion about something completed or persisting. In such cases, which are frequent enough to merit our attention, laws cannot be functions (preliminaries) of propositions but are already propositions in their complete form. At least one significant use of law has been excluded from consideration in the Positivistic doctrines.

---

[1] Similar to B. Russell's doctrine that a thing is " a certain series of aspects " (*Our Knowledge of the External World*, 1914, pp. 106-7) save that Russell can, or could at that time, think of a thing as being an infinite series of appearance, whereas this view, recognizing the improper use of infinite series in connection with empirical things, chooses to substitute " law " for series.

SUMMARY OF PART II

The problems of methodology in science which have been treated by the Positivists most completely have been concerned with the nature of probability, of induction, and of law. The probability-calculus was reduced to a branch of Logic by defining the concept of probability in terms of the relations among Spielräume, i.e. relations among propositions within each of which there was an admissible degree of variation. The essence of the application of probability to nature is the calculation of prior probabilities with the use of a metric to determine what, in fact, constitutes equal probability. The agreement or disagreement of observed distributions with calculated probabilities determines the existence or non-existence of law and chance in the world. The prior probability is therefore a measure which we apply to empirical data in order to determine the existence of dependencies among events. We hold this assessment constant whatever the actual frequency may turn out to be. It is thus an ideal from which we judge the shortcomings of the actual. Probability, therefore, is not a bridge between knowledge and ignorance, but rather a gauge by means of which knowledge is measured when it is obtained. If, for example, the prior probability and the subsequently observed frequency agree, then we know something about the events which we did not know and could not have known until this comparison was made.

It was likewise found that a law was considered to be an invariant formula upon the basis of which predictions were made. It is not an assertion but the structure of certain assertions. In so far as a law is progressively and continually satisfied we know that some regularity obtains in the course of events. In its manner a law, too, is a fixed ideal structure by means of which the facts are described, measured, and judged in respect of their variations from the ideal norm.

These theories of law and probability were necessitated

by some of the logical principles essential to the contemporary positivistic Weltauffassung. In particular, these doctrines were :—

(1) That every general proposition was an explicit truth-function of a specified, and therefore finite, set of elementary propositions.

(2) That there was no method *a priori* of inferring the unknown from the known.

(3) That all inference is *a priori*.

(4) That, consequently, induction is not a canon of inference, but a practical rule of behaviour without any logical foundation.

(5) That probability is not a method of inference.

The problem of induction was eliminated by showing that there is in science and practice no use which requires canons of inference.

In examining these results I came to the conclusion that they were not expressible in terms of the theory which necessitated them. In particular, it was found that the prescriptive principle of induction, like prescriptive principles in general, could not be expressed within a theory of language which required every significant statement to be in the indicative mood and the third person singular.[1] It was equally difficult, after we were forced by the logic of the theory to accept laws as propositional functions, to see how the preliminary form (function) of statements could occur in significant discourse. The nature of laws as propositional functions was as ambiguous in their old place as general propositions.

Beside these logical difficulties there were also the empirical difficulties of the criteria of the genuineness of predictions. I tried to show that predictions from laws or probabilities required a great number of successful instances in order to assert anything about the actual occurrences in

[1] Or reducible without remainder to such statements.

the world, and that the problem suggested by this circumstance was not satisfactorily resolved by the exponents of the doctrine for the reason that no means, within the doctrine, was adequate to the task.

This concludes the Positivistic theory of scientific method. There remain to be considered the elimination of metaphysics and the theory of knowledge.

PART III

THE ELIMINATION OF METAPHYSICS
AND
THE POSITIVISTIC THEORY OF KNOWLEDGE

In the preceding sections I presented the first part of the programme of the Viennese Circle, the establishment of the foundations of science by logical methods. Now I turn to the elimination of metaphysics. By the logical analysis of significant discourse, metaphysics will be shown to be meaningless.

The principles on which this elimination depends are the same as those used for the logical foundation of science, namely (1) the sense of a proposition is the method of its verification, i.e. the possible fact on which its verification depends (2) the sense of propositions containing defined signs depends on the sense of propositions in which the signs occur by means of which the aforementioned signs are defined, (3) the truth of non-elementary propositions depends on the truth-value of the elementary propositions from which they are derived, (4) true elementary propositions exist, and therefore the atomic facts which render them true exist.

The determination that a given series of signs alleged to express a proposition is significant depends on the reduction of the group of signs to elementary propositions by tautological transformations, definitions, and other methods of logical syntax.

If a propositional sign can be dealt with in this fashion it is significant. Otherwise it is not. It is easy to see, therefore, how metaphysics is to be eliminated from significant discourse. No way of determining the method of verifying

173

metaphysical assertions can be given either by syntactical rules or by an empirically possible test. This is the thesis of Logical Positivism.

In this part we shall observe the attempted demonstration of the thesis in the treatment of specific examples of metaphysical propositions. I shall present one of Carnap's examples and then one which I have selected by way of contrast.

The principles which are used to demonstrate that metaphysics is nonsense lead to two rather catastrophic consequences so far as Positivism is concerned. First these very principles contain " metaphysical " assertions, i.e. assertions which cannot be verified by the methods of Positivistic logic. Second the principles render much of science nonsensical by implying a solipsism of language.

These difficulties lead to a first revision of the principles to eliminate the metaphysical assumptions and to avoid the solipsism. This is what I have called the Theory of Knowledge of Positivism. It is really Rudolf Carnap's system of the *Logischer Aufbau der Welt*. I shall present and criticize this system in the third chapter of this part.

CHAPTER VI

ELIMINATION OF METAPHYSICS

In this chapter I shall follow the accounts of Carnap, Schlick, Frank, and other members of the Circle, together with the doctrines of Wittgenstein which I considered in previous chapters.

The first question that confronts us is: What is metaphysics? If metaphysical assertions are to be eliminated from significant discourse by means of logical analysis, it is important to know the distinguishing characteristics of metaphysical assertions. It is easy enough to recognize what Positivists regard as a metaphysical statement. For example, "one substance cannot be produced by another substance," [1] "To be is to be perceived," [2] "The ' I think ' must be able to accompany all of my representations," [3] " Actuality is the unity become immediate, of essence with existence, or of inward with outward," [4] are all metaphysical assertions. It is more difficult to determine what they have in common.

According to the Logical Positivists all assertions of metaphysical character are non-empirical. In other words no empirical method of determining the truth of metaphysical assertions is given. This is, I believe, a true characterization of metaphysics. Unfortunately it is also a characteristic of many of the doctrines of Logical Positivism.

A metaphysical statement, then, is a non-empirical proposition with existential import. The Positivists hold that such statements are pseudopropositions. The principal

[1] Spinoza, B., *Ethica*, Prop. vi, part i.
[2] Berkeley, G., *Principles of Human Knowledge*, i, 2.
[3] Kant, Immanuel, *Kritik der reinen Vernunft*.
[4] Hegel, G. W. F., *Encyclopaedie I Theil*, 142.

175

ground of this contention is that neither logical demonstration nor any method of experiment can reveal the facts enunciated in such statements. Beyond the methods of apodeictic reasoning and experimentation there is no third method of ascertaining meaning and truth.

Metaphysicians would hardly be inclined to question the ascription of non-empirical character to their assertions. The sources of the alleged metaphysical truths are, therefore, non-empirical criteria of meaning. It is impossible to enumerate all of these criteria here but some of the better known may be mentioned.

Some metaphysical systems are constructed by a combination of intuitive and deductive methods. Such are the great rationalistic systems of modern philosophy, those of Descartes, Spinoza, and Leibniz. Certain concepts are presented as luminously clear and distinct, therefore absolutely simple, and hence as providing a point of departure for the deduction of the general features of reality.

Other systems are possible schematic structures into which experience may be fitted. The claims made for such theories are: (1) that they consistently account for all varieties of experience, (2) that, while the theory itself is not *a priori* necessary, some theoretical presupposition of experience must be posited, and (3) the theory in question is probably true.

Still other methods of metaphysical construction could be listed here, but these are sufficient to bring out my contention. Whatever method is used, metaphysics is unquestionably a body of assertions which do not admit of empirical verification. The meanings of such assertions are, therefore, not determined by a method of verification which is empirical or experimental in character.

In a system of metaphysical assertions which are deduced from a set of axioms, two characteristics may be noted. In the first place the axioms must not be postulated arbitrarily or simply believed. They must rather be evidently certain truths. The truth of a metaphysical axiom must, that is, be seen from the mere examination of the axiom. The definitions must contain no concepts save those whose meanings are clear whenever they are presented. In the second place truths deduced from such axioms coincide with necessities of logic, and falsehood becomes self-contradiction. Whatever is called " possible " or " contingent " must accordingly be the result of doubt or the privation of ignorance. This is the character of mathematical systems, the axioms of which are considered to be *a priori* certain. *A fortiori* it is the character of deductive metaphysical systems. This shows that empirical or experimental determinations of truth and meaning are excluded from such systems as certainly as they are from mathematical systems.

In a system of metaphysical assertions which are not deduced but constructed in some other way, it is equally evident that an empirical test of meaning and truth is out of the question. Two possibilities arise : (1) the assertions made by a philosopher are determined empirically in respect of truth and meaning. In this case the assertions are simply true or false and coincide with branches of the natural sciences, (2) the assertions are not empirically determined as to truth and meaning, but are, nevertheless, existential in import. In this case a method of verification, i.e. a criterion of significance, is used which is not empirical. No metaphysical assertion, therefore, is empirically determined in respect of meaning and truth.

It is the non-empirical character of metaphysics which is the principal target for the attacks of Logical Positivism. Significant assertions are limited to the empirically verifiable ; metaphysics is non-empirical and, therefore, nonsense.

The anti-metaphysical part of the Positivist programme consists of two steps : first the demonstration that all propositions are reducible to the elementary propositions which are immediately verifiable in experience ; second the demonstration that errors in logical syntax are responsible for metaphysics. Although I have given the essentials of the first step in the first chapter, I shall repeat them in a slightly different form to recall the principal ideas which are essential for the present purpose.

According to Carnap [1] and other Positivists, logical analysis of meanings, while it consists in relating propositions to the empirical world, is not an empirical activity and its accomplishment does not require the presence of any empirical data. Logical analysis of meaning is conducted within the sphere of language and consists of (1) the reduction of complex meanings to simple ones by means of definitions, tautological transformations, equations, and other rules for manipulating symbols, (2) the presentation of the forms of propositions in order to reveal the essential, internal properties of the symbols in so far as the *rules* of symbolism have not already made this clear, and (3) demonstrative elucidations.

The principle on which this procedure depends is : The meaning of a proposition is the method of its verification. It is important that this principle should not be misunderstood. It is not to be interpreted as signifying that the meaning of a proposition is its verification. This would lead to two absurdities : (1) a proposition could not have sense unless it was verified, (2) false propositions would have no sense. On the other hand, it is clear that if a proposition can be verified at all it must have sense prior to its actual verification. The phrase " method of verification " must be taken to mean " what would be the case if the proposition was true ". As Schlick has expressed it, the meaning of a proposition is the possibility of the state of affairs which it represents.[2]

A slight digression will suffice to explain what possibility means in Wittgenstein's theory. The " possible " as a modal predicate is, of course, excluded from the theory at

[1] Carnap, R., " Überwindung der Metaphysik durch logische Analyse der Sprache," *Erkenntnis*, Bd. ii.
[2] Schlick, M., " Meaning and Verification." Forthcoming article in the *Philosophical Review*.

*cf. Coplestons exclusion of other possibilities = meaning

the outset. " Certainty, possibility, or impossibility of a state of affairs are not expressed by a proposition but by the fact that an expression is a tautology, a significant proposition, or a contradiction." [1] Possibility can best be understood in this way : Given a set of facts which have some common constituents and some common components, it is seen that a certain constituent, say " a ", occurs in several different facts, F_1, F_2, F_3. . . . It is clear, then, that a fact of the same structure as any one of the set, F_1, F_2, F_3 . . ., and containing " a " is a possible fact. " Possibility " is thus a term indicating that a fact is imaginable or constructible because it has the form and constituency of facts which have occurred. For example, it is known that a specific hue ϕ_1 has occurred as the colour of several different objects, and that a given object is a coloured object. Then, although ϕa may never have occurred, the fact is imaginable, i.e. constructible, because all the constituents and the component of such a fact are known to have existed. The " possible " fact is the subject-matter of a proposition perhaps not known to be true but known to contain names of objects arranged in a way which has been realized in true propositions.

When the sense of a proposition is described as the possibility of the state of affairs which it represents, what is meant is that the *kind* of fact represented by the proposition has existed. A proposition may, therefore, also be described as the construction of a possible fact for the purpose of experiment.[2]

It is not necessary, of course, to have an " image " of the alleged fact which is asserted by a proposition in order to understand the sense of the proposition.[3] It is simply necessary to know the method by which the proposition would be verified ; possession of a mental image of the alleged fact is only one of several ways of knowing the method. Another way would be to know the logical form

---

[1] Wittgenstein, op. cit., *supra*, 5.525.   [2] Wittgenstein, 4.031.
[3] So it is said, at least. But it would seem necessary to the understanding of the elementary proposition to be able to imagine its referent, and, without an image, it is difficult to see how this could be the case.

of the proposition, and this is given in the definition of the terms of the language in which the proposition occurs. It is clear, then, what is meant by the statement that the sense of the proposition is the method of its verification.

For the sake of convenience I shall adopt Wittgenstein's terminology and speak (1) of the meaning of names and other ingredients of symbols, whereas when propositions are in question I shall speak generally of their *sense*. It is then possible to give an exhaustive list of all kinds of symbols, signs, etc., in order to explain the logical syntax of language as Wittgenstein conceives it. The logical language of the *Principia Mathematica* is the model from which Wittgenstein derives his own system of language.

The categories of Wittgenstein's symbolism are as follows :—

(I) Undefined primitive signs.

(a) Names of objects. (An object is any ingredient of a fact ; a name is the designation of an object.)

(b) Functions of the names. (These represent the manner in which names are composed and thus the structure of the fact.)

(c) The logical constants or operations. (Only one is required since all logical constants are definable in terms of this one, namely the stroke " / ", interpreted either as mutual rejection [neither . . . nor . . .] or as incompatibility [. . . is incompatible with . . .].)

(d) The elementary proposition. (This is a combination of names in some quite definite way, the way being indicated by the functional sign.)

(e) Forms of elementary propositions and general forms of functions and operations.

(II) Defined signs.

(a) Any truth-functions involving the primitive truth-functions, " / ".

$$\text{e.g. } P \text{ implies } Q = df. \ \overline{P/P/Q}$$
$$P \text{ implies } Q = df. \ \text{not-}(P \text{ and not-}Q).$$

(b) Any truth-function of a specific form of propositions.

e.g. $aR|S\,c = df\,a\,R\,x\,.\,x\,S\,c$

Relative product of two relations = logical product of $aRx.xSc$.

(c) Any truth-function limiting the scope of an apparent variable.

$$(x)\phi x = df.\ \phi a.\phi b.\phi c.\phi d.\phi e$$
$$(\exists x)\phi x = df.\ \phi a v \phi b v \phi c v \phi d v \phi e$$

(d) Specific instances of the application of operational schemata or forms.

$$\text{e.g. } \Omega^v\,{}^{\cdot}\Omega^{\cdot}\chi = df.\ \Omega^{v+1}\,{}^{\cdot}\chi$$
$$N\,{}^{\cdot}N^v\,{}^{\cdot}P = df.\ N^{v+1}\,{}^{\cdot}P.$$

This list (perhaps not entirely complete) may be summarized as follows : Language consists (1) of names, the use of each of which is predetermined by those elementary propositions in which a given name occurs : (2) of the elementary propositions thus formed ; (3) of truth-functions of the elementary propositions all of which are defined in terms of a single primitive function, the stroke ; (4) of definitions of truth-functions ; (5) of real variables which exhibit (a) the structure of facts or (b) the structure of sign-complexes ; (6) of nominal definitions of sign-complexes.

The meaning of the names is determined by the sense of the propositions in which the names occur. The sense of any truth-function of a group of elementary propositions is determined by the sense of the elementary propositions and by the way they are combined in the truth-function. Hence the sense of any complex proposition presupposes the sense and truth of the elementary proposition, whereas the sense of elementary propositions presupposes only the way in which the objects are possibly or actually combined with one another. All defined signs signify in and through the signs by which they are defined. Ultimately these signs occur as parts of the elementary proposition or as forms of the elementary propositions. Everything in symbolism finally depends, therefore, on the elementary propositions and these depend on the empirical structure of the world. It is consequently impossible to say anything which is not finally connected with some possible or actual empirical fact or other.

The elimination of metaphysics by means of logical analysis simply consists of showing that, within a correctly constructed language, metaphysical (i.e. non-empirical) terms occur only in such sentences as cannot be reduced to the elementary propositions. The application of the rules of the language (nominal definitions and demonstrative symbols [1]) would always show that some error in the construction of symbols had occurred whenever metaphysical sentences or terms were found in the language. These sentences or terms would be, therefore, without any significance.

Thus the Viennese Positivists divide sentences into two mutually exclusive groups, namely significant sentences or propositions and non-significant sentences or pseudo-propositions. Significant sentences or propositions are capable of verification. This is a tautology, since, by definition, a capacity for verification constitutes the significance of the propositions. Non-significant sentences are not capable of verification. In this latter case the incapacity of verification is not merely a practical impossibility. When it is said that a proposition is theoretically unverifiable, this means that no method of verification can be given in the nature of the case. It may be that a given proposition is significant even though there is no method at present by which it may be verified. The lack of means of verification in this case is not a theoretical lack but a practical one. We do not, for example, possess the instruments necessary to verify statements about the other side of the moon or about the interior of the stars. This inability is simply the lack of technical facilities. Verification is, therefore, out of the question because of the lack of these

---

[1] What Schlick, op. cit., calls " deictic definitions ".

technical devices. Nevertheless, we can formulate the rules by means of which such a proposition as " There is a mountain on the dark side of the moon " would be verified. It is altogether otherwise in the case of theoretical incapacity of verification. It is impossible to formulate the rules by means of which verification would proceed in this case. For example, it is theoretically impossible to verify the statement " Adjectives love analysis ". It is likewise impossible to verify the statement " The Babig is green ". Again, " 'Twas brillig and the slithy toves Did gyre and gimble in the wabe " is incapable of verification. In all these the syntax of the propositions is not known. There is, therefore, no method of determining what would be the case if these alleged propositions were true. This is true not only of these cases of obvious nonsense, but also of all non-empirical assertions.

The Cartesian resolution of doubt is a capital illustration of the metaphysical misunderstanding of the logical syntax of language. For the Continental rationalists, two of the most important sources of knowledge were intuition and deduction. The *cogito ergo sum* may be interpreted either as the expression of an immediate intuition or as a deduction. Either interpretation reveals the senselessness of the statement. On the hypothesis that it is the expression of an immediate intuition, it would be necessary to show that " I think, therefore, I exist " was composed entirely of names representing objects. This cannot be done because what is given here is the immediate presentation of a feeling. From such a feeling the proposition " this is a thought-feeling " may be formed. The other words occurring in the cogito, viz. " I ", " therefore ", " exist ", cannot possibly be fitted into the context of an elementary proposition. This refutes the hypothesis that the cogito expresses a primitive fact of intuition. On the hypothesis that the cogito is an inference (which Descartes and Spinoza expressly deny) it would have the form :—

" I think " implies " something thinking exists ". But

the antecedent must be changed to " something thinks "
from the consideration just mentioned. We have, then :—

" Something thinks " implies " something thinking
exists ". This, in logical symbolism, is $\phi u . \supset . (\exists x) \phi x$, which
is a tautology. Tautologies assert no facts because, as has
been shown above (Chapter II), they are entirely concerned
with symbols. In this case ϕu is one way of saying $(\exists x) \phi x$.
Nothing has been demonstrated about the world. On this
hypothesis, the cogito is a deduction but it presents nothing
new, and, moreover, does not demonstrate what Descartes
attempted, i.e. that a simple, identical, substantial, and
spiritual entity exists.

The important thing to notice about this treatment of the
cogito is the elimination of the first person from the proposition. The means of determining the sense of " I think "
cannot be given, so that, in this form, the proposition is
meaningless, whereas if it is changed to " something thinks ",
the deduction " a thinking thing exists " is evidently
no new information. Consequently nothing metaphysical
could be intuited or inferred from the proposition.

I believe that the method of logical analysis as it is
applied to eliminating the pseudoassertions of metaphysics
may best be shown in some more detailed cases. Carnap
has given a good illustration of the analysis of some pseudo-
propositions. I shall add to this an analysis of faulty
deductive procedure in metaphysics.

According to Carnap (in agreement with Wittgenstein,
Schlick, and others), the logical syntax of a language fixes
the meaning of every word and the sense of every proposition in the language. Errors of interpretation of meaning
and sense can, therefore, be traced to two principal sources :

(1) words are used in propositions which have no
determinate meaning.

(2) a word which possesses a meaning in the context of
certain propositions is used in the context of other
propositions in which it has no meaning.

" 'Twas brillig and the slithy toves," etc., is an example of the first sort of error. (I have not forgotten that Carroll supposed that we could make words mean whatever we wished. The Positivist denies just this thing.) " Adjectives love analysis," " Cæsar is a prime number," and " Substance is essence including its own existence," are all examples of the second species of error.

To show how metaphysical nonsense arises and also how it can be corrected, Carnap selects some passages from Heidegger's " Was ist Metaphysik ? " The most important of these passages is the following : " Only the existing is to be studied, and otherwise—nothing ; the existing alone and further—nothing ; the existing uniquely and beyond this—nothing. What about this *nothing* ? Is there *nothing* only because there is *not*, i.e. *negation* ? Or is it just the converse ? Do *negation* and *not* exist only because *nothing* exists ? We assert that *nothing* is more primitive than *not* and *negation*. Where do we seek for *nothing* ? How do we find it ? We know it. Care reveals *nothing*. Why and wherefore we experience care is ' essentially ' *nothing*. In fact, *nothing* itself—as such—was there. What is the condition of *nothing* ? The *nothing* itself nothings." (This is not a complete connected passage but is selected from several different sections of Heidegger's essay.)

Carnap then proceeds to analyse this passage in order to show that it consists almost wholly of senseless series of words, that is sentences with which no sense is combined and which, as a consequence, are pseudopropositions. The pseudopropositions arise because of the violation of the rules of logical syntax. The errors in syntax are, in general, of one or both of the kinds mentioned above, viz. the use of words which have no determinate meaning of any kind, or the use of words in a context to which they are wholly unsuited, even though the words have meanings in some contexts.

" In order," writes Carnap, " to show that the possibility of constructing pseudopropositions rests on a logical misunderstanding of language, let us set up the following schema :—

I. SIGNIFICANT PROPOSITIONS OF ORDINARY LANGUAGE	II. GENESIS OF NONSENSE FROM SIGNIFICANCE IN ORDINARY LANGUAGE.	III. LOGICALLY CORRECT LANGUAGE

A. What is outside ?
     outside (?)
     Rain is outside
     outside (rain).
	A. What is outside ?
	     outside (?)
	     Nothing is outside
	     outside (nothing).
		A. There is not something which is outside.
		     $\sim(\exists x).x$ is outside.

B. What about this rain ?
     (i.e., what is the rain doing, or what more can, be said about the rain ?)
     ? (rain)
	B. What about this nothing?
	     ? (nothing)
		B. None of these forms can be constructed.

(1) We perceive the rain.
     perceive (rain).
	(1) We seek the nothing.
	     We find the nothing. We perceive the nothing.
	     perceive (nothing).	

(2) The rain rains.
     rains (rain).
	(2) The nothing nothings.
	     nothings (nothing).
	     (3) There is a nothing only because . . .
	     exists (nothing) . . .	

" The propositions in I are grammatically as well as logically free from objection, hence, significant. The propositions in II (exception B (3)) stand grammatically in complete analogy to those in I. The propositional forms, IIA (a question and answer), do not satisfy the requirements placed upon a logically correct language but they are, nevertheless, significant, since they can be translated into correct language ; this is shown by the fact that IIIA has the same sense as IIA. The unsuitable character of the propositional form IIA is shown by the fact that we can be led from it to the senseless propositional form IIB by grammatically unobjectionable operations. . . . The formation of the proposition (in IIB) simply rests on the error that the word ' nothing ' is employed as the name of an object since one is bound to employ it in this form in order to formulate a negative existence-proposition in ordinary language. In a correct language, on the other hand, a certain logical form of the proposition (IIIA) serves the same purpose without introducing an especial name.[1] In proposition IIB (2) something new is introduced, namely the formation of the meaningless word ' to nothing ' ; hence the proposition is senseless on two counts. We have shown above that the

[1] i.e. negation of existence is expressed by the prefix $\sim(\exists x)$ . . . rather than by the substantive " nothing ".

meaningless words of metaphysics usually arise in this way, that a meaning is assigned to a significant word by its metaphorical employment in metaphysics. Here, on the contrary, we have one of the infrequent instances of a new word being introduced which has no meaning to begin with. Proposition IIB (3) is likewise to be rejected on two counts. It agrees with the foregoing propositions in the error of using the word ' nothing ' as the name of an object. Moreover, it contains a contradiction. Even if it were permissible to introduce ' nothing ' as the name or description of an object, the existence of this object would be denied by its definition but would be asserted again in proposition B. This proposition, if it were not already senseless, would be contradictory and thus meaningless.[1]

" In view of these logical howlers, which we find in the proposition IIB, we might entertain the suspicion that perhaps the word ' nothing ' has a meaning in the treatise cited completely different from other usages. This suspicion is further strengthened if we read further that care (*Angst*) reveals the *nothing* ; that, in care, nothing itself is present. Indeed, here it seems that the word ' nothing ' is to designate a certain intuitive conception, perhaps of a religious sort, or something which lies at the foundation of such an intuition. If that were the case then the logical errors mentioned in regard to the proposition IIB would not occur. However, the beginning of the passage quoted shows that this interpretation is out of the question. From the comparison of ' only ' and ' and nothing further ' it follows definitely that the word ' nothing ' has here the usual significance of a logical particle, which serves for the expression of a negated existence-proposition. Then this introduction of the word ' nothing ' is followed directly by

---

[1] Carnap would now distinguish between " unsinnig " and " widersinnig ". A contradiction is not " unsinnig " but rather " widersinnig ". For this see Husserl, E., *Logische Untersuchungen*, 2. Bd., p. 326, and also Wittgenstein, *Tractatus*, 4.461, " Tautology and contradiction are without sense (*sinnlos*)," 4.4611 " Tautology and contradiction are not, however, senseless (*unsinnig*) ; they are a part of the symbolism just as " 0 " is a part of the symbolism of arithmetic."

the principal question of the treatise 'what about this nothing ? ' . . . Hence we find a good corroboration of our thesis." [1]

Carnap suggests that the other metaphysical usages of the word " nothing " such as, e.g., Hegel's assertion that " Pure being and pure nothing are the same ", can be treated with the same kind of analysis and likewise shown to be nonsense.

The principal points of interest in Carnap's analysis reveal the way in which pseudo-propositions, *qua* propositions, arise in discourse. Most metaphysics involves the use of another kind of error not explicitly treated by Carnap in the article from which I have just quoted. This is the faulty deductive procedure characteristic of most rationalism and idealism. I think it not out of place to present some application of positivistic analysis to this type of error.

As everyone knows, the fundamental presupposition of rationalism is the doctrine that ratiocination is somehow capable of discovering the truth about the world. The qualification that every specific truth may not be discovered is, as has been frequently pointed out, not to be regarded as an essential limitation of the rationalistic method. This limitation depends, it is said, on the temporal limitation of human understanding, rather than on the power of the rationalistic method itself. It is supposed to be sufficient if the *general* features of reality are adumbrated. I shall not question this point.

The principal difference between rationalistic and empiristic theories in respect of meaning and truth are, as I have noted above, the following :—

(1) For rationalism (especially deductive rationalism), the criterion of the meaning of a concept is to be found in the concept itself or in some other concept which contains the meaning of the concept in question.

[1] Carnap, " Überwindung der Metaphysik," *Erkenntnis*, Bd. ii, pp. 229–232.

For empiricism (here I restrict myself to Positivistic empiricism) the meaning of a concept is to be found in other concepts which determine its meaning and, finally, in the reference of the concepts to the data (i.e. something not conceptual at all).

(2) For rationalism, the truth of an assertion is either evident from the nature of the assertion or is deducible from other assertions.

For empiricism the truth of an assertion depends either on the truth of other assertions or on the correspondence of the sense of the assertion with the data which lie beyond discourse altogether.

Truth, in rationalistic systems, thus becomes identified with evident or deductive necessity, and falsehood with evident or deductive impossibility. In empiristic systems the truth of assertions cannot be determined by an examination of the assertions as such ; truth can only be established, in the final analysis, by a comparison of an assertion with its alleged datum. These observations make it abundantly clear that rationalism insists on our capacity to deduce or intuit the truth about the world.

One further observation is necessary before I proceed to analyse the method of rationalism. The species of deductive method employed by rationalistic philosophers differs radically from that employed by empiristic philosophers. Empiricism requires the extensional logic, whereas rationalism requires a logic of intension. The essential difference between these two logical systems consists of the relation in which concepts stand to one another. The relation of the subject and predicate of assertions in the two logical systems reveals the difference as well as any other example. Let S stand for the subject of an assertion, P for the predicate, $\subset$ for inclusion. Then, $S \subset P$ in extension, whereas $P \subset S$ in intension. The syllogism in Barbara is likewise differently interpreted in the two logics. Thus " $A \subset B$ and $B \subset C$ implies $A \subset C$ " in extension, whereas " $B \subset A$ and $C \subset B$ implies $C \subset A$ " in intension. The difference in syllogistic meaning is even more marked when a negative premise is introduced. Thus, in intension, " A includes B and B does not include C does not imply A excludes C," whereas, in extension, " A is included in B and B is not included in C implies A is not included in C."

This difference shows how it is possible, granting the validity of intensional inference and the legitimacy of the claim that certain simple concepts ostensibly contain a whole group of other concepts, to deduce the general features of reality from a concept sufficiently rich in comprehension. It also shows how such a concept may be derived by the converse procedure, namely the derivation of the "fullest" concept from relatively empty ones by demonstrating their dependence on other concepts and the latter on others until the ultimate and independent concept is attained.

This method was pursued by, for example, Spinoza, who derived reality from the concept of substance. I do not mean to give the impression that Spinoza did not employ many axioms and definitions ostensibly different from the concept of substance. The point is that some of the definitions are redundant, while others are contained in the concept of substance. Other definitions are simply the correlatives of the essential properties of substance. Thus " cause of itself " and " substance " are redundant, " free " is a part of " substance ", " finite in its kind " is a correlative of " infinity ". It is true also that " postulates " are introduced at several points. But these postulates are entailed by the general nature of reality, i.e. they follow from the concept of substance implicitly or ostensibly. Similar, though not identical, methods are used by idealistic philosophers. In Spinoza's case it is easy to establish the erroneous character of such a deduction. Complex concepts entail all the simpler concepts composing them. From a simple concept, however, more complex concepts cannot be derived by deductive procedure (nor, in fact, by any procedure). Now the concept of substance is either simple or complex. If it is absolutely simple, nothing can be deduced from it, whereas if it is complex only those concepts can be deduced from it which are contained in it as constituents. In the former case the derivation of any feature of reality is impossible ; in the latter the concept of substance is composed of a group of concepts which determine its meaning. Whatever is deduced in *this* case is already contained in the concept *ex hypothesi* and nothing is revealed that was not already known. The intensional logical method is an attempt to avoid this result. Accordingly it is supposed that concepts may enter into other concepts in another way than by composition. It is then possible to maintain (1) that a concept is simple and (2) that it contains other concepts. This is, it must be admitted, difficult to maintain, except in a very restricted class of cases which are irrelevant to the present issue, e.g. " x is red entails x is coloured ".

If it *is* maintained, another difficulty is encountered from which there is no escape. If the concept is simple it will not be possible to ascertain what concepts are derivable from it. This difficulty is not overcome simply by the doctrine that one concept can contain other concepts in another way than by composition. Not only is the latter doctrine wholly unexplained but also, even if accepted, the doctrine cannot tell us what we can derive from the simple concept. Thus the intensional logic presents two dogmas without any supporting evidence : (1) that a concept can contain other concepts without being a composition of them, and (2) that deductions can be made from the simplest concept.

The only way out of these difficulties is to admit that the whole rationalistic procedure is a mistake. Whenever deductions are made from propositions, the deduced proposition is wholly or partially identical with the original. In either case nothing has been proved about the world. If $P \supset P$ then the same thing is merely repeated. If $P \supset Q$ (necessary, i.e. tautological, implication is meant), then P must be composite and Q must be one of its parts. Here less is said in Q than was said in P. Again, nothing is proved.

If this is true then the intensional method is based on the

erroneous supposition that a concept or an assertion can contain other concepts or assertions in some other way than by being complexes of the latter. With the elimination of this error, the entire structure of rationalism falls. The statement of Hume—that the sort of rationalistic argument which has been considered is " nothing but a mere imperfect definition "—definitely settles the whole matter. The deductions of rationalistic logic, i.e. intensional logic, are deductions from implicit definitions. As long as the rationalist refuses to define his original terms, he is subject to the criticism which Positivists bring against metaphysics, namely that the meaning of its concepts and the sense of its assertions cannot be made determinate. If, however, the terms in question are defined, the deductions from them are purely tautological transformations of the definitions and thus establish nothing.

Similar considerations obtain for the method of rationalism. It depends, as I have said, on two unjustified theses : (1) That intuition is a form of knowledge through which simple concepts may be known and (2) that a mode of reasoning is possible which is distinct from the extensional method of logic.

*   *   *   *

These illustrations suffice to show the method of positivists in eliminating metaphysics. All metaphysical problems may be treated in this way. The analysis of causation, of the alleged freedom of the will, of the concept of existence, and so on, can be accomplished by similar applications of logic.[1]

The point at issue between Positivist and metaphysician is now clear and can be stated without reference to any particular problem. Is there any method of explaining the world of science and everyday experience other than the reduction of propositions (which allegedly provide such an

---

[1] See Frank, P., *Das Kausalgesetz und seine Grenzen*, Wien, 1932, for an analysis of causation ; Schlick, M., *Fragen der Ethik*, Wien, 1930, pp. 105–111, for an analysis of the concept of free-will ; *Principia Mathematica*, vol. i, 14, for an analysis of the concept of existence.

explanation) to the elementary propositions whose sense is completely determined by the real or possible empirical facts with which they are concerned ? The metaphysician answers affirmatively and claims a special method whereby the meaning of non-empirical concepts and the truth of non-empirical propositions is revealed to him. The Positivist claims that syntactical analysis makes it logically impossible that such a method exist. The grounds for the metaphysician's claim have been, generally speaking, intuition, deduction from intuitively certain propositions, and similar non-empirical sources of knowledge. The Positivistic grounds for rejecting the validity of this claim have been the establishment of a logical language ultimately based on the elementary propositions, in which metaphysical speculation is logically impossible. In this language metaphysical sentences can be given no sense. The rejection of metaphysics is, I believe, fundamentally sound. It is in place, however, to ask whether the Positivistic principles on which it is based are wholly sound in themselves. Does the Positivistic analysis contain any metaphysics ? If not, does it contain anything equally objectionable ?

In the first place it seems best to put aside a petty objection to the Positivistic treatment of language. While it is true that no language has been constructed which is logically perfect (complete, demonstrably consistent, etc.), it is an admissible fiction to assume the existence of such a language if the general rules for its construction are known. Moreover, ordinary language is of such a character that rigorous logical analysis cannot be carried on within its limits. One of the many reasons for this is the following : In a logically perfect language the sense of every proposition is determined by the elementary propositions to which it is reducible. The rules for such reduction are explicitly given in the proposition. For example, the sense of " a is north-west of b (in a flat map) " is determined by its translation or reduction into " a is north of x and x is west of b ". In a language in which the rules determining the sense of propositions are not explicit, the following situation might arise [1] :—

Assume that there are two languages, S and S', such that every proposition of S corresponds to a proposition of S' (with the same sense as the proposition of S) ; the converse does not obtain. It would then be possible (1) that a proposition P of S would be translatable into a proposition P' of S', (2) that P' of S' could be transformed into some given P'_1 of S', (3) that, however, no translation could occur between P of S and P'_1 of S' or between any proposition of S and P'_1. Thus :—

(1) P is identical in sense with P' and a rule to show this exists.

(2) P' is identical in sense with P'_1 and a rule to show this exists.

(3) By syllogism, if $P = P' . P' = P'_1$ we should have $P = P'_1$,

but since there is no rule by which P or any other expression of S is translatable into P'_1, $P = P'_1$ cannot be asserted. Hence S is an incomplete language because there are propositions in S' equivalent to propositions of S which cannot be expressed in S. Another way of saying the same thing is that some of the rules for the determination of sense are implicit or latent in S. As long as this is the case, logical analysis cannot be successfully carried out in respect of S. The language of everyday life and even the language of *Principia Mathematica* are incomplete in this sense. It is, therefore, an admissible fiction to suppose that a language exists in which every sense is determined by explicit rules. Consequently it is a petty and ineffective criticism to urge that ordinary language does not have the structure required to eliminate metaphysics. The possibility of such a perfect language has been, in essentials, shown to be genuine because we can state the conditions which such a language would have to fulfil.

[1] This example is from Ajdukiewicz K., " Sprache und Sinn," *Erkenntnis*, Bd. 4, Heft 2, p. 120.

There are, nevertheless, two serious objections which may be raised against the theory of language through which metaphysics is allegedly shown to be nonsense. First, the criterion of sense depends on an assumption for which there is neither logical nor empirical justification. Second, the theory of language which depends on the criterion of sense cannot be expressed. Thus there is the paradox of a theory of logical syntax which cannot be formulated.

In the first chapter I showed that the doctrine of logical atomism could not be proved by Wittgenstein's argument about the infinite regress of meaning. It is impossible to demonstrate the existence of ultimate simples by means of the assumptions about language (in particular, about the sense of propositions) ; conversely, the assumption of logical atoms cannot prove that language is absolutely unambiguous in Wittgenstein's sense. The univocality of sense depends on the simple nature of objects, yet the simple nature of objects is not a sufficient reason for the existence of univocal propositions. Nothing can be satisfactorily demonstrated either way from the logical point of view.

If the existence of elementary propositions, that is propositions the sense of which is univocally and immediately determined by the atomic facts, cannot be demonstrated, the doctrine that the meaning of all concepts is grounded in the empirical world remains unproved, assuming that empiricism involves atomism as some Logical Positivists evidently assume. The elimination of metaphysics, however, depends on this unproved dogma. Metaphysics, therefore, cannot be eliminated from significant discourse by this method.

It must not be thought that this result saves metaphysics, for there are other methods of eliminating it. All that my argument proves is that Positivism cannot wholly eliminate metaphysics by its own methods. If another meaning is given to the statement " The sense of a proposition is determined by the method of its verification ", it is still possible to show that metaphysical assertions cannot be established or refuted by any experiment.

The second objection results from Wittgenstein's doctrine that the structure of the facts is shown or mirrored *in* the propositions but is not expressible *by* propositions. The pictorial relation which obtains between the proposition and its objective, being a presupposition of the possibility of representation, cannot, in its turn, be represented. Now the most important branch of logical syntax should treat of the structure of the elementary propositions because it is upon them that the entire significance of language depends. (This obtains without prejudice from the preceding objection, inasmuch as *every* language, including relativistic ones, will have elementary propositions.) If Wittgenstein's limitation of language to the expressible is valid, the logical syntax of the elementary propositions cannot be expressed but must be shown. But a logical syntax which cannot be expressed is a contradiction in terms. It is a misnomer to call the " deictic " definitions and operational rules of elementary propositions by the name " *logical syntax* ". All statements *about* the entire structure of language must therefore be regarded as nonsense.   ? unswern vs. Sinlos

This final result may be illustrated in some examples. A proposition about the syntactical relations obtaining within a given language might have the following form : " P_1 " $= df.$ " ' P_2 ' means what is meant by ' P_3 ' ". It is easy to show that the criterion of the truth of P_1 cannot be given without circularity. In order to know whether P_1 is true it is necessary to understand the meaning of P_2 and P_3 (assuming, of course, that P_2 is not a nominal equivalent of P_3), whereas in order to understand the meaning of P_2 and P_3 it is necessary to know that P_1 is true.[1] The syntactical assertion P_1 has no significance since

---

[1] This derives from Juhos, B., " Kritische Bermerkungen zur Wissenschaftstheorie der Physikalismus," *Erkenntnis*, Bd. 4, Heft 6, p. 401. The circle which he presents is not identical with what I have given here, although the same principle is involved. Juhos gives the following : Let $P_2 = df.$ A understands $P_1 \equiv A$ behaves in such and such a way.

the method of its verification cannot be given. The identity of meaning of two expressions cannot be asserted but must be shown, i.e. that two expressions signify in the same way must be seen in the inspection of the expressions.[1]

Again, let it be assumed that an elucidation (deictic definition) could actually explain the meaning of a name occurring in an elementary proposition. For example, take " aRb " and suppose the elucidation has the form : " The ' a ' in ' aRb ' means . . ." In order to explain the meaning of the primitive sign " a ", the elucidation must include mention of " a ". It is not possible to understand the meaning of a proposition unless the meaning of each part is understood. Since the elucidation in question contains " a ", it can only be understood when the meaning of " a " is known. Wherefore it is superfluous and circular, and thus, on both counts, meaningless.

Another example of the attempt to formulate a syntactical principle makes it clear again that the syntax of Wittgenstein's language is not formulable. The syntax of a language would classify words in groups such as adjectives (= functions), nouns (= names), etc. Adjectives would also be grouped as colour-words, sound-words, etc. There would therefore be a syntactical proposition of the form : " ' Red ' is a colour-word ". In order to verify this proposition one of two methods would have to be employed : (1) it would be necessary to know all the propositions in which " red " was used and also to know that " blue " could replace " red " in these propositions without making nonsense ; or (2) it would be necessary to see from an inspection of several propositions involving " red ", " blue ", etc., that they possessed a particular kind of structure. Now (1), besides being factually an impossible task, would presuppose that the common structure could somehow be

Now P_2 is not equivalent with P_1. Therefore one must, on the one hand, know that P_2 is true in order to understand P_1, whereas, on the other hand, one must have already understood P_1 in order to determine the truth of P_2. This is an obvious circle.

[1] Wittgenstein, op. cit., *supra*, 6.2322.

intuited, whereas (2) is an admission that intuition rather than expression is necessary to understand how " red " occurs in propositions. In either case " ' Red ' is a colour-word " becomes a pseudoproposition, for no way of verifying it can be given.

On Positivistic principles no syntactical proposition asserts anything. As a consequence " The meaning of a proposition is the method of its verification ", which itself is a syntactical proposition, is nonsense. It is reasonable to reject any account of meaning which is self-stultifying and, on this ground, if no other, the Positivistic theory of meaning should be abandoned. The logical elimination of metaphysics depends on the theory of logical syntax which I have described here. Since this theory fails, the assertions of metaphysics cannot be shown to be absurd by *this* method.

It might be urged as a reply to the foregoing criticism that there are two kinds of nonsense. First there is the nonsense which results from the use of words which have no meaning at all, or of words which have a meaning in some contexts but not in the one in which they are used in the nonsensical case in question. Then there is the nonsense which results from the attempt to say what can only be shown. The latter is important nonsense in so far as crude verbal attempts of this kind may orient us so that we can see the inexpressible. This is, I think, an evasion of the issue. If there are two kinds of nonsense it must be possible *discursively* to distinguish them by pointing out what differences exist between them. *Ex hypothesi* this is out of the question. If a sentence is nonsense it is impossible to say anything about it ; consequently it is impossible to say wherein two different nonsenses differ. This is reinforced by the fact that we cannot, on Wittgenstein's principles, express any significant sentence about " the sense of propositions " ; *a fortiori*, it would be impossible to say anything significant about " nonsense ".

Thus, within the very limits set by this theory of logical

syntax, intolerable contradictions and other fallacies occur which render it unacceptable. There is, as I have pointed out in Part II (Chapters II and III), another difficulty which lies outside these limits, but is, nevertheless, important. The Positivistic criterion of meaning includes all prescriptive formulæ and all theory in the realm of pseudopropositions. There is no possibility of verifying a direction or command. Sentences expressing directions and commands are meaningless. Ethical principles and directions in scientific manuals are thus kinds of nonsense. Theories are groups of propositional functions (usually axiomatically arranged). There is no possibility of verifying a propositional function. Therefore, theories are nonsense. I am sure that Positivists are not prepared to admit quite all of this.[1] Nevertheless, a consistent adherence to the criterion of meaning entails the elimination of prescriptions, theories, and other indispensable devices of science and practice. This, then, is a further count against the method of Logical Positivism.

* * * *

It is now clear that Logical Positivism cannot eliminate metaphysics without destroying itself, and that it cannot establish the logical foundations of science without alteration of the principles absolutely essential to its teaching.

However, even if it is assumed that Positivism could somehow survive all these objections, certain consequences of its criterion of meaning constitute a permanent barrier to the establishment of the foundations of science. I shall assume, for the sake of argument, that the elimination of metaphysics has been accomplished successfully by means of the criterion of meaning. I shall then show that this criterion leads to a result which is wholly inimical to science. This demands a special chapter.

[1] See however, Karl Popper's communication to *Erkenntnis* (Bd. iii, pp. 426–7), and his *Logik der Forschung*, Wien, 1935, in which the same point is forcibly argued.

Chapter VII

✓ LINGUISTIC SOLIPSISM

If the sense of propositions depends on the possibility that certain empirical facts exist, then no significant statement can be made about inferred entities such as physical objects and other minds. The significance of language is thus limited to the realm of possible experience. This leads to the astounding result that significant propositions are incommunicable, which is what may be called linguistic solipsism.

This comes about in the following way. All significant propositions are truth-functions of the elementary propositions. The sense of the elementary propositions taken collectively is determined by the totality of possible empirical facts. This is, I suppose, a finite, because explicit, totality, but it is boundless. There is a sense in which language is limited in the kind of application it may have. This limitation is determined by the empirically possible.

Nothing significant could be said, therefore, about any reality which *ex hypothesi* remains outside the limits of possible experience. This is a kind of solipsism. Statements about the " experience " of another person would then have to be interpreted so as to be statements about experience in the proper sense. If a person, A, is said to see a triangular spot of a blue hue at time t_0, this state of affairs must be described in empirical terms. Consequently, if the statement " A sees a blue triangular spot at t_0 " is made, and if I make a similar statement " There is a blue triangular spot now ", the analysis of these statements in terms of my experience will yield quite different results. The former statement will reduce to a statement about the behaviour of A, the latter is a statement about immediate data.

There is no way to avoid the ultimate difference between these two kinds of propositions. Assertions made by what I call " a human being " occur in my language (i.e. the language of experiential facts) in the form of indirect discourse and cannot be transformed into direct discourse, without altering the significance of the statements. Thus " *A* says that it is 30° C." is, for me, not a statement about temperature, but a statement about *A*. On the other hand " It is 30° C.", is a statement about temperature and not about me. But " I say it is 30° C." is a statement about my behaviour and not about the temperature.

It is not difficult to see why this is the case. Symbols, in the final analysis, have either a direct reference to facts of experience or are not symbols. If I utter a series of sounds or write a series of marks, any sense attached to these series is directly related to my experience, real or possible. The signs used by another must always be interpreted as facts of his behaviour as long as I cannot suppose the signs to refer to my experience. Indeed, what is called " another person " is a configuration of the facts of my experience. I cannot even imagine what the meaning of the experience of another might possibly be on such a view.

It is, of course, a misnomer to speak of *my* experience. Experience is simply whatever atomic experiential facts there happen to be. It is quite impersonal and is not mine in any sense. In fact, except in the sense that " I " am a certain configuration of experience, the word " I " has no significance. The solipsism resulting from Wittgenstein's theory is not a metaphysical egoism. The ego or metaphysical substance is as much a pseudoconcept as any other metaphysical idea. " The thinking presenting subject ; there is no such thing. If I wrote a book ' The World as I Found It ', I should have to report therein on my body and say which members obey my will and which do not, etc. This then would be a method of isolating the subject or, rather, of showing that in an important sense there is no subject : that is to say, of it alone in this book, mention could not be made. The subject does not belong to the world but is a limit of the world. Here we see that solipsism strictly carried out coincides with pure realism, the I in solipsism shrinks to an extensionless point and there remains the reality co-ordinated with it." [1] Elementary experience is not enclosed within an ego in any sense. The individual facts are independent of one another and could not, therefore, form a closed totality. There is, moreover, no fact of experience corresponding to the experience of an ego. Hence there would be no sense in affirming or denying the existence of such an entity.

What solipsism means cannot be expressed by language, but it is shown by the fact that language has significant application to the empirical facts alone. Nevertheless, I do not see any way to explain what is meant by this solipsism of meaning other than to refer to the difference between statements made by *myself* and those made by others.

Statements in the form of direct discourse are directly about experiential facts, whereas statements in indirect discourse containing proper names of individuals are about the behaviour of the individuals in question. This result depends on two principles one of which may be valid, the other of which, as I have tried to show, is not.

The first principle has already been discussed in Chapter I of this study. One proposition can enter into a larger proposition only as a base of the truth-operation which produced the larger proposition. Thus " P ", in " PvQ ", is a base of the operation " v " which produces the logical sum " PvQ ", whereas " P " in " A says P " is not a proposition at all since " A says P " is not a truth-function of P. In this case P must be a fact in its own right for it certainly cannot occur symbolically in this usage. Therefore, from a logical standpoint, the statements contained in statements of indirect discourse are not symbols at all.

The second principle is simply that whatever sentences

[1] Wittgenstein, op. cit. *supra*, 5.621–5.64. Cf. Popper-Lynkeus, J., *Erkenntnis*, Bd. iii, pp. 309–314.

cannot find interpretation in terms of possible experience are nonsensical sentences. Now, since the statements made by A cannot find an interpretation in terms of my possible experience, such statements, *qua* statements, are nonsense for me. " A says P " may, nevertheless, be interpreted as a fact of A's behaviour, because, in such an interpretation, it does have significance in terms of my experience (i.e. possible experience).

Objects, in the sense of inferred physical entities, are evidently in the same position. The object which lies beyond my experience is a pseudo-object, for no significant assertion could possibly be made concerning it.

There is thus a complete solipsism in the significance of language. This leads to a difficulty which is even more serious. Language is not a means of communication among individuals, for if there is no sense whatever in talking about experiences which, *ex hypothesi*, are excluded from my experience, there is certainly no sense in talking about communication. Nevertheless, the subject is important because it is a necessary condition of objectivity in science. Moreover, some Positivists have written as though they regarded " communication " as a significant term.[1]

Now it is easy to show that, whether the Positivist admits the significance of the statement that " several groups of experiences are logically possible " or whether he denies this possibility, communication is out of the question.

On the first hypothesis there would be a group of experiences X associated with a group of symbols S, another group of experiences X' associated with a group of symbols S', and so on. This would be a kind of monadology in which the monads would be *groups* of experience (or perhaps it would be better to say experiential facts) rather than *substances*, the predicates of which were perceptual states. We could make one of three assumptions here.

[1] Schlick, M., " Erleben, Erkennen und Metaphysik," *Kant-Studien*, Bd. 31, pp. 146–158.

A 1. X and X' have no common members, i.e. no members qualitatively identical.

A 2. X and X' have some members qualitatively identical but differ in others.

A 3. X and X' have all members qualitatively identical.

It is clear that the members would be numerically different in any case; otherwise X and X' would fall together wholly or partially.

Communication would be impossible on any of these auxiliary hypotheses. The symbols S associated with X have meaning only in respect of X; likewise, the symbols S' have meaning only in respect of X'. There would be no means whereby communication considered as a *causal* process could be effected save by way of a kind of pre-established harmony. Even supposing this (for it is a *logical* possibility) communication as a logical interchange of meaning between X and X' is still out of the question.

I shall suppose that a proposition P which is significant in respect of some member x [1] of X is given to X'. Then, since the meaning of P is the method of its verification, and since the verification of P could occur only in respect of x in X, no member of X' could supply a meaning for P in X'. This is immediately evident from A 1. It also obtains for A 2 and A 3. Suppose that x and x' are qualitatively identical but numerically distinct. (x and x' are facts and, in a sense, since facts are individuals, it may be thought that individuals cannot differ *solo numero*. In our fictitious universe this may be neglected. Mere numerical difference is a logical possibility for any two or more ingredients of several facts, therefore it is possible for all the ingredients. Thus two facts can differ *solo numero*.) A proposition is verified, not by a type of fact, but by a specific fact. Hence although x and x' are the identical kind of fact, x alone verifies P. Consequently, meaningful propositions cannot be

[1] x here means some fact of experience of the subject X.

interchanged between X and X . This much, then, for the first theory.

On the second theory it is nonsense even to speak of a group of experiences which lies altogether outside " my " possible experiences.   Communication between " my " group and any other group is *a fortiori* nonsensical.

It is also possible to represent the matter in another way. Wittgenstein says : " That the world is my world shows itself in the fact that the limits of the language which I alone understand mean the limits of my world." [1]   This results from the logic of the theory as follows : The propositions are truth-functions of the elementary propositions. All these truth-functions have the same fundamental structure in common (the general form $\{\bar{P}, \bar{\xi}, N\,'(\bar{\xi})\}$ mentioned in Chapter II) and this structure owes its significance to the propositions which fall under it.   Therefore the important problems of structure and meaning pertain entirely to the elementary propositions.   Now an elementary proposition is a structure whose terms are names.   It pictures a fact composed of objects in immediate combination.   I cannot understand a proposition unless I know the meanings of the names composing it, and, since the names are logically proper names (i.e. immediate designations of simple objects), they are indefinable.   What is indefinable cannot be communicated by definition or by demonstrative gesture. The names have meaning only in the context of an elementary proposition. The way in which the names occur in such a proposition is its structure. The meaning of structure cannot be expressed *by* language, since it shows itself *in* language and is presupposed in the expressiveness of language. In other words, the structure cannot be analysed in a definition since analysis, in so far as it distinguishes parts, would destroy the structure. Neither the names nor the structure of elementary propositions can be defined or otherwise explained. The sole function of language is to

[1] Wittgenstein, op. cit., *supra*, 5.62.

picture what cannot be expressed. Since the pictures relate solely to possible experience and since their sense can only be shown, communication of the senses of propositions is impossible.

There should, therefore, be no doubt about the linguistic solipsism to which the positivist criterion of meaning inevitably leads. There is another serious result of the Positivistic system, which is an aspect of the same solipsistic situation.

The physical reality, i.e. the realm of physical events, must be a logical construction within the realm of experience. It will therefore be nonsensical to use the term " physical object " except in the sense of a law of certain occurrences of experiential facts. The idea of a physical universe existing independent of experiential facts, which as I have pointed out in Chapter V seems to be an indispensable assumption in science, is eliminated by Positivistic principles. A system which purports to establish the logical foundations of science thus excludes the two indispensable conditions of science, namely intersubjectivity founded on communication and objectivity.

The justification for these conditions is found in the simple fact that without them no satisfactory interpretation of the physical world is possible. Any instances of discrepancies between two accounts of the same physical event (i.e. what is *presumably* the same event), of lacunæ in experience, etc., suffice to show that even the experience of a solitary individual is not sufficiently complete and well-organized to be systematically interpreted. The objective and inter-subjective character of science remedies these defects.

The Logical Positivists have fully recognized that the solipsistic consequence of their analytic methods must be mitigated. In order to establish a system in which scientific objectivity can be achieved two courses are open. Either some of the postulates of the system must be altered so as to eliminate metaphysical ideas from Positivism itself (in this way the general position may be retained and the objectivity of science may be attained), or if this method fails the whole system of Logical Positivism will have to be abandoned and an entirely new method of attacking problems will have to be adopted. Carnap's attempt to derive scientific objectivity is an instance of the first way.

Can have practical interpretation of results of experiment

CHAPTER VIII

THE POSITIVISTIC THEORY OF KNOWLEDGE

In the last chapter I indicated that the explanation of experience required an objectivity which science, as an existent body of knowledge, supplies. My use of explanation is twofold. Things and events are said to be explained : (1) When there is no obscurity in the meanings of the propositions which describe the things and events, and (2) when the causal relations in which things and events stand have been given. My contention is, then, that the linguistic solipsism to which the fundamental principles of Logical Positivism inevitably lead (1) introduces obscurity in the meanings of propositions describing physical events, and (2) does not explain the causal connections of physical events with experience.

A method of explanation in philosophy should be uniform. It is necessary, that is, not only to avoid contradictions in explanation of the world, but also necessary to avoid the use of different principles among which no connection is, or can be, given in the system of explanation. In this sense, monism is superior to dualism. Consequently, whatever principles are added to or subtracted from the foundations of Logical Positivism, no principle can be added which has no relation to the general body of doctrine, and nothing can be removed which would substantially alter the doctrine. I shall examine Carnap's *Logischer Aufbau der Welt* with the foregoing remarks in mind. Does Carnap's system explain the intersubjective and objective nature of scientific principles ? Doe it remain within the limits of Logical Positivism in so far as certain postulates are altered or omitted ?

The principal objections which I urged against linguistic

solipsism were : (1) that the realm of physical events independent of precepts (i.e. data of experience) was not satisfactorily accounted for ; (2) that the " experience of other persons ", is, according to Positivistic principles, a meaningless phrase ; (3) that communication is impossible on the theory.

It seems to me that all these are distinct issues and should not be confused so as to give the impression that, in replying successfully to one issue, the remaining issues are likewise explained. Therefore, before I proceed, I wish to explain what seems to be the crucial point of the criticism.

Let it be supposed that (1) the physical event could somehow be satisfactorily explained as the laws of the occurrence of certain experiences (as explained in Chapter V) and that (2) the world of the " psychically foreign " or " other persons " could be explained as a construction of (my) experience. I do not believe that such satisfactory explanations are possible, but I wish to show that a fundamental problem still remains which cannot be solved by these and similar methods.

If I use a set of marks or noises which I have arranged according to certain rules to symbolize some fact of experience, this set of marks or noises is a significant proposition in terms of (my) possible experience. Three distinct cases for consideration thus arise.

I. " I say : ' There is a green tree.' " Let this sentence be P.

II. " John says : ' There is a green tree.' " Let this be P'.

III. " There is a green tree." Let this be Q. Now P and P' are on the same level. Both, according to Positivistic logical theory, express facts about behaviour; P about the behaviour of that construction which is called " I ", P' about the behaviour of that construction called " John ". Q expresses a fact about a tree, i.e. a fact about a certain experience, whereas P and P' are not about trees but about persons uttering sentences containing the word " tree ".

There is an essential difference here to which everyone will assent. It is fallacious to regard P and P' as being similar to Q.

Now, if I use Q to express a fact about trees, Q is a significant symbol. If John uses Q to express a fact about trees, I can use P' as an attempt to say what is involved in John's usage but, although P' will be significant to me, as my expression of John's behaviour, Q, as used by John, is not significant to me. What is more important, it will be impossible for me to explain how these " constructions ", of which John is one, could apparently use significant symbols. There is no escape from this conclusion, as I tried to point out in the preceding chapter. I do not see how Logical Positivism can possibly overcome *this* objection. Since the assumption or proof that communication is possible and significant is a necessary condition of the objectivity of science, the failure to include such an assumption or proof is a mark of the incompleteness of a philosophy, and the inability to include it, is an immediate refutation. With these considerations in mind, I turn to Carnap's theory of knowledge.

There are, as mentioned above, certain differences between the fundamental theses of the *Logischer Aufbau der Welt* and those of Wittgenstein's *Tractatus*.

(1) In Carnap's system no realm of atomic facts is assumed. Elementary experiences form the basis of the system of concepts. They are, however, not assumed to be absolutely simple entities in the logical sense ; on the contrary they are the unanalysed point of departure for the construction of a hierarchy of concepts used in the description of the world.

(2) Concepts or objects (no distinction between the two is made) are constructed in a synthetic manner from a primitive relation among elementary experiences. This method is called " quasi-analysis ". The difference between quasi-analysis and genuine analysis will be explained later.

(3) A principle which makes it possible to equate two

propositional functions which have the same extension although different " contents " is deduced from the doctrine of extensionality (which is, as discussed in Chapters I and II, that every function of a proposition is a truth-function). This makes it possible to maintain that two concepts are logically equivalent in meaning even though they are epistemologically distinct in content.

(4) The range of values of a propositional function is not limited to a specified set. Thus there may be functions of elementary propositions which have an infinite number of values. In this way functions of higher order may be introduced into the system.

These differences require some discussion. The first difference (1) is a distinct advance over Wittgenstein's logical absolutism. Instead of atomic facts, there is simply the realm of elementary experiences which is taken as the basis of the system. The " given ", that is to say, are " the experiences themselves in their totality and closed unity. Their ingredients down to the final elements are to be derived from these experiences by establishing relations and comparisons among them ; in short, the ingredients of experience are to be derived from experience by abstraction. This abstraction is, at least in its simpler stages, already achieved in prescientific thought or by intuitive means, so that we are accustomed to speak of a visual observation and a simultaneous aural observation as if they were two different ingredients of experience. The facility with which such analysis is accomplished should not conceal the fact that abstraction is already involved in the procedure ; *a fortiori* this applies to elements to which attention is first drawn by scientific analysis ".[1]

Carnap then makes it clear that no assumptions of psychological atomism are involved in the theory. " If the elementary experiences are selected as the primitive elements, it is not assumed thereby that the stream of experience is composed of discrete elements. On the

[1] Carnap, R., *Der Logische Aufbau der Welt*, Berlin, 1928, p. 92.

contrary, it is presupposed only that assertions can be made about certain parts of the stream of experience to the effect that one such place stands in a definite relation to another, etc. ; however, it is not assumed that the stream can be univocally divided into such places." [1]

With these qualifications Carnap proceeds to explain how the world of perception and physics (and also psychology and social science) is to be developed from the basis of the elementary experiences. Thus all the objects of perception are to be derived by forming logical constructions out of elementary experience. Any such construction must be of one of the following kinds :—

(1) Classes of the primitive elements (*Cl'el*) or relations (*Rel'el*) among the primitive elements.

(2) (a) Classes of classes, i.e. *cl'Cl'el* or classes of relations, i.e. *cl'Rel'el*.

(b) Relations among classes of type (a), i.e. *Rel'cl'el*, or relations among relations, i.e. *Rel'Rel'el*.

Hence it will never be possible to regard the *basic* or *primitive elements* of a system of logical construction as being capable of being treated as logical constructions. As a consequence the elementary experiences are not to be analysed in the system in question. They are, relative to the system, to be regarded as irreducible unities.

(2) Hence a different method of analysis is involved. " In analysis properly so-called, irreducible unities or points without any characteristics are not dealt with ; on the contrary, genuine analysis treats of objects which have various ingredients or characteristics. This analysis consists of deriving these ingredients, which are at first unknown, from other statements, e.g. from a relational description. If a relational description is given such that the relation signifies an agreement (among objects) in at least one ingredient, then the method of genuine analysis consists in the fact that a circle of similarities is formed in respect of the relation." [2]

[1] Op. cit., *supra*, p. 93.   [2] Op. cit., *supra*, p. 96.

Quasi-analysis is similar to genuine analysis save in this respect, that the basic objects are not assumed to be reducible to their constituent parts by means of the analysis. The quasi-analysis proceeds to construct classes and relations among the basic elements by means of isolating *groups* of them which are similar. The group of similar elements (in the present case a group of elementary experiences) is itself treated as if it were an ingredient. It is thus a quasi-ingredient. This makes it possible to refrain from analysing those elements which are *ex hypothesi* not analysable or which are *ex hypothesi* not to be analysed. The difference between these two kinds of analysis may be illustrated by the following example. Beginning with the " felt whole " of experience we can assert that any statement about the experience is reducible to statements about its constituent parts. Thus we could say " The table is mahogany " is reducible to " the table is a logical construction out of the data x, y, z . . . and is characterized by ϕ ". This would be genuine analysis. On the other hand, we could agree to regard the experience as unanalysable in this way and form groups of experiences which were remembered to be similar. We would not analyse tables into sense-data but rather construct colours, figures, etc., out of groups of experiences by means of isolating those experiences which were remembered to be similar. Thus tables would be constructed from classes of elementary experiences rather than from discrete data. This would be a kind of synthesis. The group of experiences itself may then be treated as a kind of ingredient of the experiences which form the group. A colour would then be a relation or class of similar experiences.

In this way no mention is made of experience. The whole system of objects and events of the world is a system of logical constructions which are quasi-objects and quasi-events.

(3) The system must be of such a character that objects constructed from different groups of elementary experiences will agree in structural properties. They may then be con-

sidered as logically equivalent even though the psychological conditions differ in the several cases. The method of establishing such agreement is based on the thesis of extensionality and is deduced from that thesis as follows :—

Every function ϕ involving another function f is a truth-function of f. If a function ϕ of f is equivalent to another ϕ' of f, ϕ and ϕ' have the same meaning, i.e.

$$(f)\phi f. \equiv \phi' f. \ \equiv \ .\phi = \phi'.$$

Although the psychological associations or content of ϕ and ϕ' differ, they are logically equivalent and mean the same thing.

(4) The system of construction is a system of classes and relations of several different types (see Introduction for an explanation of " type "). Now a class of objects presents no especial difficulty. When, however, classes of classes are in question, it is necessary to assume that the number of members of the class of classes is unlimited. This makes it necessary to assume that the number of objects is unlimited for otherwise the infinity of classes would collapse. Thus if k is a class of classes α, and if $N \subset {}'\alpha < \aleph$, some given α_1 and some given α_2 would contain the same members and hence would not be distinct classes. It is necessary, therefore, to assume the axiom of infinity or to assume the unlimited scope of the prefixes of generality (which is almost the same thing). This is opposed to Wittgenstein's doctrine ; but inasmuch as Wittgenstein's arguments are based on considerations explicitly rejected in the first thesis, (1) mentioned above, it would seem to be possible, by assuming the axiom of infinity, to construct classes of higher types.

These are the basic theses of the *Logischer Aufbau der Welt*. Before I attempt any criticism, I shall develop the consequences in so far as the specific problem of objectivity and intersubjectivity is concerned. At first sight there seems to be no way to avoid solipsism or subjectivism, inasmuch as the realm of the " psychically immediate " is taken as the basis of the system of constructions. Carnap understands

" objectivity " in two senses ; knowledge is objective in so far as it is limited or constrained by certain conditions (the facts) over which arbitrary will has no control ; again, knowledge is objective in so far as it is independent of the judging subject and holds for other subjects.[1]

I suggested that there are two senses in which the linguistic solipsism may be understood, namely as the solipsism which limits the world to (my) possible experience, and the phenomenalistic monadism of the several " groups " of experience. In either sense intersubjectivity cannot be derived by comparing two distinct streams of experience or by communication. Carnap believes that there is a third way which leads to success. This is the method of logical construction.

If it is true that all knowledge is structural (i.e. pertains to the structural properties of the world and not, in any sense, to content), then if it is possible to regard a part of the construction-system as " another person " and the behaviour of this other person as his " world ", then the structural properties of objects and events which are the same for " my world " as for " the world of the other " will be an intersubjective world. Objectivity, in Carnap's sense of the word, will then be certified.

The *Logischer Aufbau der Welt* is an attempt to construct a system of concepts hierarchically arranged in which all scientific meanings can find a place. This system is called a " Konstitutionssystem ". The higher stages of this system can be constructed from the lower stages and conversely they are reducible to the lower stages. These terms must be accurately defined. One preliminary definition is required.

(1) A propositional function exclusively about the objects $a, b = df.$ a propositional function which contains no non-logical constants excepting " a ", " b ".

(2) An object a is reducible to $b, c = df.$, for every propositional function L exclusively about a there is a propositional function L' exclusively about b, c such that $L \equiv L'$. This

---

[1] Carnap, op. cit., *supra*, pp. 90–1.

definition depends on the principle of analytic equivalence mentioned above (under (3)).

(3) A concept (object) a is constructed from concepts (objects) $b,c = df.$ there is a constructional definition such that sentences containing "b,c" can be replaced by sentences containing "a" without alteration of truth and meaning.[1]

The construction of the world from the elementary experiences is divided into three stages : (1) the construction of the private-psychical realm, (2) that of the physical realm, (3) that of the psychically foreign realm (i.e. other persons).

The construction of the " private-psychical " proceeds as follows :—

The fundamental relation is that of " Ähnlichkeit-serinnerung ", remembrance of similarity (*Er*). This is the relation holding between two elementary experiences. It is asymmetrical. The terms of the relation are introduced separately in a constitutional definition. Partial similarity of experience is defined as the logical sum of *Er*, *the converse of Er*, and *Er when its terms are identical*. The relation of partial similarity is symmetrical and reflexive. A range of similarity with respect to partial similarity is called an *Ähnlichkeitskreise*, i.e. a range of similarities.

A quality-class a of elementary experiences is a class of elementary experiences such that a is contained in γ if, for every γ which is a range of similarity, the number of members of a and γ divided by the number of members of a is less than $1/2$ and such that, for every x which is not a member of a there is a δ such that δ is a range of similarity and a is contained in δ and x is not a member of a.

Two elementary experiences are partially identical if there is a quality-class to which they both belong. Two quality-classes are similar if every element of the one is partially similar to every element of the other. Similarity of qualities is symmetrical and reflexive.

The abstraction-class of the powers of the relation

[1] Carnap, op. cit., *supra*, p. 35.

" similarity of qualities " is a sense-class. The visual sense embraces each quality class in which a sense-class has the dimension number 5 with respect to " quality-similarity ". An ordered pair of an elementary experience and a quality-class to which the elementary experience belongs is called a sensation. Two sensations are simultaneous if they belong to the same experience. A place in the visual field is a class of qualities of the visual field such that it is not an empty class and embraces all those elements of a similarity-range of qualities identical or different. Two qualities are said to be in the same place if they belong to the same classes of places. Classes of places are neighbouring if a quality-class of the one is similar to a quality-class of the other. The class of such neighbourhoods is the visual field. This kind of definition is employed to define every element and component of the various sense-modalities together with the co-ordination of the several sense-modalities.

The next important set of definitions constitutes the construction of physical objects. The special details are interesting but present technical, logical, and scientific problems with which a general discussion has nothing to do.

A complete construction of the physical world might seem to presuppose and involve the construction of all the sense modalities. A theoretically complete and perfect system may, actually, involve as much as this. Carnap, however, is content with less than this and constructs the physical world from the visual world. The first step is the temporal series of visual fields occurring in experience. The world of sight is produced by the ascription of colours to the spatio-temporal points. Definite parts of this physical-visual world constitute physical objects and processes.

A significant element of this constructed world is the object known as " my body ". It can be uniquely characterized by certain permanent characteristics, viz. (1) My body is always in the proximity of my eyes (visual fields).

(2) Qualities (local signs) of the sense of touch correspond to the places of the surface of " my body ", etc. The total class of the " private-psychical " events and things constitutes the ego.

The observational world is constructed out of the visual world by the ascription of qualities to the common senses. The genuine physical world stands in contrast to the visual and observed physical world in so far as numbers, instead of qualities, are ascribed to the positions in the four-dimensional class of positions.

Propositions about the genuine physical would have advantages over propositions about the observed world in that (1) the former is intersubjectively valid in an unambiguous manner, and (2) exact laws obtain therein.

All this having been accomplished, we can characterize all the physically differentiable processes and things in the physical world as, e.g. organisms, and, more particularly, " other persons " (strictly, other persons' bodies and actions).

The construction of the intersubjective world requires the constitution of (1) the expressive relation and (2) the psycho-physical relation. (1) The expressive relation is the connection between a movement, facial expression, verbal utterance, etc., and the psychical processes of which this movement, etc., is the " expression ". (2) The psycho-physical relation is the connection between the psychical process and the parallel or corresponding process of the central nervous system.

Having constituted the " bodies of others ", we can constitute the psyche of others by means of the expressive-relation. A psychically foreign object is a logical construction made from correlations between psychical and physical processes in the " body of another person ". The expressive relation makes this correlation possible.

The *expressive relation* is the relation between a sign and what is designated by the sign. It is clear that it cannot be the relation between a symbol and what is designated by the symbol. Thus if the verbal behaviour of an individual x is described, all that can be said is " x uses the sentence p to designate the object a ". This means that it has been observed that x co-ordinates p with a on the occasion of a's occurrence. All this is a logical construction within my experience, so that the sentences of x are simply constructions, i.e. facts, but in no sense symbols. The verbal report of x is not a communication to me of the experiences of x, but rather an indication of his behaviour.

Psychical processes in respect of " another person " do not have the significance which we would ordinarily expect. The psychically-foreign is a logical construction from the physical world. No statement can be made about the " elementary experience of another person ". All that can be understood in connection with the psychically-foreign is the class of behaviour processes of " another human body ". But this is not so serious because no statement is made about elementary experience as such in any case. Only the structure comes to verbal or written expression.

From the construction of another person M, we can constitute the " world of M ". The totality of M's actions and words is the basis of this world.

The two connections between the " world of M " and " my world " are (1) the relation of analogous construction of my world with M's world ; (2) the intersubjective co-ordination between empirically similar objects in M's world and my world.

The construction of the intersubjective world is most important for our purposes for in it we shall find the professed transcendence of solipsism. We must expect only so much as can be derived from an ordinal similarity between various elements of the private worlds of many persons. As this is of paramount importance, I give the translation of the section devoted to it.

" From the above-mentioned kind of constitution of the world of M it follows that a certain analogy exists between this world and ' my world ' ; more exactly : there is an analogy between the whole constitution-system(s) and the

' constitution-system of M ' (Sm). But Sm is only a sub-system within S ; the world of M is constituted within my world. It is not to be conceived as constructed by M but rather as constructed by me for M.

" The analogy between S and Sm signifies a very extensive but still not a complete agreement. Now for every construction of S there exists a corresponding construction in Sm which possesses an analogous form of definition, and the indication of it is made by the index M . . .

" Now the . . . physical things within S do not agree with the corresponding things in Sm (for the things standing in definite spatial connection to my body do not, generally speaking, stand in the same connection to M). But now an agreement of a new kind if discovered : between the physical world in S and the physical world in Sm there exists a one-one correspondence such that between the physical world-points of Sm the same spatio-temporal . . . relation obtains as between the world-points of S co-ordinated with the former. This co-ordination we shall call ' intersubjective co-ordination '." [1]

The intersubjective world is the world of all intersubjective agreements between the world S, Sm, Sn, etc. This is the world of science, i.e. the real world. An object is " real " if it is intersubjective ; more exactly, an object is real if (1) it belongs to a comprehensive, legitimately constructed system, (physical, psychical, etc.), (2) if it is intersubjective or yields means for the construction of an intersubjective object, and (3) if it has a place in the temporal order.

A review will serve to indicate how solipsism has been apparently avoided. The criterion of truth and meaning makes it necessary to assume a methodological solipsism. The realm of elementary experience is, therefore, a necessary point of departure. Nothing is said (or can be said) about the " nature " of individual elementary experiences. These are simply taken as indivisible unities and we proceed to discover and express the relations obtaining among them.

[1] *Logischer Aufbau*, sec. 146.

Classification of these relations leads to a hierarchical set of classes and relations and this constitutes the logical construction of the *private-psychical realm*. Further constructional definitions make it possible to define and erect all the objects and processes of the physical world. In this world there occur "my body" and "other human bodies". From the co-ordination of "my world" with the "world of another" we have a set of agreements which we call the intersubjective world. This is an objective world in the sense that it is freed from the particularities of the private subjective world. It becomes the gauge of what experiences I am to call "real" and what "illusory".

The result is that an analysis can be given to the statement that another human being exists, and the like. All of the propositions which we regard as true and significant presumably can be analysed in some way in Carnap's scheme. Nevertheless, I do not think that he has succeeded in escaping from solipsism.

In the criticism of this system it must be conceded at the outset that, assuming the logical methods to be unobjectionable, intersubjectivity and objectivity seem to have been established in the sense in which Carnap defines these terms. The propositions about the objects and events of the physical world are not determined by the caprice of an individual nor are they limited by the experience of an individual. The physical world has been constructed so that it is intersubjectively valid. Propositions about the intersubjective world must, therefore, be constructed so that my individual experience or the immediate constructions from it are not the sole criteria of their truth and meaning. Other constructions in my experience must agree with the proposition which I assert about a given object or event. This provides objectivity and inasmuch as the other constructions (which, together with mine, determine the truth of a proposition about a given object or event) are what are called "other people", an intersubjective world has been established.

It is quite irrelevant, on Carnap's theory, that I associate psychological presentations with my constructions different from those which I associate with the objects and events of the " world of the other " (*Fremdpsychische*). For suppose that $f(x)$ occurs as a subconstruction of the world of M and $g(x)$ occurs as a subconstruction of my world. Then if $f(x)$ and $g(x)$ are formally equivalent they are analytically equivalent, since f and g contain no non-logical constants. Therefore $f(x)$ and $g(x)$ are identical in logical content even though I may associate certain presentation y with $f(x)$, which I do not associate with $g(x)$.[1]

This same result obtains for the description of the psychological processes of other people. If I assert that M is hurt, this must mean that M behaves in such and such a way, for M is a logical construction from my world (ultimately from my elementary experiences) and I cannot mean more than can be significantly asserted about M and M's behaviour. Whatever else I may associate with the assertion " M is hurt ", *this* is all that can significantly be asserted. The residue of my psychological presentations is wholly irrelevant and cannot be expressed.

My concession that the intersubjective world has been established is intended only to apply to Carnap's definition of intersubjectivity.[2] I do not think that his meaning of intersubjectivity is actually the one required by objective science. Moreover, I do not think that his method is wholly unobjectionable from the technical point of view. It is expressly stated in the *Logischer Aufbau der Welt* that the " whole sequence of experience of other people consists of nothing else than an arrangement of my experiences and their ingredients ".[3] Thus the intersubjective world common to all men is an organization of some of the ingredients of my experience. Let the following symbols serve in an explanation of what is involved.

---

[1] Carnap, R., *Scheinprobleme in der Philosophie*, Berlin, 1928, pp. 31–3. Cf. Petzäll, Åke, *Logistischer Positivismus*, Goteborg, 1930, pp. 28–9.
[2] Carnap, *Logischer Aufbau der Welt*, pp. 90–1.
[3] Carnap, *Logischer Aufbau der Welt*, p. 186.

Wm = my world.

Wn = the world of n.

Wi = the intersubjective world.

Om = a physical object in Wm.

On = a physical object in Wn.

Oi = a physical object in Wi.

The relations among these can then be given as follows :—

Wn is undoubtedly a part of Wm for it is a system of construction within the total system Wm. Om is a construction in Wm not included in the construction Wn. By analysing the behaviour of n in connection with Om I construct the object On as a part of Wn. Likewise for other individuals n_1, n_{11}, n_{111}, etc., until there are Om, On, On_1, On_{11}, etc. The characteristics in which the O's agree together constitute Oi and the class of Ois together with the relations among them constitute Wi. Evidently Wi is included in Wm, since it is an organization of the system of construction from my experience.

If I wish to make an intersubjectively valid assertion about an object it must be made about Oi rather than Om. The determination might, therefore, easily become circular in particular cases because the determination of what is objectively valid depends upon a system of " checks and balances " within my experience. Thus a statement about Oi may depend upon statements about Wn, whereas statements about Wn may depend on Oi. I do not assert that this is necessary, but I see no way to exclude it as a possible result. I shall not insist on this, however. I rest my criticism simply on the observations (1) that intersubjectivity as a genuine communication of agreements among the experiences of several persons is impossible on Carnap's terms because meaningless, and (2) that the existence of objects independent of my experience has not been established.

The object Om is represented by a symbol of my Konstitutionssystem. The object On is not represented by a symbol in the system of n, but is constructed from n's behavioural responses. Among these responses are the verbal acts of n. These verbal acts cannot be regarded as significant symbols by me. Hence the object On is constructed from n's designations of the object Om. For me, therefore, " Om " is a significant symbol for an object, whereas " On " is my symbol, not for an object, but for a part of n's behaviour. There is an essential difference between Om and On which could be avoided on the assumption that real communication occurs but which is unavoidable on Carnap's theory.

The intersubjectivity actually required in the establishment of scientific principles depends, in my opinion, on the genuineness of communication. Communication by symbols which are significant for more than one individual is the necessary condition for objectivity and intersubjectivity in science. Inasmuch as communication is impossible on Carnap's theory, that theory fails to provide a satisfactory basis for science.

If this is questioned it is still true that the apparent existence of communication cannot be accounted for. How can it be explained that n and I use the same marks to designate objects and facts when, on the theory, a propositional sign, " p," is a symbol for me when used by me, whereas it is never a symbol for me when used by n. Nothing is clearer than the fact that other people employ a set of signs identical in form with my sign-language. An explanation of this patent fact is impossible within the Konstitutionssystem.

In other words " There is a tree " and " n says ' there is a tree ' " have identical marks but different meanings. The first expresses a fact about a tree, the second expresses a fact about n. n's verbal usage must always be expressed in my language in the second way while mine, in the significant occurrence, must be expressed in the first way. Inasmuch as these two ways are not logically equivalent it is evident that an intersubjective symbolism is out of the question.

Linguistic solipsism cannot be avoided by the method of logical construction. Therefore one fundamental meaning of " intersubjectivity " remains unexplained and this meaning is as essential to science as any other. There are only three ways out of this difficulty.

The first way consists in eliminating the distinction between language and the world and confining discussion to language alone. A public language will then have to be constructed from the protocols of the private languages of individuals.

The second way consists of eliminating the distinction between language and the data but differs from the first way in treating all linguistic utterances as public, i.e. inter-subjective *ab initio*, and as expressions of the form :—

A says " *p* ", *B* says " *p* ", etc.

The third way consists of retaining the distinction between language and data, while requiring a public theory of language. Carnap in his first system of Physicalism has adopted the first method, and Otto Neurath has adopted the second. This new system has several advantages over the theory of Logical Positivism, either in Wittgenstein's or in Carnap's formulation. The elimination of metaphysics and the avoidance of solipsism through Physicalism do not present the difficulties encountered in the former views of the Viennese Circle.

PART IV

RADICAL PHYSICALISM

Radical Physicalism and the syntactical doctrines on which it is based represent an emendation of the doctrines of Logical Positivism. Carnap in particular has attempted to preserve the empiricism and anti-metaphysical direction of Logical Positivism while he seeks to avoid the difficulties of the older doctrine. Radical Physicalism and the theories of language on which it is based purport to be a philosophy of language; hence it is allegedly restricted to a logical analysis of the meaning of discourse, i.e. it is neither a branch of natural science nor an epistemology. *formal language*

The difficulties of Logical Positivism result, as I have indicated, from a kind of empiristic absolutism which is hardly in the spirit of a non-metaphysical and scientific philosophy. The absolutistic doctrine of atomic facts, the rigid distinction between discourse and empirical reality, and the various prohibitions of certain kinds of linguistic expression (such as, for example, the prohibition of the use of unlimited operators), all depend on assumptions which cannot be demonstrated, and lead to results which tend to eliminate much of what goes by the name of science. If we were to select the theses which seem to lie at the foundation of this unsatisfactory doctrine we would perhaps choose these: The ultimate and exclusive referents of discourse are the empirical atomic facts, and discourse represents these facts pictorially by an identity of structure of the representation and the represented; this identity of structure, as being the presupposition of the possibility of discourse, cannot be expressed in discourse; all propositions are explicit truth-functions of the elementary propositions. The theory of mathematics and natural science

227

logically follow, in part, from these doctrines, but it is difficult to avoid the impression that many concepts and propositions of natural science have been somewhat distorted so as to fit into this scheme, while others have been summarily dismissed as being metaphysical without a genuinely fair hearing. It is clear, therefore, that an emendation of Logical Positivism will have to dispense with such theses and such cavalier methods.

Dr. Carnap in his recent essays has attempted to do this. The metaphysical atomism is simply abandoned as being without proof, and the distinction between discourse and reality has been dispensed with in favour of a purely discursive theory of truth and meaning. It is no longer necessary, that is, to distinguish between discourse and fact because everything is expressible, and thus the ground for the distinction disappears. This alteration of procedure has profound consequences. Logical syntax of language may now be formulated in a significant way. The prohibition of certain kinds of expression disappears, so that the unlimited operators, essential to the formulation both of mathematics and of natural scientific laws, may be re-introduced. And finally, the syntactical investigation of the inter-translatability of various kinds of sentences provides a key to the problem of intersubjectivity.

In what follows I shall describe the doctrines of logical syntax which make possible these innovations. It is to be observed that Carnap's syntactical theories are extremely systematic, and provide means whereby the difficulties which we have hitherto encountered *may* be solved.

The most interesting doctrine is that of Radical Physicalism, although perhaps Carnap would not place most emphasis upon it now. According to this doctrine all sentences (excluding those of pure syntax and pure logic) may be translated into a universal language which is similar in form to the language of contemporary physics. The assertions about unobserved objects and events as well as the records of personal experience may, on the basis of certain known laws and experimental findings, be translated into this intersubjective language of physics. The methodological solipsism and the extreme empiricism which prevented Positivists from formulating a satisfactory account of scientific objectivity are thus simply avoided without the re-introduction of metaphysical principles.

I should like to indicate here the relations of dependence in which Carnap's various recent doctrines stand. The logical syntax of languages is, it seems to me, quite autonomous and must be approached from a purely logical point of view. The theory of Physicalism, on the other hand, depends partly on specific syntactical theses and partly on empirical considerations. And thus the refutation of Physicalism does not imply a refutation of the syntactical doctrines on which it is based, although a refutation of the latter would imply the untenability of the former. Moreover, a solution of the problem of intersubjectivity can occur via syntactical doctrines and principles in other ways than Physicalism, so that a possible refutation of Physicalism need not give any occasion for despairing of a solution of the problem of objective science.

According to Carnap there are two kinds of syntax, logical syntax which treats of the logical properties of language and which consists solely of analytic sentences, and descriptive syntax which treats of the physical properties and relations of linguistic expressions. In the following account of Physicalism both kinds of syntax will come into consideration. Certain sentences, for example, about the thesis of Physicalism will be pure syntactical sentences, whereas others will be descriptive. To say that " sentences S and S' are physicalistically equipollent " is a statement of pure syntax, whereas to say that " sentence S is uttered by John Smith " is a statement of descriptive syntax.

Pure syntax is a branch of mathematics, more exactly of arithmetic. If we assign certain numbers to the logical constants and others to non-logical constants then the properties of expressions, sentences, and transformation of sentences may be characterized in terms of the properties and relations of numbers, sequences of numbers, sequences of sequences of numbers, etc. And thus, for a given language the logical rules of which are known, syntax is formulable without taking account of the meanings of the expression of that language, i.e. account may be taken only of the arithmetical properties of the term-numbers, series numbers of sentences, and so on. In this way it is possible to answer certain questions of philosophical analysis without introducing any mystical or inexpressible features of meaning.

The great advantage of such a method, if it proves to be successful, is plain. The problems of meaning and of the nature of truth can be solved without any recourse to intuition or to showing what cannot be said. Many philosophical issues will become problems of pure mathematics. *What what? philosophy of scientific world*

In the first chapter of this part I shall develop the theory of logical syntax, and in the second I shall apply this theory to some of the problems of mathematics and natural science which I discussed in connection with Wittgenstein's doctrines. The third and fourth chapters will be specifically concerned with Physicalism, with especial reference to the problem of intersubjectivity. I shall try to indicate the places in which Physicalism seems to fail as an account of scientific method. The systematic syntactical theory of Carnap, although it seems to require emendation in important respects, seems to me to be the most original and consequent philosophical work of our time. My criticism, therefore, should not mislead the reader into believing that there is anything essentially unsound in the general method of Carnap's syntactical studies.

Chapter IX

LOGICAL SYNTAX OF LANGUAGES

An extension of the theory of definition and meaning so as to permit the expression of every connection in the empirical world and in the realm of discourse is the initial step required in overcoming the difficulties of the views which I have hitherto discussed. It is necessary, that is, to devise a language in which the names of unanalysed terms may be discursively explained, and in which the meanings of sentences may be discursively determined. Depending partly on the metamathematical researches of Tarski, Gödel, and others, but to a large extent through original work, Rudolf Carnap has shown how such a language may be constructed. As this syntactical work of Carnap is fundamental to the new system of ideas of which Physicalism is perhaps most important, I propose to devote some space to the delineation of its principal aspects.

Carnap distinguishes, in the first place, between the object-language and the syntax-language and we may best construe this distinction as follows : The language of everyday usage contains words and sentences the referent of which is the empirical world. Other words and sentences, however, refer to the physical or logical properties of the empirical or object-language. No sharp line is drawn between these two kinds of words and sentences in ordinary discourse. It is not difficult to show that antinomies break out as a result of this laxity in ordinary discourse which can only be eliminated if we are careful to observe the difference between *using* a language and speaking *about* a language. And in order to establish general rules, for the avoidance of such antinomies the structure of languages must be formalized, i.e. definite principles must be established according to which sentences of a given language may be *formed*, and according to which sentences may be *transformed* into other sentences. In this way the antinomies which result from confusing the object-language and the syntax-language may be avoided.

The object-language, then, is the language of the natural sciences and mathematics. The syntax language is a discourse the subject-matter of which is the structure and constituency of the object-language. It is possible to formulate the syntax of a language within the limits of the means of expression given in the object language. Certain syntactical sentences cannot be tested, and certain syntactical terms cannot be defined within the limits of the means of expression of the object-language but many of the important terms and sentences of syntax may be treated without difficulty.

Within the limits of the object-language, moreover, every characteristic of the empirical world can be expressed via nominal definitions, ostensive definitions, and reductions.[1] As a consequence of the general expressibility of everything with which the object-language and the syntax-language are concerned, it is no longer necessary to differentiate between discourse and empirical reality. The antinomies and metaphysical pseudo-sentences which result from the duplication of terms such as " object " and " name ", " fact ", and " sentence ", " discourse " and " reality ", can be eliminated either by speaking only of objects, facts, and realities, or by speaking only of names, sentences, and discourse. For the purpose of clarity as well as for technical reasons it is best to adopt the latter alternative, i.e. to speak only of names, sentences, and discourse.

There are, then, two modes of expression, the connotative mode which speaks of objects and facts, and the formal mode which speaks of terms, expressions, and sentences. There is no objection to the connotative mode if it is used

---

[1] This term will be explained later on. Briefly stated, a term is reducible to other terms if there are empirical sentences, the acceptances of which entails the acceptance or rejection of the sentence in which the reducible term occurs.

exclusively and consistently, although the possibility of expressing matters logical and syntactical is, of course, excluded. The use of a mode of expression containing a mixture of the other two modes leads to needless duplication and to pseudo-sentences such as occur in discussions of the psycho-physical problem and the linguistic solipsism of Wittgenstein's doctrine. The formal mode is thus to be preferred.

It might seem as if antinomies would break out in the formulation of the syntax of a language whether the language be scientifically constructed or whether it be one of the ordinary historical languages. Tarski, Lukasiewicz, and Carnap have, however, shown that this is only true of ordinary languages. It is instructive to see how these antinomies break out in the latter kind of discourse.

I shall take an example from Tarski.[1] Let there be a language, such that there is a single name for every sentence of the language; such that the following sentence :—

" x is a true sentence if and only if p "

is recognized as true when a specific sentence replaces " p " and the name of this sentence replaces " x "; such that an empirically established sentence of the kind (α) in the example following is regarded as true ; and such that the laws of logic obtain for this language. Every such language will then be inconsistent. For if " C " is an abbreviation for " the sentence prefixed by ' I ' on this page ", and we find :—

I. " C is not a true sentence," then we have :—

   (α) " C is not a true sentence " is identical with C, and
   (β) " C is not a true sentence " is a true sentence if and only if C is not a true sentence.

(α) . (β) ⊃ C is a true sentence if and only if C is not a true sentence. This is a contradiction. It is not difficult to find the source of this contradiction, but it is practically impossible to add a general syntactical rule to the existing

[1] Tarski, Alfred, " Der Wahrheitsbegriff in den formalisierten Sprachen," *Studia Philosophica*, Lemberg, 1935, vol. i, pp. 270–1, 278–9.

body of rules in ordinary discourse which would automatically exclude the possibility of such antinomies.

It is correct, I believe, to find the inconsistent character of ordinary discourse in the circumstances (1) that ordinary discourse has no fixed syntactical principles which would absolutely limit the kinds of expressions which can occur in it, and hence (2) that ordinary discourse contains object-sentences and syntactical sentences without any precise distinction between them, treating all sentences alike. As a consequence syntactical terms and object-terms occur in the same sentences, and connotative and formal expressions duplicate one another, the occurrence of antinomies is thus naturally to be expected. The potential number of syntactical antinomies in ordinary discourse is almost unlimited and should convince the reader that a formalization of language is indispensable in any philosophical investigation.

I shall now turn my attention to the structure of some simple object languages in order to show the manner in which its syntax may be formulated without paradoxical or circular statement. For this purpose I shall consider Carnap's Languages I and II.[1] Language I contains predicates of n-argument-places and functors of n-argument-places, together with the values of these argument-places. In addition there are the logical constants " $\sim$ ", " v ", " . ", " $\supset$ ", " $'$ ", " $=$ ", " $\exists$ ", and " K ", the logical punctuations " (", ") ", and the constant number-expressions " 0 ", " 1 ", " 2 ", " 3 ", . . .

The " $\exists$ " is an existential operator of limited scope occurring in sentences such as " $(\exists x)5(\phi x)$ ", where " 5 " indicates the x numbered 5. The " K " is a descriptive operator which occurs in expressions (not sentences) such as " $(K_x)5(\phi x)$ ", and in sentences such as $\psi[(K_x)5(\phi x)]$.

Finally, the " $'$ " is stroke-expression which occurs in number-expressions such as " $0'$ ", " $0''$ ", " $0'''$ ", " $0''''$ ", etc. The other operations are already familiar. The use of

[1] R. Carnap, *Logische Syntax der Sprache*, Wien, 1934.

numbers in this object-language must, however, be briefly explained. The numbers are used as the names of places, times, temperatures, etc., so that the language is correctly called a co-ordinate language. The places, predicates of the places and functors could, therefore, all be given by numbers. Thus " a adjoins b " could be rendered " cent. distance $(5,6) \gtrless 3$ " where " 5 " and " 6 " are names for " a " and " b ", and the sentence is rendered " the centimeter distance from 5 to 6 is not greater than 3 ". There are at least three notable advantages of a co-ordinate language, more generally of a language in which numbers replace names. In the first place the number of fundamental kinds of expression is potentially determined, so that with finitely many fundamental expressions any denumerable number of expressions may be constructed. Secondly, there is the possibility of ostensive definition of a nominally undefined term of the language, so that the expressiveness of the language is extended to *discursive* characterization of every property or relation of the empirical world (thus leaving no inexpressible realm over and above what may be stated in discourse). Finally the inclusion of arithmetic in language makes it possible to construct the syntax of a language in the language itself (1) without circularity and (2) as a system of analytic sentences. A further advantage of an arithmetical language is the fact that it may be easily adapted to translation into a physicalistic language. This need not concern us at this stage.

The kinds of definition in this language are : (1) ostensive, (2) explicit, and (3) recursive. An ostensive definition would have the symbolic form " $x = df. (K_v)\eta$ (spatio-temporal co-ordinates of $x = [a, b, c, d])$ " ; in words " the x is the individual which occupies such and such a spatio-temporal position ".

The explicit definition of an n-place predicate has the form : " $\Phi_1^n(x_1, \ldots x_n) \equiv P.$ " For example, " x is between y and $z \equiv x$ is to the left of y and x is to the right of $z.$ "

The explicit definition of an n-place functor has the form :
" $\Psi_1^n(x_1, \ldots x_n) = Y$." For example, " the successor of $x = x + 1$." The recursive definition of a functor has the form :—

$$(a) \text{ " } \Psi_1^n (0, x_1, \ldots x_n) = Y_1 \text{ "}$$
$$(b) \text{ " } \Psi_1^n (x_1', x_2, \ldots x_n) = Y_2 \text{ "}$$

Predicates may always be explicitly defined, functors are either explicitly or recursively defined.

Although the strictest development of syntactical principles would seem to require arithmetization, it is possible, for explanatory purposes, to make the distinction between expressions of the object-language and those of the syntax-language by using Gothic or Clarendon type for the latter. This avoids the excessive use of quotation-marks, and is also advisable on other grounds.[1]

Consequently Carnap uses the following syntactical symbols :—

> $\mathfrak{S}$ for " sentence "
> $\mathfrak{a}$ for " any expression "
> $\mathfrak{z}$ for " number-variables "
> $\mathfrak{nu}$ for " the sign ' o ' "
> $\mathfrak{pr}$ for " predicate "
> $\mathfrak{pr}^n$ for " n-place predicate "
> $\mathfrak{fu}^n$ for " n-place functor "
> $\mathfrak{verfn}$ for " logical connective "
> $\mathfrak{Z}$ for " number expression "
> $\mathfrak{A}$ for " any expression "
> $\mathfrak{A}_d$ for " descriptive expression "
> $\mathfrak{A}_e$ for " logical expression "

With this apparatus it is then possible to define all the logical syntactical and descriptive syntactical properties of the Language I. It is to be observed that this language is a *definite* language inasmuch as unlimited operators are not employed. In order to express unlimited generality either of mathematics or of natural science in this language free

---

[1] Cf. Tarski, Alfred, op. cit., *supra*, pp. 268–9.

variables are used. A natural law, for example, would be expressed as "$\phi x \supset \psi x$", where the absence of a prefix indicates the unlimited generality of the law. The existential sentences of unlimited scope in mathematics cannot be expressed in Language I.

Carnap defines number-signs, stroke-expressions, number-expressions, and sentences as follows :—

(1) A number-sign ($\mathfrak{z}\mathfrak{z}$) of Language I is either nu or $\mathfrak{z}$ or a defined $\mathfrak{z}\mathfrak{z}$.

(2) A stroke-expression ($\mathfrak{S}t$) of I is either nu or nu′ or nu″ or . . . etc.

(3) A number-expression ($\mathfrak{Z}$) of I is either $\mathfrak{z}\mathfrak{z}$ or $\mathfrak{Z}'$ or $\mathfrak{fu}^n(\mathfrak{Arg}^n)$ or $(\mathfrak{K}_{\mathfrak{z}1})\mathfrak{Z}_1(\mathfrak{S})$.

(4) An argument-expression ($\mathfrak{Arg}^n$) is recursively defined : $\mathfrak{Arg}^1$ is a number expression, i.e. a $\mathfrak{Z}$; $\mathfrak{Arg}^{n+1}$ has the form $\mathfrak{Arg}^n$, $\mathfrak{Z}$.

A sentence ($\mathfrak{S}$) of I is an expression of one of the following forms :—

1. $\mathfrak{Z} = \mathfrak{Z}$ (i.e. " Equation ").

2. $\mathfrak{pr}^n(\mathfrak{Arg}^n)$ (i.e. an n-placed predicate with n-filled argument-places).

3. $\sim \mathfrak{S}$ (i.e. negation of 1, 2, 4, or 5).

4. $(\mathfrak{S})\,\mathfrak{verkn}\,(\mathfrak{S})$ (i.e. a junction of expressions of the forms 1, 2, 3, 4, or 5).

5. $\mathfrak{A}_1(\mathfrak{S})$ where $\mathfrak{A}_1$ is a prefix either $(\mathfrak{z}_1)\mathfrak{Z}_1$ or $(\mathfrak{H}\mathfrak{z}_1)\mathfrak{Z}_1$ and $\mathfrak{S}$ has one of the forms 1, 2, 3, or 4.

These are the <u>principal definitions</u> which determine the *formative rules* of the Language I. When they are given the expressions which belong (potentially) to the language are fixed. It is, however, also necessary to determine the transformative rules of a language in order to set the limits within which permissible sentence-forms may be transformed into other permissible sentence-forms. This necessity is not a metaphysical one but principally exists so that a language may be *used*. A contradictory language is evidently useless since any sentence which can be formed in it can be both proved and refuted and any two predicates of the language will be synonymous. The result of such a state of affairs is plain. Nothing can be uniquely expressed in such a language and there would be no distinction between the acceptable and the unacceptable sentences.

The formative rules depend upon the undefined signs and the admissible kinds of definition ; the transformative rules depend upon the primitive sentences and the inferential rules of the language. It is not necessary to set forth the primitive sentences of Language I here in complete detail. The axioms of the sentential calculus are those given in the introduction to this essay, the axioms of limited operators are peculiar to an arithmetized co-ordinate language. There are two axioms of identity, namely (1) $\mathfrak{z}_1 = \mathfrak{z}_1$ and (2) if $\mathfrak{z}_1 = \mathfrak{z}_2$ then any sentence in which $\mathfrak{z}_1$ occurs implies the sentence which results when $\mathfrak{z}_1$ is replaced by $\mathfrak{z}_2$. The arithmetical axioms are : (1) $\sim (\mathfrak{nu} = \mathfrak{z}')$, i.e. the null-sign is not identical with any number-sign involving a stroke-expression, (2) if $\mathfrak{z}'_1 = \mathfrak{z}'_2$ then $\mathfrak{z}_1 = \mathfrak{z}_2$. These are familiar and require no discussion. There is an axiom governing the use of the descriptive $\mathfrak{K}$-operator which need not be given here.

It is now possible to give some of the most important concepts of syntax, those of derivability and provability. A sentence $\mathfrak{S}_3$ of I is *immediately derivable* from another sentence $\mathfrak{S}_1$ or from $\mathfrak{S}_1$ and $\mathfrak{S}_2$ if one of the following results obtains : a substitution of a number expression in $\mathfrak{S}_1$ yields $\mathfrak{S}_3$; $\mathfrak{S}_3$ results from $\mathfrak{S}_2$ via the following equivalences : $\mathfrak{S}_1 \equiv \mathfrak{S}_4 \supset \mathfrak{S}_5$ and $\mathfrak{S}_3 = \sim \mathfrak{S}_4 \vee \mathfrak{S}_5$ or, conversely, $\mathfrak{S}_1 \equiv \mathfrak{S}_4 . \mathfrak{S}_5$ and $\mathfrak{S}_3 \equiv \sim(\sim\mathfrak{S}_4 \vee \sim \mathfrak{S}_5)$ or, conversely, $\mathfrak{S}_1 \equiv \mathfrak{S}_4 \equiv \mathfrak{S}_5$ and $\mathfrak{S}_3 \equiv (\mathfrak{S}_4 \supset \mathfrak{S}_5) . (\mathfrak{S}_5 \supset \mathfrak{S}_4)$ or conversely : $\mathfrak{S}_2$ has the form $\mathfrak{S}_1 \supset \mathfrak{S}_3$; $\mathfrak{S}_1$ is what results from $\mathfrak{S}_3$ when a number-sign ($\mathfrak{z}$) is replaced by the null-sign ($\mathfrak{nu}$), and $\mathfrak{S}_2$ has the form $\mathfrak{S}_3 \supset \mathfrak{S}_3$ [when a $\mathfrak{z}$ is replaced by its immediate successor]. These rules are already familiar to the reader under the names " substitution ", " mutual replaceability of equivalences ", " inference ", and " mathematical induction ". In short, a sentence $\mathfrak{S}_3$ is immediately derivable from another sentence $\mathfrak{S}_1$ or from two other sentences $\mathfrak{S}_1$ and $\mathfrak{S}_2$ if $\mathfrak{S}_3$ can be obtained from $\mathfrak{S}_1$ or from $\mathfrak{S}_1$ and $\mathfrak{S}_2$ via the inferential rules of the language.

A *derivation with the premises* $\mathfrak{S}_1$, $\mathfrak{S}_2$, ... $\mathfrak{S}_n$ (the number of premises being of any finite length from o to n) is a series of sentences such that every sentence in the series is either a premise, a definition, or is immediately derivable from some sentence or sentences preceding it in the series. A sentence $\mathfrak{S}_m$ is *derivable* from $\mathfrak{S}_1$, ..., $\mathfrak{S}_n$ if there is a derivation the premises of which are $\mathfrak{S}_1$, ..., $\mathfrak{S}_n$ and the terminal sentence of which is $\mathfrak{S}_m$.

The primitive sentences and the inferential rules of a language are not to be regarded as premises. We can, with this convention, then define *provable sentence* as follows : A sentence $\mathfrak{S}_1$ is *provable* if it is derivable from the empty series of premises and hence from any series of premises. This is equivalent to saying that a provable sentence is one which can be obtained solely from the primitive sentences of a language with the aid of inferential rules. A proof, accordingly, is a derivation without premises, and the terminal sentence of such a derivation is a *provable* sentence. This is merely a variant expression of the definitions just given. A sentence $\mathfrak{S}_1$ is *refutable* if there is a sentence $\sim \mathfrak{S}_2$ which is provable and which results from $\mathfrak{S}_1$ via the substitution of all free variables in $\mathfrak{S}_1$ by stroke-expressions. If $\mathfrak{S}_1$ contains no free variables then it can be simply said that $\mathfrak{S}_1$ is refutable when $\sim \mathfrak{S}_1$ is provable. A sentence which is neither provable nor refutable via the methods of proof allowed in a given language is said to be *irresoluble* (*unentscheidbar*).

In order to make the distinctions between analytic, contradictory, and synthetic sentences it is necessary to give the definition of " being a consequence of ". In the Language I a sentence $\mathfrak{S}_1$ is an *immediate consequence* of a class of sentences $\mathfrak{K}_1$ if $\mathfrak{K}_1$ is finite and there is a derivation the terminal sentence of which is $\mathfrak{S}_1$, or if $\mathfrak{K}_2$ is the class of sentences which result when the number-sign $\mathfrak{z}$ in $\mathfrak{S}_1$ is replaced successively by $\mathfrak{nu}$, $\mathfrak{nu}'$, $\mathfrak{nu}''$, etc. *Consequence* is a simple generalization of *immediate consequence* via the following definitions.

$\mathfrak{K}_2$ is an immediate consequence-class (in I) of $\mathfrak{K}_1$ if every sentence of $\mathfrak{K}_2$ is an immediate-consequence of a subclass of $\mathfrak{K}_1$. A consequence-series (of I) is a series of sentence-classes such that every such class is an immediate consequence-class of the class immediately preceding it in the series. Carnap then defines : $\mathfrak{S}_n$ is a *consequence* of $\mathfrak{K}_1$ (in I) if there is a consequence-series of which the first class is $\mathfrak{K}_1$ and the terminal class is the class whose only member is $\mathfrak{S}_n$.[1]

It is clear that " consequence ", " derivable," and " provable " (in language I) cannot be defined in I because they involve in their definitions the unlimited operators which do not form a part of this language.

A sentence $\mathfrak{S}_1$ is *analytic* (in I) if it is a consequence of the empty class of sentences (hence a consequence of every class of sentences), *contradictory* if every sentence is a consequence of $\mathfrak{S}_1$, and *synthetic* if it is neither analytic nor contradictory. With the aid of all of the foregoing definitions, of which the most important is that of " consequence ", it is possible to define the logical content (*Gehalt*) of a sentence, $\mathfrak{S}_1$, or a class of sentences $\mathfrak{K}_1$ (in I), as the class of all non-analytic sentences which are consequences of $\mathfrak{S}_1$ (in I).

This important definition of logical content requires some

---

[1] These definitions are verbally rather prolix and are perhaps more comprehensible if stated in a mathematical form :—

Immediate Consequence $(\mathfrak{S}_1 \ \mathfrak{K}_1) \equiv \left\{ \mathfrak{R}_c \ '\mathfrak{K}_1 \ \mathsf{z} \ n \ \binom{n}{\text{finite}} \cdot (\exists \mathfrak{R}) \right.$ Deriva-tion $(\mathfrak{R})$. Premises " $\mathfrak{R} = \mathfrak{K}_1 . \text{terminus} \ '\mathfrak{R} = \mathfrak{S}_1 \right\}$ v $\left\{ (\exists \mathfrak{z}_1) \ \mathfrak{K}_1 = [\mathfrak{S}_1 \binom{\mathfrak{z}_1}{\mathfrak{nu}}), \ \mathfrak{S}_1 \binom{\mathfrak{z}_1}{\mathfrak{nu}'}, \ \ldots \ \mathfrak{S}_1 \binom{\mathfrak{z}_1}{\mathfrak{nu}''} \ \ldots \ : \right) \right] \right\}$.

Immediate Consequence class $(\mathfrak{K}_2, \quad \mathfrak{K}_1) \equiv (\mathfrak{S}) \mathfrak{S}_\epsilon \mathfrak{K}_2 . \supset . (\exists \mathfrak{K}_3) \mathfrak{K}_3 \subset \mathfrak{K}_1 .$ Immediate Consequence $(\mathfrak{S}, \ \mathfrak{K}_3)$.

Consequence series $(\mathfrak{K}_1, \ \ldots \ \mathfrak{K}_n) \equiv (\mathfrak{K}_m) \ \mathfrak{K}_m \ \epsilon \ [\mathfrak{K}_1, \ \ldots \ \mathfrak{K}_m] . (\exists \mathfrak{K}_{m-1}) \ \mathfrak{K}_{m-1} \epsilon \ [\mathfrak{K}_1, \ \ldots \ \mathfrak{K}_n]$. Immediate Predecessor $(\mathfrak{R}_{m-1}, \ \mathfrak{K}_m)$. Immediate consequence class $(\mathfrak{K}_m, \ \mathfrak{K}_{m-1})$.

Consequence $(\mathfrak{S}_n, \ \mathfrak{K}_1) \equiv (\exists \mathfrak{R})$ Consequence series $(\mathfrak{R})$. $\mathfrak{K}_1 = \text{first}$ $'\mathfrak{R} . [\mathfrak{S}_n] = \text{terminus} \ '\mathfrak{R}$.

explanation. If we consider a sentence $\mathfrak{S}_1$ it is readily seen that $(\mathfrak{S}_n)$ (analytic $(\mathfrak{S}_1) . \supset .$ consequence $(\mathfrak{S}_1, \mathfrak{S}_n))$, i.e. an analytic sentence follows from any sentence.

The content of one sentence would always partially overlap that of another if the analytic consequences were included in the logical content of sentences. The definition of content must therefore exclude analytic consequences. There are, in fact, four distinct cases for consideration.

I. Analytic sentences which are consequences of analytic sentences, e.g. "$p \vee \sim p$" as a consequence of the axioms of this language for the sentential calculus.

II. Non-analytic sentences which are consequences of non-analytic sentences, e.g. "$p \vee q$" as a consequence of "$p . q$".

III. Non-analytic sentences which are consequences of analytic sentences. This case is vacuously satisfied because from analytic sentences only analytic sentences follow.

IV. Analytic sentences which are consequences of non-analytic sentences. This case is universally satisfied since *per definitionem* analytic sentences follow from any sentence.

Case I belongs to pure logic. Cases III and IV are expressions in the formal idiom of the fact that nothing empirical is expressed by analytic propositions; in other words, there are no non-analytic consequences of analytic sentences. Case II alone ·yields synthetic consequences of synthetic sentences, and it is only in such cases that we may speak of logical content.

It might be objected at this point that some sentences have no non-analytic consequences (excepting trivial ones such as "$\mathfrak{S}_1$ is always a non-analytic consequence of itself"), and hence have no content whatsoever. This objection may be dealt with at a later stage when I come to consider the nature of the protocol sentences. But this much may be said here. The case is similar to the verification of those sentences the truth of which depends upon an experiment. If we abandon the logical atomism of earlier doctrines, then no synthetic sentence is finally and ultimately verified or falsified. Yet for a given language-system, and within the limits set by a given experimental problem, it is permissible to speak of the complete verification of a sentence. By convention it is decided that certain sentences are tentatively to be accepted if they fulfil certain experimental conditions. The acceptance is conventionally fixed, tentatively made, and only in reference to a given problem in natural science. It is similarly the case with content. There is no theoretical limit to the analysis of sentential content although in practice we do in fact terminate this analysis. Ordinarily we terminate the analysis when we are intuitively satisfied that the meaning of a sentence is clear to us. In scientific languages we terminate the analysis when we obtain sentences which are composed of nominally indefinable predicates, functors, or arguments of such predicates and functors. But nominal indefinability is evidently relative to a given language and is by no means an ultimate limit. Consequently the objection loses much of its force when it is considered that potentially every sentence has content, although actually some contents are never fully delineated.

*   *   *   *

Corresponding to the concept of content of sentences we have the meaning of non-sentential expressions, but this need not be separately treated, since the various kinds of definitions take care of the meanings of such terms. It is advantageous, however, to have a definition of synonymity corresponding to the definition of identity of content. Carnap therefore defines synonymity with the aid of identity of content. And thus two sentences are identical in content if and only if they are consequences of one another. An expression $\mathfrak{A}_2$ is synonymous with an expression $\mathfrak{A}_1$ if every sentence $\mathfrak{S}_1$ in which $\mathfrak{A}_1$ occurs is identical in content with a sentence $\mathfrak{S}_2$ which results from $\mathfrak{S}_1$ if $\mathfrak{A}_1$ is replaced by $\mathfrak{A}_2$.

In many respects the Language I corresponds to the requirements of Wittgenstein's language. If, that is to say, we were to operate with this language alone, we would have atomic sentences upon which the truth and meaning of all other sentences of the language would depend. The absence of unlimited operators renders every sentence an explicit truth-function of the atomic sentences inasmuch as the limited operators in sentence of the forms $(\mathfrak{z})$ $\mathfrak{Z}$ $(\mathfrak{S})$ and and $(\mathfrak{Z}\mathfrak{z})$ $\mathfrak{Z}$ $(\mathfrak{S})$ are mere abbreviations for junctions of definitely many atomic sentences. It would follow that natural laws would have to be expressed by sentences containing free variables (i.e. what Russell calls propositional, and Carnap calls sentential, functions). Consequently also the transfinite ordinals and cardinals would have no meaning in this language, since it would be impossible to define the inductive numbers and hence impossible to define non-inductive cardinals. And thus number is presented in terms of a general variable form and not defined (specific numbers are, of course, defined. e.g. " $2 = 0''$ ". But this is also true of Wittgenstein's language). The Kaufmann-Wittgenstein programme for mathematics finds its formal expression in the object- and syntax-language I. It is clear that while it is possible to limit scientific and mathematical concepts to such as may find expression in a *definite* language, it is disadvantageaous and undesirable to do so. And Carnap is quite correct, I believe, in maintaining that, without the absolutistic and untenable arguments of Wittgenstein there is nothing but a conventional ground for so doing.

In an unpublished essay Carnap has given methods (partially based on investigations of Karl Popper) which allow the introduction of unlimited operators in natural scientific systems. I shall consider some of these in a later chapter. It is sufficient to remark here that the demand for the complete verification of all sentences of a language is simply a consequence of Wittgenstein's absolutism and is unnecessary in a non-absolutist theory of language.

Carnap has therefore constructed a language whose means of expression is enriched by the introduction of unlimited operators together with the various technical rules governing their uses. He has called this " Language II ". It contains Language I as a sub-language.

Language II thus differs from Language I principally in the following ways :—

1   In Language I there are no unlimited operators ; in Language II there are operators of the form $(\mathfrak{z})$ $(\mathfrak{S})$, $(\mathfrak{Ez})$ $(\mathfrak{S})$.

2.   In Language I there is no hierarchy of types since there are no variables save number variables of nullth type.   In Language II there are predicate and functor variables and hence a hierarchy of types is necessary.

3.   In Language I the mathematical concepts of real, complex, and other more complicated kinds of numbers cannot be defined.   Language II contains all classical mathematics.

4.   Physical Laws are expressible as general sentences in Language II, but are not expressible as sentences in Language I.

5.   There are further primitive logical sentences in Language II of two kinds : (1) Those which form the axioms of the unlimited operator calculus and the calculus of descriptive operators ; (2) the mathematical axioms : induction and the multiplicative axiom.

6.   There are axioms in Language II which assert the identity of functors and predicates which have the same values of their arguments.

The greater richness in means of expression of Language II alters some definitions in the direction of greater generality. I shall only indicate this in connection with the most important syntactical concepts.   The definition of " sentence " is enlarged so as to limit the types of arguments which predicates and functors may take as values. $\mathfrak{S}_2$ is a consequence of $\mathfrak{K}_1$ (in II) if the class composed of $\mathfrak{K}_1$ and the class whose only member is $\sim ( )(\mathfrak{S}_2)$ is a contradictory class ; symbolically : Consequence (in II) $(\mathfrak{S}_2, \mathfrak{K}_1) \equiv \mathfrak{K}_1 \frown [\sim ( ) (\mathfrak{S}_2)]\ \epsilon$ Contradictory. The logical content of a sentence $\mathfrak{S}_1$ is the class of non-analytic sentences which are consequences of $\mathfrak{S}_1$. " Consequence " (and thus " Content ") in Language II differs from Consequence (in I) in so far as no limitations of finitude occur in the definition.

It is possible to increase the expressiveness of Language II by creating another language of which Language II is a part. This may be done in various ways ; for example, by including more complicated kinds of operators. It is also possible to devise a richer language by including among the primitive sentences general physical laws. This latter method is a most important innovation.

Before I discuss Carnap's theories of generalized syntax, however, I wish to consider the following questions : Is it not possible that in the formulation of logical or descriptive syntax some syntactical terms and sentences will refer to themselves ?   And if this self-reference occurs do not circular definitions and antinomies break out which render the formulation of syntax meaningless ?

In an *indefinite* language (i.e. one in which unlimited operators occur) which contains the arithmetic of the natural numbers it is possible to construct a syntactical sentence $\mathfrak{S}_x$ which, connotatively speaking, asserts that $\mathfrak{S}_x$ is not provable in that language. Kurt Gödel has shown how this can be accomplished. Roughly speaking the construction is as follows : Every sentence in arithmetized syntax has a number associated with it which is obtained by calculation. And thus the sentence : $\sim$ Provable Sentence II (r,x) $\equiv$ ' $\sim (\exists r)\{$ Proof (r). terminus ' $r = x\}$ i.e. " x is unprovable in II " has a series number. There will also be a series number for " x ". The sentence is then formed which results from " $\sim$ Provable Sentence II (r,x) " when the syntactical description of the number of " x " replaces " x " ; thus :—

(1) "$\sim$ Provable Sentence II (r, subst $[x, 3, \text{str} (x)]$) "
is formed. Furthermore, the sentence can be formed
which results from (1) when the syntactical description of
the number b of (1) replaces "x" in (1). And thus a
sentence is formed :—

(2) "$\sim$ Provable Sentence II (r, subst $[b, 3, \text{str} (b)]$) "
which in verbal language says that the sentence the series
number of which has the syntactical description subst
$[b, 3, \text{str} (b)]$ is unprovable. And this sentence is (2) itself.

Thus, without any circularity,[1] it is possible to have
sentences which refer to themselves in a perfectly
unambiguous manner. Is such a sentence self-contradictory ?

Carnap and others have shown that this is not the case.
A sentence can be unprovable and yet analytic ; unrefutable
and yet contradictory ; and there is no incompatibility
between these pairs of concepts.[2]

The attempt to prove or refute the sentence "$\sim$ Provable
Sentence II (r, subst $[b, 3, \text{str} (b)]$) " in II (i.e. the language
in which it is formulable) leads to a contradiction. Hence,
assuming II to be free from contradiction, "$\sim$ Provable
Sentence II (r, subst $[b, 3, \text{str} (b)]$) is an irresoluble analytic
sentence. The presence of irresoluble and self-referring
concepts of pure syntax does not involve contradiction.
The attempt to resolve irresoluble sentences, however,
produces contradictions as is evidently to be expected.

Is it possible to construct a contradiction via syntactical
self-referring sentences ? If the concept "analytic" is
assumed to be definable in the language to which the
concept applies we can form a sentence which asserts :—

(3) $\sim$ Analytic Sentence II (subst $[a, 3 \text{ str} (a)]$, i.e.
if a is the series number of (3), then (3) asserts : (3) is

---

[1] There is no circularity because the number of (2) does not occur in
(2) but only a description of this number occurs therein.
[2] Cf. Carnap, R., *Logische Syntax der Sprache*, pp. 93–5, and " Die
Antinomien und die Unvollständigkeit der Mathematik," *Monatshefte
für Mathematik und Physik*, 41 Band, 2 Heft, Leipzig, 1934, pp. 264–272.

contradictory. That this is a self-contradiction follows from the considerations—

(α) (3) is either analytic or contradictory because it is a logical sentence (i.e. contains no descriptive expressions).

(β) Assuming (3) is contradictory it follows that whatever (3) asserts is connotatively false ; hence—

(γ) ∼ (3) is contradictory.

(δ) A logical sentence which is not contradictory is analytic ; hence (3) is analytic, i.e. whatever (3) asserts is connotatively true ; therefore—

(ε) (3) is contradictory.

(β) and (γ) are logically incompatible, likewise (δ) and (ε). This is, therefore, a genuine vicious-circle contradiction. Hence the assumption that " analytic in language S " is definable in S is false. The contradiction is avoided by the discovery that for every language S there are concepts of S which cannot be defined within the limits of the language,[1] and thus the syntax of a language can, to a large extent, be formulated within the language itself, and wholly formulated within a language richer than itself in modes of expression. And thus no contradictions arise.

For the purpose of discussing syntactical questions relating to philosophy and scientific method, a generalization of the syntactical concepts which I have already discussed is required. The principal generalization is, as I have already remarked, the addition of physical principles to the logical axioms of a language. This addition makes it possible to establish physical equipollency (i.e. identity of content) of sentences as a parallel of logical equipollency, an innovation which is required for the possibility of inter-subjectively testable sentences.

Carnap [2] first introduces the idea of validity. A class of

---

[1] Cf. Gödel, K., " Über formal unentscheidbare Sätze der Principia Mathematica und verwandten Systeme. I," *Monatshefte für Mathematik und Physik*, 38 Band, 1 Heft, pp. 173–198, and Carnap, R., op. cit., *supra*.

[2] *Logische Syntax der Sprache*, pp. 126–7.

sentences, $\Re_1$, is *valid* if it is a consequence-class of the empty class and hence of every class. For logical languages (i.e. languages in which the only axioms are logical sentences) *valid* coincides with *analytic* ; whereas for languages containing physical axioms this is not the case. (Analytic sentences of the latter kind of language are valid, but the converse does not obtain.) Similarly a class of sentences, $\Re_1$, is *contra-valid* if every sentential class is a consequence-class of $\Re_1$. Sentential classes which are either valid or contra-valid are said to be *determined*, if neither valid nor contra-valid, sentential classes (and hence sentences) are *undetermined*.

Carnap [1] then defines the content of a sentence $\mathfrak{S}_1$ or class of sentences, $\Re_1$, as the class of non-valid sentences which are consequences of $\mathfrak{S}_1$ or $\Re_1$. Two sentences $\mathfrak{S}_1$ and $\mathfrak{S}_2$ are equipollent if all non-valid consequences of $\mathfrak{S}_1$ are also non-valid consequences of $\mathfrak{S}_2$ and conversely.

If a language contains physical principles (general laws as well as particular experimental sentences) it is necessary to differentiate between logical equipollency and physical equipollency. And thus $\mathfrak{S}_1$ and $\mathfrak{S}_2$ are physically equipollent if they are equipollent but not logically equipollent. Whether two sentences are physically or logically equipollent will, in general, depend upon whether physically valid sentences or logically valid sentences are employed in delineating their non-valid consequences.

Just as it is determined by convention whether unlimited operators are to occur in a language, it also depends on convention whether physical sentences are to be included among the axioms of a language. And we must agree, I believe, with Carnap that no absolutistic *a priori* arguments exist which could determine our decision. As against Carnap, however, it could be urged that a convincing basis for selecting some given physical sentences rather than others is to be found in the privileged character of

---

[1] *Logische Syntax der Sprache*, pp. 128–9.

experimental or experiental sentences. However this may be, it is clear that no valid *a priori* arguments could decide the case, unless, indeed, the privileged character of experimental records be such an argument.

As this chapter is intended principally to be descriptive, I shall introduce no critical consideration here. Indeed, most of the principles of logical syntax as developed by Tarski, Gödel, and Carnap seem to be unquestionable. My only questions, which I shall defer until the next chapter, are concerned with the adequacy of the formal idiom for expressing the character of natural science. And this objection while it is fundamental to the thesis of Physicalism does not affect the syntactical studies with which the present chapter has been concerned.

Chapter X

PROBLEMS OF SCIENTIFIC METHOD AND PHILOSOPHY IN TERMS OF LOGICAL SYNTAX

In this chapter I shall discuss Carnap's syntactical treatment of some of the problems of scientific method and philosophy with especial reference to the earlier Positivistic doctrines on the same subjects.

I

In Wittgenstein's theory of language the truth and sense of propositions ultimately depend on the complete verifiability of the elementary propositions. That this should be the only possible construction of truth and meaning follows from an absolutism for which no convincing arguments can be given. If it is desirable to retain some essential feature of empiricism in the new or amended doctrines, the way to accomplish this is plainly a revision of our conception of the nature of general and singular statements. It is then necessary to demand of general sentences simply that they be *incompletely* verifiable, or incompletely testable in Carnap's terminology.[1] It is a matter of decision which determines whether sentences of a language are to contain unlimited operators or not. If they are introduced, however, the rules governing their usage exclude the possibility of their replacement by any set of singular sentences. And thus " $(x)(\phi x)$ " is not replaceable by " $(x)n(\phi x)$ ", i.e. " $\phi x_1.\phi x_2. \ldots \phi xn$ " is never an analytic or valid equivalent of " $(x)\phi x$ ". An expression of this is sometimes given in the statement that the universal

---

[1] For the preliminary remarks in this chapter I am indebted to Dr. Carnap who has kindly allowed me to read an unpublished paper on " Testability and Meaning "

affirmative sentences have no existential import, but such a formulation only states a part of what is required.

The generalizations involving unlimited operators having been radically distinguished from any sets of singular sentences, the question remains—what connection exists between the general statements and the singular statements which record experimental findings? This question is simply answered by regarding general statements as being incompletely testable by singular statements of such and such a required form. Any consistent interpretation of generalization is possible and our choice is determined by whatever seems to be the most advantageous form of language for scientific purposes. There is therefore no objection to interpreting the general statement : " All planets move in elliptical orbits " as meaning " no planet moves in a circular or parabolic, or . . . . or rectilinear path ". This statement is unilaterally testable by means of the occurrence of experiment records of such and such a form. The statement, that is to say, will be refuted by an experiment-sentence which states or implies the existence of a path excluded by it. It is incompletely testable because experiment can decide the fate of such a sentence by condemning it, but never by acquittal. And there would seem to be no objection to regarding natural science as an organized body of hitherto unrefuted generalizations and hitherto unquestioned experimental records. This is, then, a simple but effective solution to the problems of induction and of the nature of scientific law which I discussed in earlier chapters.[1]

It is possible to generalize this notion. Wittgenstein and Kaufmann have forbidden the use of what they have called accidental generality in mathematics and have maintained that the generality of mathematics is something which must be shown by presenting general mathematical forms rather

[1] This treatment of general assertions is due to Karl Popper (see his *Logik der Forschung*, Wien, 1935). It has been stated in a more general form by Carnap in the unpublished essay on testability.

than by asserting general statements. What remains of this conception when its absolutistic basis is left out of account is simply this : On the one hand the operators " $(x) \ldots$ " and " $(\exists x) \ldots$ " are interpreted as definite and explicit truth-functions of the elementary functions, thus excluding them from the unlimited generalization required in mathematics ; on the other hand, mathematical generality is given in the presentation of variables. It is plain that it is neither necessary nor advantageous to proceed in this way. For the interpretation of generalization, which Popper and Carnap have suggested, permits the use of unlimited operators in mathematics and natural science as before. What cannot be said in Wittgenstein's language becomes expressible simply by the introduction of unlimited operators.

An example here would be instructive. Wittgenstein gives the general form of the series of natural numbers by the formula $[0, x, x + 1]$, whereas Russell and Whitehead define the natural numbers as the posterity of zero in respect of the relation *immediate predecessor*. Wittgenstein then states that the series of numbers is ordered by an internal relation which must be shown because it cannot be expressed. It is not difficult to see that the relation is expressed by the Frege-Russell definition of the ancestral relation. And Carnap has explained that internality of certain relations is expressible in terms of logical syntax. The " interlocking " of two numbers one of which immediately precedes the other in the series of natural numbers *is* expressed by saying that the relation between these numbers is an analytic predicate. And thus the inexpressible essential features of mathematical terms and sentences become expressible by enriching the object-language by unlimited operators, a typal hierarchy, etc., and by formulating a syntax language in which analytic predicates are defined.

The principal innovation, then, seems to be the introduction of unlimited operators. This yields one general kind of generalization which may be employed *indifferenter* in natural science and mathematics. The distinction between logical generality and scientific generality is made in a syntax-language in which distinctions are made between analytic (or logical) predicates, etc., and descriptive (or synthetic) predicates, etc. As this study is not concerned with the nature of mathematics, the reader must be referred to Carnap's essays for further details.[1]

The meaning and truth of general sentences is incompletely determined and testable via the singular statements. The form of the singular statements is then partially determined by convention, and partially determined by the general statements of which the singular statements are tests. There must be a determination for the meaning and truth of the singular statements, which avoids the absolutism of Wittgenstein's theory.

According to Wittgenstein and his followers in the Viennese Circle, the sense of elementary propositions is determined by what is the case if they are true or by what is the case if they are false. A clear distinction between truth and meaning is out of the question here. It would then be a matter of dispute whether the method of verification or the fact the existence of which is verified determines the sense of propositions. Carnap, in a hitherto unpublished paper, has given a definition of verification (complete testability) which clearly distinguishes between these various aspects of verification in a perfectly precise manner.

Carnap's general principle is that any significant statement is testable. Those sentences which are completely testable are dealt with in the following manner: Let T be the test-condition-sentence of the sentence S which is to be tested, T' be the truth-condition-sentence of S, and M be the test-sentence of S. Then $M . \equiv : T \supset (T' \equiv S)$, i.e. the test-sentence of a sentence S is the sentence which states that *if* the test-condition of S is established *then* the

---

[1] Carnap, R., *Logische Syntax der Sprache*, Wien, 1934, especially pp. 41–3, 230–1.

truth-condition of S is equivalent to the truth of S. For example, if it is asserted that the temperature of a given spatio-temporal area x is 100° C., the test-condition consists of placing a mercury thermometer at x, the truth-condition depends upon the coincidence of the top of the column of mercury and the mark " 100 " on the scale, and then we can say : " If a mercury thermometer is placed at x, then the coincidence of the top of the mercury column and the ' 100 ' mark of the scale implies S and the non-coincidence implies not-S." The logical conditions of any such test sentence require the validity of the whole sentence M, the non-contravalidity of the test-condition-sentence T, and the testability of the truth-condition-sentence T'. In other words, the test-sentence must be a consequence of the logical or physical axioms of the language, the test-condition-sentence must not violate the logical and physical axioms of the language, and finally it must already be known that the truth-condition-sentence is testable.

This schematism requires some further consideration. Whether a sentence is completely testable depends, in the first instance, upon whether it is in accord with the laws of physics and logic which constitute the foundation of the language system in which it is formulated. The test sentence M must therefore be not simply non-contravalid (i.e. it is not sufficient that it stand in the relation of simple consistency with the logical and physical rules). On the other hand it must be determined, on the basis of physics and logic, that M is a necessary and sufficient test for S, and this will be the case if and only if M follows from the axioms. The experimental situation which is created in order to test S, however, may be any situation which does not violate the logical and physical rules, i.e. any situation which is neither logically nor physically impossible. And finally the truth-condition T' of S must be completely and directly testable, that is to say, its truth or falsity must be revealed directly and completely to the observer by an observation.

The implications of the direct and complete testability

of truth-condition sentences are very far-reaching. It would seem to be the case that some sentences must exist in any language the meaning and truth of which is exclusively and exhaustively determined by concrete data. And this would violate the formal idiom as well as the relativism which characterizes Carnap's doctrines.

It is plain that the relativism of the doctrine may be preserved, although I cannot see how the circumstance that directly and completely testable statements must lie at the foundation of scientific experiments is expressible in the formal idiom. As Carnap has said, every sentence may be considered as a hypothesis so that the completely and directly testable sentences may be abandoned if further experiment seems to demand it. And it is also true that sentences the contents of which seem to be completely and directly determinable by means of ostensive definitions may, under further analysis, be reduced to other sentences. And this effectively avoids any abolutism of truth and meaning of sentences. But how are we to express the fact that for a given language-system or in respect of a given scientific problem certain sentence-forms must be conventionally taken to be completely and directly testable and ostensively determined in respect of content ? This means, it would seem, that the referent of certain sentences is in an extra-linguistic realm ; it means that the referents of certain sentences are concrete data. The introduction of the phrase " concrete data ", however, violates the formal idiom which speaks only of sentences, terms, and the like. I shall return to this point in the terminal chapter of this essay, but a few further remarks are in place here.

Carnap's system of logical syntax allows us to distinguish between the object-language and the syntax language. Sentences which contain a mixture of object-terms and syntactical terms are called, and rightly, pseudo-object sentences. Thus, e.g., the sentence " A rose is a thing " is a pseudo-object sentence, and must be transformed into " The word ' rose ' is a thing-word " in order to be significant. A descriptive syntactical sentence may be formed, however, which asserts " Sentences of the atomic form as correlated with data immediately presented " There are several ways in which this sentence may be interpreted :—

(1) As a synthetic statement of psychology. In this sense the sentence is simply a natural scientific hypothesis.

(2) As a sentence of methodology. In this sense the determination of the meaning and truth of atomic sentences is given as a necessary principle.

The first sense is irrelevant to the present purpose. The second, however, seems to violate the formal idiom which would only permit a negative formulation such as " The truth and content of atomic sentences is not determinable by reference to other sentences of the language ". And thus, although it is admitted that everything is expressible and that all sentences are hypothetical, the distinction between discourse and concrete data cannot be eliminated and yet escapes expression in the formal idiom. The problem of determining the truth of the atomic sentences of a language remains essentially unsolved.

The other problems of scientific method, in particular the problem of the testability of general sentences, is treated in a far more satisfactory manner. If unlimited operators are permitted in a language and if incomplete testability of sentences prefixed by such operators is sufficient guarantee that they are related to the empirical world, then the problem of induction disappears. For this problem arises only in a system in which complete testability of general sentences is demanded. The meaning of sentences involving reference to complex objects is determinable in a similar manner.

The constitution of complex physical and empirical objects in terms of classes and relations after Russell's method of logical construction was seen to be unsatisfactory. An object, such as a table, cannot be characterized epistemically in terms other than empirical, yet the supposition that a table is a logical construction out of sense data fails to account for the existence of the table between moments of observation and fails also as a sufficient description of the table. On the one hand, we must assume that tables can exist without being observed and, on the other hand, no enumeration of empirical qualities ascribed to tables necessarily exhausts the possible empirical qualities of tables. This may be expressed formally by saying that the sentences " $Q_1(a)$ ", " $Q_2(a)$," ... " $Q_n(a)$," are collectively not equipollent with the sentence " a is a table ". For all of these sentences may be true and " a is a table " false, whereas " a is a table " may be true while some of the sentences $Q_1(a)$ ", " $Q_2(a)$," " . . . $Q_n(a)$ " may be false. And for reasons discussed in Chapter V (Natural Law), it cannot be granted that objects are replaceable by scientific laws. It is possible, in Carnap's new doctrine, to explain sentences about objects which will effectively avoid these difficulties.

Sentences involving reference to empirical objects or objects of physical science (such as atoms) are *reducible* to sentences involving reference to concrete data, where *reduction* means that the former sentences are testable by the latter. Thus " a is a table " is not equipollent with any set of atomic sentences, but, nevertheless, is testable by means of the verification of certain atomic sentences. Carnap, therefore, characterizes tables and atoms as hypothetical entities. The necessary conditions for the existence of such objects are given in atomic sentences the verification of which would falsify the sentences asserting such existence. The content of a sentence about an object would then be determined by the atomic sentences which, if true, would falsify it. This solution of the problem is due to Karl Popper, and Carnap essentially agrees with it.

A slightly different definition of content of sentences would seem to be required here. The content of sentences is, in general, defined as the class of non-valid sentences which follow from it. Some sentences are thus equipollent with the class of their non-valid consequences. Sentences involving objects, which are unilaterally testable by the atomic sentences which follow from them are not usually equipollent with their consequences since the consequences assert less than the original sentences. This difference, however, does not involve any considerable alteration of the general definition. It is only necessary to differentiate between sentences. with reductive contents and those with contents (without qualification).

II

The present attitude of Carnap (and his followers in the Viennese Circle) toward philosophical investigations is somewhat different from the radically anti-metaphysical doctrines of Wittgenstein and Schlick. Some of the allegedly philosophical problems belong to the realm of pure or descriptive syntax, others are questions of psychology or other branches of natural science, while still others are either syntactically or empirically meaningless.

Carnap suggests, however, that the term " logic of science " replace the ambiguous word " philosophy " and he explains that the logic of science is to be regarded as the syntax of the language of science.[1]

As I explained above, Carnap traces some of the most widely discussed problems of the logic of science to a confusion of terms of the object-language with those of the syntax-language which results in sentences containing object-terms and syntactical terms or containing object-terms and terms of the connotative (or material) mode of expression.

It will be impossible to discuss all kinds of problems here, but a few will be sufficient to illustrate the method. We may begin with a sentence of arithmetic : " Numbers are classes of classes of things " or " Numbers are functions of functions of things ". Carnap regards these sentences as being in the

[1] *Logische Syntax der Sprache*, pp. 207–210.

material idiom, perhaps as being pseudo-object sentences. He proposes that they be replaced by " number-expessions are class-expressions of the second level " or " number-expressions are one-place predicates of the second level (i.e. $\mathfrak{z}\epsilon^2 pr^1$)". Whether this syntactical statement is to be accepted depends wholly upon what language-system happens to be chosen for the expression of mathematical concepts and sentences. And I feel that this would successfully close the debate (between, e.g., logistic and formalistic mathematicians) were it not for the fact that it is possible to express the allegedly " philosophical " sentence— " numbers are classes of classes of things " in a perfectly precise manner in the object-language, for example, as Russell does. Thus it would seem legitimate to define the number of a class a as the class of classes similar to a. In Russell's notation, of course, no mention need be made of " class " and we may say more correctly : " The cardinal number of $a = df$ the β's, such that β is similar to a." The question, therefore, as to the nature of number *may* be construed as a syntactical question, but it also may be regarded as a question of analysis of mathematical terms to be dealt with in the object language.

Another example from the empirical realm will serve to indicate more clearly the danger of over-simplifying problems. Carnap asserts that whether " every colour is in a place " depends upon the form of the language we have chosen to employ. And thus this sentence is translatable into the syntactical sentence " A colour expression always occurs in a sentence in combination with the designation of a place." This sentence will be either a pure convention or a physically valid sentence, in any case a sentence of syntax. But I do not believe the matter is so simple as all that. If we choose, " colour " may be the common designation of a syntactical category. It is possible, however, to regard " colour " as a term of the object-language as Carnap does in *Die Logische Aufbau der Welt* (§ 108 ff.) or as W. E. Johnson does in his *Logic* (vol. i on the Determinable).

Under such circumstances the question is one for empirical science to decide, and it is conceivable that a negative decision might result.

On the other hand, many logical problems of meaning (if not all) are quite correctly and satisfactorily treated by Carnap's syntactical method. In particular, terms such as the " possible ", " the impossible ", " the necessary ", etc., are plainly connotative expressions for the syntactical predicates "undetermined ", " contra-valid ", " valid ". Likewise the question whether there need be intensional functions of sentences is correctly answered by Carnap in terms of the possibility of constructing a language with only extensional functions of sentences.

The assessment of these views may be summarized. The thesis that problems of methodology may be entirely construed as problems of logical syntax of the language of science seems to obtain for all those questions (1) concerning the relation between general sentences and singular sentences, (2) concerning the meaning of sentences. On the other hand, (a) it can hardly be granted that the truth of directly and completely testable sentences is treatable syntactically. (b) And again it is hardly a matter of convention whether certain logical definitions and certain empirical sentences depend upon the language-system which we have chosen.

(a) The truth of atomic sentences depends, as Carnap would grant, I believe, upon observation. The characterization of the truth of such sentences likewise involves reference to extra-linguistic entities. And although I do not see any wholly satisfactory way in which this could be stated, it seems to be required for a complete explanation of scientific method, that the co-ordination of sentences with empirical data be taken into consideration. The expression of the meaning of atomic sentences wholly within discourse by means of ostensive definitions does not entail the characterization of the truth of these sentences wholly within the realm of discourse. It appears to be an obvious point that psychological presentations (i.e. images) cannot be brought into sentences.

(b) I am inclined to think that whether sentences such as " Every colour is in a place " belong to the object-language or to the syntax language does not depend upon our decision, but rather that, in such cases, our decision will depend upon empirical investigations. And it is hardly a solution to say that the problem is either a matter of pyschology or a matter of syntax. For in the sense that all the sciences depend finally upon observation, psychological laws of behaviour as well as the physical axioms depend thereupon. What language system we employ, and what valid psychological principles we admit, will in some sense depend upon our observations. It cannot, therefore, be wholly a matter of decision or convention that certain physical axioms and psychological laws are adopted.

CHAPTER XI

THE PHYSICAL LANGUAGE

In the last chapter I tried to show that the characterization, the test of atomic sentences, seemed to escape expression in the formal idiom. The thesis of Neurath and Carnap known as Radical Physicalism is *inter alia* an attempt to overcome this difficulty. It is, however in a larger sense a thesis which provides a solution to the problem of inter-subjectivity.

Radical Physicalism has undergone several reformulations since its first systematic presentation. It will be instructive to present the doctrine in its original form before discussing any of the revised versions.

In " Die physikalische Sprache als universale Sprache der Wissenschaft " [1] Carnap has devised a method in which an intersubjective language is developed from the protocol language of individuals. The protocol language consists of all sentences which are written by an individual as an account of his personal experience. It is incorrect to explain the protocol language in this way, since we have agreed to speak only of sentences and never of " experience ". This definition is therefore only a provisional aid for understanding what is meant. It is more correct to say that the protocol is the direct " report " of an individual. From the several reports of individuals an intersubjectively valid group of sentences will be developed. First it is necessary to introduce some definitions.

A language is said to be universal if every sentence can be translated into it (if it describes any fact whatsoever) ; a language which is not universal is a partial language. A protocol language is one that is not derived from any other language. This does not mean that it is impossible to

[1] *Erkenntnis*, Bd. ii, pp. 432–465.

derive any given protocol sentence by indirect methods. It means that it is a record written in terms such that the individual terms cannot be derived from other propositions by explicit definitions. This may be better explained in another way. Carnap writes: " The simplest sentences of a protocol language are those which are the basis of the verifications of all more complicated sentences. (The simplest sentences of the protocol language are related to the given ; they describe the immediate content of experience or phenomena.) '

The kind of words which occur in the protocol sentences cannot be determined with exactitude at present. The philosophy of elements (Mach) would perhaps say that they would be of the form " blue here, red there ". (Elements of the given are simple sensations and feelings.) The gestalt psychologist would undoubtedly say that we always have " now a red circle here ". (There are configurations of the sense-modalities ; the indiviual sensations are abstractions.) This debate does not affect the doctrine presently to be delineated. The sentences of the protocol have a form similar to one or both of those just cited, so that it is not necessary to determine exactly what form they possess.

The sentences of a system of science are not directly derived from the protocol. They are derived in a circuitous manner from it. Within a scientific language we have to differentiate between singular sentences and laws. A singular physical sentence is concerned with an individual circumstance which is entirely expressible in physical terms. A law is a general non-enumerative sentence which has the character of an hypothesis in regard to the singular propositions. It cannot be derived from any given class of the singular sentences, but is said to be confirmed by them. Likewise the singular physical sentence has the character of an hypothesis with regard to the protocol sentence from which it is derived. Conversely, from a sufficiently large and extensive class of singular physical sentences the protocol sentences can be derived. This last-mentioned fact is the key to Carnap's solution of the problem of solipsism. This point will be developed later. If a given sentence P can be reduced to a protocol language of a subject S by known rules of transformation, it is said to be understood by S, i.e. S knows all the consequences of P. Otherwise, when a determined set of rules of derivation is not available S cannot understand P. If a sentence P has a derivative connection with the protocols of more than one subject, then P is said to be significant for all of these subjects. A language is said to be intersubjective if it has a derivative connection with the protocols of many subjects. An inter-subjective sentence is said to be intersubjectively valid if it is valid for all of these subjects, i.e. is verified to a sufficient degree by each of them. Carnap wishes to prove that the language of physics is an intersubjective language, that it is a universal language of which the protocol language is but a part.

The physical language is characterized by the fact that sentences of the simplest form ascribe a definite value or range of values of a co-efficient of a physical state to a specific set of co-ordinates. Every sentence of physics is to be so formed that every protocol sentence which may be translated in it is contained in it. The language of physics is a universal language in that every sentence can be translated into it.

The concepts of physics are quantitative. But as being quantitative they possess a further characteristic which is important here. They are abstract, and free from qualitative determinations. In the formal mode this means that the rules for translation from the physical language into the protocol language are of such a kind that a given word of the physical language is never correlated with words of the protocol language of only one definite sense-modality (e.g. only colour-determination, tonal determination, etc.). From the physical determination protocol determinations of every sense-modality can be derived; the physical determinations are intersensorial.

A physical sentence which contains a tonal determination is not only co-ordinated with sentences which contain that determination of the tonal realm but also, under definite conditions, it is co-ordinated with sentences containing determinations of other sense-modalities.

Two kinds of determinations are possible under the circumstances revealed in the foregoing.

1. Personal determination. S can determine what physical determination is co-ordinated with a definite qualitative determination of the protocol language (under what physical conditions he experiences a definite quality). " The fundamental possibility of this kind of determination rests upon the happy circumstance, which is not logically necessary but only occurs empirically, that the protocol (the content of experience) has a certain property of order which holds for each sense-modality." [1] Thus, e.g., a series of gradually increasing tuning forks present a visual, tactual, and aural order. Any ordinal similarity between visual and tactual or visual and aural modalities yields examples of structural properties common to the perceptions of the several senses. The physical determinations hold inter-sensorially.

2a. Foreign determination. A subject S (e.g. a psychologist) can determine in another subject S_1 what physical determination is co-ordinated with a definite qualitative determination of the protocol language of S_1.

2b. Foreign determination by different subjects. If the investigation of S_1 occurs when there is more than one investigation subject, say, S_1, S_2, . . ., the same result as above is attained. This is conditioned as follows : The determination of the value of a physical magnitude for a concrete case in not only independent of the sense-modality employed but also independent of the investigating subjects. Here again the happy circumstance occurs, which is not logically necessary, to wit, a certain property of order of the protocols of the different subjects in comparison with one

[1] Carnap, *Erkenntnis*, Bd. ii, " Die physikalische Sprache, usw.," sec. 4.

another. Hence the physical determinations are inter-subjectively valid.

Beyond the language of physics there is no inter-subjective language known. Science is a system of inter-subjectively valid sentences. Therefore the physical language is the language of science.

It is also a universal language. The first place in which doubts might arise is in regard to biological phenomena. Many claim that biological phenomena cannot be reduced to physical laws. However, the doctrine of the universality of the language of physics has nothing to do with this problem. It only asserts, in this connection, that biological phenomena can be described in physical terms, that is that the concepts of biology are reducible to the language of physics.

The second doubt would most naturally occur in the field of psychology. But the Physicalistic doctrine, in this connection, only asserts that all sentences of psychology can be translated into physical language, both the singular and the general sentences ; otherwise stated the definition of every psychological determination leads back to physical determinations. The same thing holds for sociology.

The case of metaphysics has already been treated. Metaphysical pseudosentences stand in no relation whatsoever to the protocol language. Either they contain words which are not reducible to the words of the protocol language or they are composed in a manner contrary to logical syntax.

We must now consider whether the sentences of the protocol language are translatable into the physical language. This is equivalent to the question whether the solipsistic point of departure can be transcended. Carnap claims that the sentence of the original protocol language are translatable into the language of physics. In the more ordinary content-mode of expression one would say that the facts of the given, the content of immediate experience, are physical facts and hence spatio-temporal processes. Carnap maintains that the objections which are raised against his thesis are only significant in the content-mode. For instance,

* purely a question of terminology whether theories of historical change and development, while described in the language of science and capable of being individually confirmed or refuted, are called 'philosophy' of history or society.

[left margin handwritten notes: Kant personal vs. third person both adequate; X; XX]

he gives the example, " The rain may be a physical process but my *experience* of rain is not." It should be clear that this objection cannot be retained if we translate it into the formal idiom. We should say that " some of the words and sentences of my protocol are ' rain ', ' falling ', ' pleasure ', . . . ; ' the falling rain pleases me ' . . . ; and these cannot be translated into the language of physics." But Carnap has shown that they can be so translated and the objection is no longer fundamentally sound.

Some of the protocol sentences of a given subject are compared with one another and found to be ordinally similar to one another. This yields an intersensory sentence. The protocol sentences of several individuals, when rendered intersensory, are sometimes found to be ordinally similar. This yields an intersubjectively valid sentence. When the sentence so obtained is translated into the language of co-ordinates and physical co-efficients we have a physical sentence. Then the physical sentence which describes the behaviour of a given subject are correlated with the protocol sentences of that subject. This may be done by the subject himself or by other subjects (e.g. observing psychologists). It is then possible to formulate certain laws which state that a set of physical sentences is formally equivalent to a given protocol sentence. Thus the protocol sentences are transformable into physical sentences and, conversely, from a sufficient number of physical sentences, a given protocol sentence can be derived. Now, by definition, the logical content of a sentence is the set of its non-valid [1] consequences. Hence the sentences of physics and those of protocols are inter-translatable. The protocol language is thus a part of the language of physics.

There is, however, a more far-reaching objection to Carnap's thesis which I must consider at some length. I shall give a translation of his essay at this point, since it cannot otherwise be expressed with greater force.

" Let P_1 be a singular sentence in the protocol of S_1,

[1] " Non-valid " is synonymous with " undetermined ", cf. p. 248 supra.

therefore a proposition about the content of the experience of S_1, e.g. *I am thirsty* or, briefly, *now, thirst*. Can the same fact be expressed in the protocol of another person S_2? The sentences of the latter protocol speak only of the content of the experience of S_2. The content of an experience is always that of a definite subject, and it cannot be the content of the experience of another subject at the same time. Now if perchance S_1 and S_2 are thirsty at the same time, then the protocol sentences of S_1 and S_2 have the same sound (appearance) but different senses, for they are related to different facts ; the one to the thirst of S_1, the other to the thirst of S_2. No sentence of the protocol of S_2 can express the thirst of S_1. . . . We say that S_2 knows of the thirst of S_1 and can express it. But what S_2 can know, strictly speaking, is only a physical condition of the body of S_1 which S_2 joins to the presentation of his own particular thirst. If S_2 says S_1 *is thirsty* then it is only verifiable in the content of the experiences of S_2 that S_1 has such and such a bodily condition. . . . If we do not understand this physical condition by the *thirst of S_1* but rather by his feeling of thirst, then the thirst of S_1 is in principle not knowable for S_2, and hence it is without sense for S_2.

" In general every protocol sentence of a given subject has sense only for this subject itself, but it is not understandable and is without sense for every other subject. Therefore every subject has a protocol language peculiar to himself. If different protocols exhibit words and sentences which sound the same the senses are, nevertheless, different and they are, accordingly, not comparable. Every protocol can only be applied monologously ; there is no intersubjective protocol language. . . .

" But a connection does exist between the language of physics and the language of experience in the case of a given subject. . . . In order to save the physical description one might make the assumption that the protocol language does not speak of physical processes but that the physical language speaks only of the contents of experience and of complexes thereof.[1] But one gets into difficulty as soon as one considers the relation between the protocol language of two different subjects and the physical language. The protocol language of S_1 speaks of the content of the experience of S_1; that of S_2, of the content of the experience of S_2. What does the inter-subjective language of physics speak of? Surely it must speak of the contents of the experience of S_1, just as it does of S_2; but that is impossible since the realms of the contents of the experiences of the two subjects do not overlap. No solution of the solipsistic predicament is discoverable by this method, which is free from contradiction. . . .

"But the contradiction disappears as soon as we restrict ourselves to the formal mode of expression. . . . If we no longer speak about 'contents of experience', 'colour-sensations", etc., but rather of " protocol sentences with colour-words', etc., there is no longer a contradiction between the protocol and the physical language.

"If we eliminate all contradictions and pseudo-problems by the use of the formal mode of expression, the question remains to be answered, how the derivative connection between the physical and the protocol languages is procured.

"We have noted above that, if a sufficiently extended class of physical sentences is available, a sentence of the protocol language can be derived therefrom. . . . This derivation has the simplest form if the physical propositions describe the physical state of the subject in question. . . .

"One might think that a derivation of this kind is Utopian and could only be realized if the physiology of the central nervous system were completely known. This is not the case, for the derivation is practicable at present and is accomplished in everyday life by the mutual agreement of people . . . it can be formulated in expressions of the physical language. We (can, for instance) designate some given physical state as *seeing of red* which is characterized by the fact that such and such physical reactions proceed from such

[1] Carnap refers here to the theory which he advanced in the *Logischer Aufbau der Welt.*

and such physical stimuli. For example, the stimulus :
verbal sound $=$ '*what do you see now ?*' and the reaction :
speech-motion $=$ ' *red* '; stimulus : verbal sound $=$ ' point
to the colour just seen,' reaction : the finger is moved to
such and such a region, etc. $(\pm\,?\,?)$ *really?*

" While we do not know the values of the physical
magnitudes which occur in such a physical state of the
subject, we know many physical processes which frequently
occur as causes. . . . Therefore (1) we can determine such a
physical state and (2) we can obtain predictions from it in
order to obtain physical processes expected in the future.
. . . . The protocol sentence P can therefore be derived from
a class M of singular physical sentence. Conversely, from
the protocol sentence P, the class M of physical sentences can
be derived. When two sentences are thus intertranslatable,
we say that they have the *same content* or are *mutually
derivable*. (For this see the definitions given in Chapter IX.)

" A correspondence exists between a given protocol
language and that *part* of the language of physics from which
it can be derived and conversely. Hence the protocol
language is a part of the language of physics.

" If we formulate this result that the given protocol
sentence and the physical sentence have the same content (P
is derivable from p), in the connotative mode, P and p
describe the same fact, we shall encounter the old objections.

" S_2 writes an account of the processes of S_1's life for
yesterday, on the bases of certain physical determinations.
Perhaps S_2 will not recognize this as a complete account of
yesterday's chapter of his life ; he will say that the account
describes his movements, gestures, etc., but that his
experiences, memories, etc., are lacking in the account . . .
because S_2 cannot determine them by physical methods.
But if S_2 could introduce definitions of the kind ' seeing
red ' $=$ oo, he could add these to his account and hence be
consonant therein with the protocol of S_1. Nevertheless,
S_1 will not recognize even this account, for he will object
that although S_2 employs expressions like ' joy ', ' red,'

' memory ', etc., he means something else by them than what S_1 means. Thus to S_2 they mean a physical condition of the body, whereas to S_1 they mean something experienced. . . . We know that his objection rests upon the confusion between having a common formal content (i.e. being mutually derivable) and having a common presentation-content.[1] The accounts of S_1 and S_2 have a common formal content, but different presentation-contents. The difference of presentation-content is not an objection to identifying formal content, for the content of a sentence means the possibility of deriving other sentences from it ; and if the same sentences can be derived from two given sentences, then these two latter sentences have the same content independent of the particular presentations which we are in the habit of combining with them . . . (the problem of illusion is treated as well as that of bodies which are not perceived). Perhaps p is not of the same content as P_1 as in the case of illusion or of an unperceived body. But still p is of the same content as another physical proposition P_2 : ' *the body of S now has a physical condition Z* ' ; and, moreover, the condition Z is characterized by *different* determinations. These are, among others : (1) the verbal report ' *a red ball on the table* ' follows from the stimulus ' *what do you see ?* ' ; (2) if a red ball is lying on the table and if S is brought in a satisfactory position then the condition Z occurs. P_1, under satisfactory circumstances, can be concluded from P_2 . . . Since P_2 can be derived from p, P_1 can indirectly be inferred from p. The usual explanation of a protocol sentence by a certain condition of the surroundings of a subject is, therefore, an indirect explanation (composed of the statement of the bodily condition of S) and a causal inference. . . .

" The result of our reflections is : not only the language of the different branches of science, but also the protocol languages of different subjects are only (partial languages) parts of the language of physics ; all sentences, those of the

---

[1] Cf. *Scheinprobleme*. For a different definition of content (Gehalt) see *Phil. of Science*, pp. 12–14, vol. i, No. 1.

protocol as well as those of scientific systems, which are constructed in the form of a system of hypotheses in connection with the protocols, are translatable into the language of physics ; this is a universal language and, since no other such language is known, the language of science." [1]

I have translated this long passage because it seems to me to present the essence of Carnap's attempt to solve the problem of intersubjectivity. We shall see, however, that certain further emendations are necessary. Before considering these emendations, it will be instructive to compare the results of Physicalism and those of the earlier positivistic formulation in respect of the problem of intersubjectivity.

Solipsism, as Wittgenstein's system presents it, is insurmountable because the limits of the language which a given subject S understands coincide with the limits of the world of S. This follows from an absolutistic empiricism which states that to understand a proposition means to know what is the case if it is true. And this, in turn, means that a proposition is verified when and only when the fact indicated by the proposition is an ingredient of experience.

In Carnap's system the language comprehensible to a given subject is more extensive than the protocol-sentences of that subject. And thus, connotatively speaking, it is possible to give some meaning to the sentence " unobserved processes now exist " or to the sentence " other people exist ". In the formal idiom we can say : if there is a language intersubjective in respect of S_1 and S_2 then the content of the protocol of S_1 is known to S_2 and conversely. In general, if S_1 and S_2 have a language more extensive than the private languages of S_1 and S_2, then their knowledge is not limited to sentences directly verifiable by S_1 alone or by S_2 alone. Sentences about physical processes and about other organic beings are now significant to anyone who knows an intersubjective language. It is therefore possible for S_1 and S_2 to communicate via the intersubjective language. Nor is this all.

[1] *Erkenntnis*, Bd. ii, pp. 453–461.

It is not necessary that *all* the sense-modalities of S_1 and S_2 function normally. For the intersubjective language is also intersensorial, so that a sentence involving visual terms may be equipollent with one involving tactual terms. It follows that verification of sentences is not limited to the protocol language of visual terms or tactual terms or aural terms, etc. Any protocol language which is sufficiently extensive to be translated into the intersensory and quantitative sentences of the physical language is a sufficient basis for verification of physical sentences.

Intersubjective communication, understanding, and corroborative verification are possible in the physical language, and the problems of verification and communication, which seemed insurmountable when stated in the connotative mode of expression, are solved without essential difficulty.

The method of " physicalizing " a language may be stated in a formal manner. Let :—

(1) P_1, P_2, P_3, ... be the protocol-sentences of a given subject S.

(2) Q_1, Q_2, Q_3, ... the protocol sentences of S'.

(3) R_1, R_2, R_3, ... the protocol sentences of S'', etc.

(4) π_p, π_q, π_r, ... be intersensorial sentences of these various subjects.

(5) ϕ_1, ϕ_2, ϕ_3, ... be singular physical sentences.

(6) L_1, L_2, L_3, ... be physical laws.

Then, given an ordinal similarity among several P's, Q's, and R's, the intersensorial sentences can be derived. A group of intersensorial sentences together form a physical sentence provided they are taken from protocols of different subjects. Thus :—

$$(P_1, P_2, P_3) \text{ yields } \pi_p$$
$$Q_1, Q_2, Q_3) \text{ yields } \pi_q$$
$$(R_1, R_2, R_3) \text{ yields } \pi_r$$
$$\text{and } (\pi_p, \pi_q, \pi_r) \text{ yields } \phi_1.$$

In this way a singular physical sentence is formed from the protocols of S_1, S_{11}, and S_{111}. The next step involves the formulation of laws from singular physical sentences.

A singular physical sentence ϕ_1 will have the form of a set of co-ordinates as a function of a physical co-efficient. Thus ϕ_1 might be $t(x_1 x_2 x_3 x_4) = z_1$, e.g. the temperature at the place defined by $(x_1 x_2 x_3 x_4)$ is 30° C. The formulation of laws would depend on a functional relationship between various singular physical sentences. Thus if $\phi_1 \supset \phi_2$ for every case of ϕ_1 and ϕ_2 in a large group of cases, the law $L_1 = (\phi_1)$ $(\phi_2) : \phi_1 \supset \phi_2$ results. The most significant laws for the present purpose are not those of classical physics. If there is a law, L_2, such that—

$$L_2 = (\exists \phi_1)(\exists \phi_2)(\pi_p) \ \phi_1 . \phi_2 \supset \pi_p \text{ or}$$
$$L_3 . L_4 : \ (\exists \phi_1) \ (\exists \phi_2) \phi_1 . \phi_2 \supset (P_1),$$

then there is a law establishing a functional relationship between a set of laws and singular physical sentences on the one side, and a protocol sentence on the other. The protocol sentences of a given sort can thus be derived. A sufficient set of laws of this kind will provide a derivation for every protocol sentence. In this way the physical language will contain the protocol language of each subject as a sub-language. The following relationship then exists :—

$$
\left.
\begin{array}{l}
\left.
\begin{array}{l}
(P_1 P_2 P_3) \\
(Q_1 Q_2 Q_3) \\
(R^1 R_2 R_3)
\end{array}
\right\} \supset \phi_1 \\
\left.
\begin{array}{l}
\cdots\cdots\cdots \\
\cdots\cdots\cdots \\
\cdots\cdots\cdots
\end{array}
\right\} \phi_2 \\
\left.
\begin{array}{l}
\cdots\cdots\cdots \\
\cdots\cdots\cdots \\
\cdots\cdots\cdots
\end{array}
\right\} \phi_3
\end{array}
\right\} \text{yield } L_1
$$

$$
\left.
\begin{array}{l}
\cdots\cdots\cdots\cdots\cdots \\
\cdots\cdots\cdots\cdots\cdots
\end{array}
\right\} \text{yield } L_2
$$

$$
\left.
\begin{array}{l}
\cdots\cdots\cdots\cdots\cdots \\
\cdots\cdots\cdots\cdots\cdots
\end{array}
\right\} \text{yield } L_3
$$

$$\Bigg\} f(L_1 L_2 L_3)$$

$$L_1 \phi_2 \pi_r \supset P_1$$
$$L_2 \phi_3 \pi_q \supset P_2$$
$$L_3 \phi_4 \pi_r \pi_q \supset P_3$$

Thus the formation of the laws from a given set of protocols does not prevent the possibility of derivation of the protocols from the set of laws, singular physical sentences, and whatever further information is required.

This whole scheme has been criticized by Stebbing, Neurath, and L. J. Russell on the following ground : A protocol-sentence of a given subject cannot possibly have the form " here red now " or " joy now " or even " there is a red book ". Protocols must contain mention of the protocolizing subject. According to Carnap, each subject *must* take his own protocol as a point of departure. If these two conditions must obtain then Carnap cannot possibly develop a public physical language from a set of private protocol languages. In the first place no two protocols contain the same statement. On Carnap's original theory this was simply an arbitrary condition. When it is amended, as Neurath and others suggest, it is a necessary condition. For S_1's protocol-sentences will always contain mention of S_1. Thus typical protocol-sentences of S_1 would have the forms :—

(1) " S_1 said ' P_1 '."

(2) " S_1 said ' $P_1 . P_2 . P_3$ imply π_p '."

(3) " S_1 said ' π_p and S_2's statement about π_q imply ϕ_1 '."

(4) " S_1 said that S_2 said π_p."

(5) " S_1 said that S_2 said that S_3 said π_r." [1]

From this it is evident that S_1 cannot develop a public sentence from his protocol or from the protocols of S_2, S_3, etc. The laws which he formulates will only occur within the statements made by him with explicit mention of himself. Carnap's hypothesis that a physical and intersubjective language is developed from private languages is therefore unjustified.

A physical language can be developed in this way but an intersubjective one cannot. A physical language is, in the

[1] This criticism, originally due to Neurath, O., *Erkenntnis*, Bd. iii, pp. 204–214, was formulated, as I have given it, by L. S. Russell in *Proc. Arist. Soc. Supp.*, 1934. I naturally owe the remarks wholly to the authors.

present usage, a language which contains no words such as would occur in the protocol of a given subject in respect of his immediate experience. Such a language could be developed by a given subject because he can transform his protocol sentences into sentences which contain mention solely of physical co-ordinates. The language so obtained will, nevertheless, not be intersubjective because every sentence in it must be written in one of the following ways :—

(1) S says. . . . .
(2) S says that S' says. . . . .
(3) S says that S' and S'' say. . . .
(4) S says that S' says that S'' says . . . and so on.

In every case the mention of S must be made. The solipsistic point of departure is therefore not transcended by the method which Carnap developed.

Neurath offers another suggestion which is perhaps somewhat more fruitful. The adoption of the formal mode of expression was occasioned by the pseudo-problems arising from the spurious dualism between language and "experience". The linguistic solipsism of the Logical Positivists originated in this dualism and the thesis of meaning and verification associated with it. The formal mode should therefore allow complete freedom from solipsism at the outset. All sentences are therefore intersubjective *ab initio*.

It might be argued as against this point of view that some sentences must exist as a point of departure in order to provide a basic set of sentences, the truth of which depends on no other sentence. This would be necessary, the objectors might say, in order to provide a solid foundation for the truth of the physical propositions derived from the protocols.

Neurath has pointed out [1] that the ' necessity ' accrues to the atomic (elementary) sentence of Wittgenstein but not to the protocol sentences of the Physicalist. The criterion

---

[1] *Erkenntnis*, Bd. ii. " Soziologie in Physikalismus," pp. 392–405 and Bd. iii, pp. 208–9.

of truth for Positivism is correspondence of propositions with the facts, whereas, for Physicalism, this is meaningless.

The system of Physicalism requires a method of comparing sentences with sentences. The structural agreements among whole groups of sentences at hand determine which sentences of the future are to be called true and which are to be called false. There is, therefore, no necessity to assume a " firm foundation " for the system of physical laws. Consequently a set of basic sentences which require no establishment (Bewährung) is a relic of the logical absolutism of Positivism and has no place in Physicalism. The methods of Carnap and Neurath appear to differ in essential respects in spite of their agreements.

Neurath's statement of his own position is very significant.[1] " Sentences are to be compared with sentences, not with ' experience ', nor with a ' world ', nor with anything else. All these senseless duplications belong to a more or less refined metaphysics and are therefore to be rejected. Every new sentence is confronted with the totality of sentences which are present and which have been brought into agreement. *Then a sentence is called correct if it can be brought into the system* (eingliedern). Whatever we cannot systematize is rejected as incorrect. Instead of rejecting the new sentences we can also, wherever we find it generally difficult to make a decision, alter the whole system of sentences until the new sentences can be included. *Within the unified science these are significant methods of transformation.* The definition of ' correct ' and ' incorrect ' given here is far removed from those customary in the ' Viennese Circle ' which centre in ' meaning ' and ' verification '. In the present theory we always remain within the realm of speech-thinking. The system of sentences is transformed. But generalized sentences, thus sentences developed by determined relations, can be compared with the totality of protocol-sentences." This is further explained in another

[1] Neurath, Otto, " Soziologie in Physikalismus," *Erkenntnis*, Bd. ii, pp. 403-4.

article.[1] " The progress of the sciences consists of the fact that sentences which were used in a certain period of time fall into disuse later, and are frequently replaced by others. Frequently their forms remain the same but the definitions are altered. *Every law and every physicalistic sentence of the unified science or one of its branches can undergo such alteration. This obtains likewise for every protocol-sentence.*"

" In the unified science we endeavour to create a self-consistent system of protocol sentences and non-protocol sentences (inclusive of laws). If a new sentence is presented to us we compare it with the system with which we are concerned and which we control in order to see whether the new sentence stands in contradiction with the system or not. We can (in case the new sentence stands in contradiction to the system) cancel the sentence as inapplicable (false) . . ., or we can accept it and then alter the system so that it remains self-consistent when the new sentence is included. The sentence is then called ' true '."

Thus in Neurath's system there is, to begin with, a group of sentences. They are divided into protocol sentences and non-protocol sentences (i.e. the singular and general physicalized sentences). The systematization of the group may consist in the axiomatic organization of the system such that any given sentence bears a definite relation to another. If a new sentence is presented it is either a consequence of the axioms, theorems, and singular sentences or it is not. If it is, it can be included in its proper place. If it is not, one of two courses is open. It may be rejected or the system can be altered. Intersubjectivity is simply assumed, whereas objective (i.e. resp. intersubjective) validity depends on the consistency of a given sentence under consideration, with the whole system.

I believe that it is incorrect to characterize this system as merely deductive. In deductive systems " being true " coincides with " being a consequence of the axioms " and " being false " coincides with " being the negation of a

[1] Neurath, O., " Über Protokollsätze," *Erkenntnis*, Bd. iii, p. 208.

consequence of the axioms ". In Neurath's system " being true " means " being consistent with the sentential system " and " being false " means " being inconsistent with the system ". " Consistency " is a more extensive term than " consequence of axioms " ; it includes all the consequences of axioms as well as any sentence which, although not consequences of the axioms, are consistent with them.

The test of the truth of a sentence or (if the phrase is better) its intersubjective validity is its coherence with the total scientific system. The system may be altered so that new sentences need not be rejected under certain conditions.

Recently [1] Carnap has indicated, in a very exact manner, that there are two different methods of physicalizing a language. The first method of Neurath is used if we decide that the protocol-sentences are outside the system-language (i.e. outside the physical language). The correlation of protocol reports with the physical states and reactions of the protocolizing subject yields rules by means of which the reports are translatable into sentences of the system-language. Any behavioural reaction can serve as a protocol report, although, in practice, verbal expressions are most important. It is possible that certain reports of a subject occur even when the environmental circumstances do not ordinarily elicit such reports. This circumstance necessitates the use of two kinds of rules of translation from protocol reports into the system-language. The first kind may be called thing-rules and yields thing-sentences. These rules are formed when the protocol reports are correlated with objects or processes which exist in the environment of the protocolizing subject. The second kind of rules constitute the body-rules ; they are derived from correlation of the reports and the physical states of the protocolizing subject. Thus protocol-reports of an event the existence of which is guaranteed by no intersubjectively valid sentences of the physical language are nevertheless explicable in the system language by body-rules. Protocol reports cannot

[1] Carnap, R., " Über Protokollsätze," *Erkenntnis*, Bd. iii, pp. 215-228.

contradict one another in this scheme, although two contradictory system-sentences may, under certain conditions, result from protocols via the thing-rules or the body-rules. Here an alteration of the rules is required in order to retain the consistency of the system-language.

The second method concerns a language-form, the protocol sentences of which are contained in the system-language. " Any concrete sentences of the system-language may serve as protocol-sentences." [1] The protocol-sentences are therefore intersubjectively comprehensible in this scheme; there are no private protocol languages. There are no sentences which are " unassailable and definitive ". The protocol-sentences are used to test the other sentences of the system language, singular as well as general. But the protocol-sentences are further testable by means of the other sentences of the language. Consistency of the language is the ultimate test of the truth of sentences. As a consequence, contradictions are to be eliminated either by altering the axioms or by altering or striking out certain protocol-sentences. It is a matter of decision guided by the desire for a most advantageous system which determines whether the axioms or the protocols are to undergo alterations.

The various methods of constructing a physical language, although differing in details have at least this in common : each method is an attempt to present rules by means of which any sentence whatsoever is translatable into a physicalistic sentence. The thesis of Physicalism is a syntactical doctrine which states that every significant statement either is, or is equipollent with, a physicalistic sentence. An intersubjectively valid and unified science results from the rigorous application of the principles of physicalization of languages.

---

[1] Carnap, *Erkenntnis*, Bd. iii, p. 223.

CHAPTER XII

CRITIQUE OF PHYSICALISM

According to Carnap Physicalism is the syntactical thesis which asserts : Every descriptive sentence is equipollent with a physicalistic sentence. Expressed in greater detail and with perhaps more exactness : There is a language-system with logical and physical formative and trans-formative rules and such valid singular sentences as to render every sentence of the language either logically or physically equipollent with a physicalistic sentence. According as we interpret this thesis as an assertion or as a proposal, different kinds of critical considerations are relevant.

As a proposal the thesis may be interpreted as being equivalent to the statement : It is proposed that a language be constructed with such valid logical and physical rules and singular scientific sentences as to render every sentence equipollent with a physicalistic sentence (i.e. a sentence involving physical magnitudes associated with spatio-temporal co-ordinates are the only non-logical constants). As an assertion the physicalistic thesis means : There are valid general and singular sentences of a language (either an existent or a potentially constructible language) which render the translation of every sentence into a physicalistic sentence a consequence (either logical or physical) of the rules of the language together with the positively tested singular sentences.

Any criticism of this thesis will have to take account of both interpretations. Considered as a proposal, it may be questioned only whether Physicalism is a construction put upon scientific theory and practice which is most useful for the solution of methodological problems (such as, e.g., the problem of intersubjectivity), for it is obviously meaningless to affirm or deny a proposal. Considered as an assertion, however, it is significant either to affirm or deny the existence of a physicalistic language, because it can plainly be questioned whether there are sufficient valid laws and non-contravalid singular sentences which would guarantee the physicalization of, for example, every psychological assertion. I shall consider both possible interpretations.

I shall assume that there are some valid physical laws which may provide the physical axioms of the language to be constructed. Language II has the minimum logical complexity which satisfies the requirements for physicalization. The protocol sentences may be regarded as physical signals (behavioural reactions) outside the system-language, or they may be any concrete sentences within the system language. In the former case intersubjective sentences are created out of the data provided by the protocol records. In the latter intersubjectivity of the basic sentences of the system-language must be assumed.

A crucial case would perhaps be furnished by an instance of neurasthenia in which the protocol record included mention of definitely localized sensations of pain. The patient has, let us say, submitted to a thorough examination, and no correlation of organic difficulties with the protocol record of specific pain can be established. It is likely, in this instance, that the behaviour of the patient (including a past history of protocol-records of an unusual character, e.g. those indicative of hypochondria) will furnish a basis for the diagnosis of neurasthenia. We know, nevertheless, that this does not always obtain, and it is a logical possibility that there are no data which would provide a basis for such a diagnosis. And thus we have a protocol-sentence which cannot be physicalized. If the proposal-interpretation of physicalism is adopted, then, under the described condition, the sentence in question is simply stricken from the system-language or neglected as a datum outside the system-language. Now, if, instead of the protocol " I feel pain in . . . place ", the protocol-sentence " The top mercury column coincides with the 100° mark of the scale " is in question, and if this sentence is neither corroborated by the sentences given by other subjects nor physicalistically explained (e.g. by the psychological statements asserting the astigmatism of the protocolizing subject), the sentence in question must be stricken from the language or the language-rules must be altered. It is a matter of *decision* whether we do one or the other.

The question then arises what distinguishes the system from other possible systems. Carnap and Neurath answer : The fact that it is adopted by the natural scientists of the present cultural epoch. In the formal idiom, this should be expressed thus : The system which contains the sentence : " All the sentences of the language L_x are accepted by the scientists, $N.N.$, $N'.N'.$, . . . etc." [1]

It is not difficult to show that this answer is inconclusive. For, in the first place, many coherent systems of sentences each of which contain the sentence " All the sentences of language L_x . . ." may exist. And in the second place, within the limits of a given language L_x the test of the descriptive sentence " All the sentences of L_x are accepted by $N.N.$, $N'.N'.$, . . ." cannot be given. Let this sentence be $\mathfrak{S}_1$, i.e. $\mathfrak{S}_1 = (\mathfrak{S})\mathfrak{S}$ is accepted by $N.N.$, $N'.N'.$, . . . $\equiv \mathfrak{S}$ belongs to L_x. $\mathfrak{S}_1$ itself must belong to L_x *ex hypothesi*.

Hence there will be a sentence, $\mathfrak{S}_2$, which is the result of replacing the apparent variable in $\mathfrak{S}_1$ by a syntactical description of $\mathfrak{S}_1$, i.e. " $\mathfrak{S}_1$ belongs to L_x $\equiv \mathfrak{S}_1$ is accepted by $N.N.$, $N'.N'.$, . . ."

$\mathfrak{S}_1$ is not analytically equivalent to $\mathfrak{S}_2$. In order to know that $\mathfrak{S}_1$ belongs to L_x it will be necessary to know that $\mathfrak{S}_2$ is true. But in order to know that $\mathfrak{S}_2$ is true it is first necessary to know that $\mathfrak{S}_1$ belongs to L_x. In order, that is, to know whether all sentences of a given kind are accepted by certain people it is necessary to know that " All sentences of a given kind are accepted by certain people " is accepted by certain people ; whereas, whether " all sentences of a given kind are accepted by certain people " is accepted by

[1] i.e. all the sentences which conform to certain conditions of testing.

certain people depends upon whether all sentences of a certain kind are accepted by certain people. This test method is obviously circular.[1]

It follows that because mere coherence or coherence plus the alleged acceptance of a system by certain people cannot uniquely characterize the " true " scientific system, the presence or absence of some extra-discursive entities is the only alternative. Try as one will, it is impossible to characterize the truth of a system within the limits of the system in question. And if one transcends the limits of the system, the difficulties of infinite process remain and prevent any discursive expression of its truth.

A further difficulty with the theory that Physicalism is a proposal may be mentioned here. Scientific laws are accepted tentatively, that is accepted until some corroborated evidence that would refute them is discovered. It is not the same with empirical evidence itself. Either an alleged bit of evidence is not sufficiently corroborated, in which case nothing can be said, or it is corroborated, in which case the hypothesis to which it is relevant is retained or rejected. The basic sentences need not be regarded as untouchable and irrefragable. But laws cannot refute data nor the sentences which record the presence or absence of data. And thus the test of hypotheses by singular sentences is an irreversible process. This is the usual view. On the Carnap-Neurath view, however, it is a matter of decision whether the system is to be retained and the basic sentences stricken from the language, or whether the basic sentences are to be accepted and the system altered. The place of experiment in such a view of methodology is undetermined ; it is impossible to distinguish the rules of the scientific game from those of the creation of legend. I agree with Popper[2] that the present view offers no *Abgrenzungskriterium* and therefore unintentionally abandons empiricism altogether.

---

[1] See von Juhos, B., " Empiricism and Physicalism," *Analysis*, vol. ii, No. 6, pp. 91–2.

[2] Popper, Karl, *Logik der Forschung*, Wien, 1935, pp. 54–5.

This brings us to the second alternative : Physicalism is the hypothesis that the intersensory agreement of the protocols of a given subject, and the intersubjective agreement of protocols of various subjects together with accepted physical laws, make possible the physicalization of every sentence of a language. Now every hypothesis, by definition, is open to possible refutation. I can see only one way in which the *hypothesis* of Physicalism could meet with refutation, namely via the absence of intersensory and intersubjective agreements of protocol sentence. This means that whether protocols are taken as signals, or whether they are integral parts of the system-language, the test of the equipollency of a physicalistic sentence with a protocol sentence will be uniquely determined by the kind of protocol sentences at our disposal ; connotatively speaking, the empirical data will finally decide the case. It is then a matter of experiment and, as Schlick [1] has pointed out, the philosopher has to consider the possibility of an arrangement of empirical data which would prevent the physicalization of all sentences. Carnap has admitted that the intersensorial and inter-subjective agreements of protocols depends on a fortunate accident which is not logically necessary ; in the formal idiom the equipollency of protocol sentences and physicalistic sentences is a consequence of the physical axioms (not of the logical axioms) of a language. This means that either a hitherto undiscovered " unfortunate accident " or known disagreements of protocols would render complete physicalization impossible. And a partial agreement of protocols presents simply a possibility of physicalistic intersubjectivity, whereas a complete theory of scientific method would demand either a complete agreement or an alternative kind of intersubjectivity in lieu of it.

Physicalism as a hypothesis may indeed be refuted ; as a proposal, physicalism renders scientific method an arbitrary game. This is simply because it is rather a

[1]·Schlick, M., " De la relation entre les notions psychologiques et les notions physiques," *Revue des Synthèse*, Avril, 1935, pp. 5–26.

characteristic of unscientific dogmatism to exclude from consideration or to " alter " that which does not fit into a prearranged scheme, than the mark of scientific procedure. Thus we are presented with two alternatives : Physicalism as a hypothesis is open to question ; as a proposal it does not allow for the pursuit of scientific method. The latter alternative becomes plainer if we consider that Physicalism could always be " saved " by *ad hoc* hypotheses and thus could effectively retard any scientific advance. The stock arguments against conventionalism obtain with equal force against the present view.

A further difficulty must be discussed which specifically concerns an ambiguity of the term " sentence ". As it occurs in pure syntax the term is clearly defined. Carnap has given precise definitions also for the terms of descriptive syntax. " Sentence," as it occurs in descriptive syntax, may mean a single physical structure, or it may mean a class of similar physical structures. In either meaning the term " sentence " is employed differently in descriptive and pure syntax. For in descriptive syntax a sentence is frequently considered as a physical signal, whereas in pure syntax the logical properties of the sentence alone are in question. Connotatively speaking, the " sentence " of descriptive syntax is a fact, whereas the " sentence " of pure syntax is not a fact but a meaning. This creates a difficulty when the relation between the protocol sentences and the system-language is in question. If the protocol sentences fall outside the system-language then they are to be considered as mere report-signals of behaviour. As such they can never be anything but the data about which singular sentences of the system-language assert something. The sentences of the system-language, however, are never to be considered as report-signals. It is, therefore, difficult to avoid the idea that the report-signals are non-discursive entities (i.e. mere data of the system-sentences), and that the question of their empirical existence is on the same level with the question of the existence of psychological presentations. On the other hand, if any concrete sentence of the system language may, by convention, be a protocol sentence, the relation between these sentences and their empirical referents comes into question. On either hypothesis the non-discursive empirical realm seems to present itself and thus to render the formal idiom inadequate.

Some mention of the circumstance that the empirical data stand in some connection with the realm of discourse would appear inescapable. I cannot see how this would reintroduce metaphysical absolutism because it is not necessary to assume anything inexpressible in order to speak of the data of immediate experience. It might, of course, be said that sentences about the data of experiences of other people are not testable and hence are metaphysical. But surely this obtains only if complete testability or complete and direct testability of sentences is demanded. If a sentence about the experience of another person is unilaterally testable (i.e. refutable merely), it may be permitted as meaningful. Ajdukiewicz [1] has, in fact, shown that we may construct sentences of this kind. A metaphysical assumption is, therefore, not required in order to speak significantly about the data of the experience of others.

It will be granted that most methodological issues can be discussed solely in terms of the relation between basic sentences and the general sentences of a scientific system. The nature of laws and their confirmation, the form of general and singular statements, the logical connections among the sentences of a scientific system, all may be discussed in terms of syntax. The relations, however, between basic sentences and their empirical referents, while entirely expressible in discourse, involve reference to non-discursive, that is to say empirical, entities.

I shall summarize these critical remarks. The general assertion that it is a matter of decision whether a basic sentence which refutes a law will be accepted, or whether the law will be retained and the basic sentence which refutes

[1] Ajdukiewicz, K., " Sprache und Sinn," *Erkenntnis*, Bd. iv, pp. 106–109.

it will be rejected, is an inadequate characterization of scientific procedure. The place of experiment in terms of such a theory is not unambiguous, so that science is not distinguishable from an arbitrarily devised game. The rules of scientific procedure, in my opinion, should distinguish science from other pursuits by giving a pre-eminent place to experiment and observation. This does not mean that sentences recording experiments are to be considered as absolutely certain truths ; rather it means that hypotheses are to be tested via non-discursive empirical entities which are not hypothetical (because non-sentential) in character.

The rule that experiment and observation are to be the sole judges of theories would then seem to involve a theory of perception which explains the inter-relations of perceptions as well as the relations between basic-sentences and the perceptions which they express. I shall not discuss this further here.

The problem of the intersubjectivity of the scientific sentences does not seem to be satisfactorily treated in terms of Physicalism. On Carnap's first theory a public language could not be constructed. On Carnap's altered theory, whether intersubjectively valid sentences exist depends on whether there is a coherent system of protocol and theoretical sentences. In order to make this more than a merely possible system, the conventional character of testing sentences was introduced which enables us to eliminate protocols which do not agree with the system. While this convention would yield a body of intersubjectively valid sentences, it violates the demands of empiricism. Thus all physicalistic attempts to solve the problem of inter-subjectivity involve conventions which are inacceptable or ignore distinctions which are important and fundamental.

An alteration of Physicalism and an extension of syntactical distinctions seem to be required before a finally valid logic of science is achieved.

PART V

CONCLUSION

Chapter XIII

AN ESTIMATE OF THE VIENNESE CIRCLE

It would be somewhat pretentious to attempt a general judgment of a philosophical programme which covers such an extensive territory of knowledge as the present system of ideas. As a consequence the remarks of the present chapter are intended simply to summarize for the reader the doctrines and criticisms which have gone before, and to distinguish what, in the author's opinion, ought to be accepted and what questioned among the views of Logical Positivism.

Wittgenstein's analysis of logic, although limited to the logic of elementary propositions, proves conclusively that the propositions of logic can neither be established nor refuted by any possible experiment. And in the same way our knowledge of the world is neither increased nor decreased by the tautologies of logic. A deductive metaphysics is therefore theoretically impossible. In so far as this doctrine of Logical Positivism is not open to question, at least a part of the anti-metaphysical thesis is definitely established. The question remains whether, beside experiment and observation, there is another mode of knowing which would provide knowledge of the world. This question is phrased in psychological terms. Logically expressed we should ask whether, beside experiment and observation, non-logical statements are decidable by some other method of verification. And it would seem that no other method is known. The meaning of a statement is inextricably bound up with the method of its verification and the factual difference its truth or falsity would make. I therefore believe that the second part of the anti-metaphysical thesis is conclusively demonstrated because it is plain that the only specifiable referent of a non-logical statement is the non-discursive realm of empirical reality. All metaphysics is therefore out of the question. The assertions of metaphysics are decidable neither discursively nor empirically, and the alternative of discourse and experiment seems exhaustive and exclusive.

The specific doctrines of Wittgenstein on which the anti-metaphysical thesis depends, are, it is true, not beyond question in their own turn ; indeed, many of them seem to be wholly untenable. However, this means simply that an alteration of Wittgenstein's logical theories is necessary. The nature of propositional meaning and verification and the character of the proposition of logic may, that is to say, have been incompletely or erroneously explained by Logical Positivists. But their work shows, I think, that no explanation of propositional meaning and truth will allow a significant place in discourse for the assertions of metaphysics. This much could have been learned from Hume and Kant were it not for the fact that Hume's arguments against metaphysics have always been identified with his unacceptable psychological principles, and Kant's analysis of the paralogisms and the alleged proofs for the existence of God have erroneously been made to depend on his architectonic scheme of the intellectual and perceptual faculties. The logical analyses of Logical Positivism provide a more satisfactory basis for antimetaphysical arguments. The fact that they require emendation is not, in itself, evidence that the rejection of metaphysics is essentially unsound. And the examination of the doctrines seemingly requiring emendation has not revealed any method whereby metaphysics can be given meaning.

The second part of the programme, namely the delineation of an acceptable and non-metaphysical theory of scientific concepts and methods, is by no means as secure as the critical contribution of Logical Positivism. A brief review of the

Positivistic theories of scientific method will recall the critical issues.

The doctrine that propositions are pictures of possible empirical facts implies that the ultimate and exclusive referents of discourse are absolutely definite complexes of simple objects. These objects are designated by the logically proper names which are the sole constituents of the elementary propositions, and the manner of their composition is shown by the logical form of the proposition (i.e. by the manner in which the names are arranged). Objects, therefore, can only be represented. It follows that the meaning of elementary propositions depends wholly on the existence or non-existence of the factual complexes for which they stand. Non-elementary propositions are explicit truth-functions of elementary propositions and no method of combining propositions save by truth-operations is admitted. And thus the connection between discourse and empirical reality is simply established by confronting propositions and facts. The propositions of logic and their negations are limiting cases of discursive expression which are important for symbolism but convey no information about the world. All this implies the meaninglessness of epistemology and metaphysics. Epistemology is out of the question because it consists of attempts to assert the relation between propositions and facts, whereas this can only be shown ; metaphysics is impossible because it asserts the existence of entities which, by definition, cannot be specified in verifiable elementary propositions.

I found that there were essential defects in this system of ideas which rendered it inconclusive as a logical schematism and unsatisfactory as a basis for scientific method. It is inconclusive from a logical standpoint because its first principle, namely the alleged demonstration of the ultimate simplicity of the constituents of facts, is a *petitio principii*. And it is unsatisfactory as a basis for scientific method because it issues in a kind of solipsism, and because the limitations it places on language are too narrow to permit a satisfactory expression of general laws and of those scientific concepts which cannot be exhaustively referred to experiential data. And the theory is self-stultifying because it includes in the scope of the nonsensical the philosophical discussions on which its own conclusions depend.

It is plain that if the conception of meaning is narrow enough all kinds of problems can be dismissed, and important concepts of natural science must be distorted to be retained. If the logical arguments for this narrow view of meaning were conclusive, the fact that a radical reinterpretation of science would be entailed might disturb practical scientists, but would convince philosophers. The logical arguments were, however, untenable. In a sense, this result could have been anticipated. Logical arguments about the ultimate structure of the empirical world are surely verbal if valid, and beg the question if not, whereas empirical arguments about the ultimate structure of the empirical world are bound to be circular if they are ostensibly conclusive, and inconclusive when they are not circular. The only alternative remaining to us is to regard discussion of meaning in terms of the consequences which we draw from linguistic rules and conventions set up by ourselves.

This does not imply that the definitions and constructions of the logical notions which I have discussed, e.g. probability, are necessarily erroneous. Wittgenstein and Waismann have given a definition which expresses one very important aspect of probability perhaps more clearly than previous definitions, and the fact that it is not universally applicable simply means that it is insufficiently general, but certainly not that it is wrong.

The Positivistic conception of natural law does not stand in so secure a position. The unlimited generality of the meaning of laws is incompatible with the limited scope of propositions (in Wittgenstein's sense) ; laws, therefore, occupy a place in the interstices of the meaningful and the meaningless. This, as I tried to show, is wholly unsatisfactory since laws are more frequently employed as complete assertions than as models or preliminaries for) propositions.

The critical arguments of Positivists against a rationale of induction are wholly convincing. Their substitutions, however, are vitiated by the fact of dependence on an unsound view of scientific laws. Since we are not forced to accept the limitation set on the possible range of propositional meaning, we must simply extend our view of meaning so as to include laws among genuine assertions, and adopt a more liberal criterion of truth.

Finally the logical syntax which cannot be formulated is a contradiction in terms that cannot be retained in a consequent system of ideas. The inexpressibility of syntax, just as the other unsatisfactory principles we have examined, follows from untenable arguments about the ultimate simplicity of the constituents of the world. On a view of meaning which is free from this absolutism, the logical syntax of our conceptual apparatus is wholly formulable in discourse.

I found that Wittgenstein's scheme of ideas issued in a kind of linguistic solipsism which, although not metaphysical, was incompatible with the objectivity and intersubjectivity of science. This was a logical consequence of the Positivistic view of meaning. If we reject that view, wholly or partially, it will be impossible to *deduce* the solipsism of language. The communication of ideas will then be possible, and this is the minimum requirement of objectivity in science.

Logical Positivism has undergone a transformation of ideas largely initiated and developed by members of the Viennese Circle themselves. Carnap has been largely responsible for this (although the stimulation of his ideas has come in part from Neurath, Popper, and some of the founders of metamathematics). Many of the difficulties of the earlier views have been gradually overcome via Carnap's syntactical investigations of the nature of meaning and verification. The points where further improvement are obviously desirable are the treatment of the intersubjectivity and the test of concrete statements. Physicalism, at least

* preconceived notion of what science is like

in its present formulations, hardly seems to have accomplished these things satisfactorily.

The investigation of logic, mathematics, and the nature of scientific systems which have been carried out by the Logical Positivists are, nevertheless, of the greatest importance. It seems safe to assert that these studies have given us the clearest view of logic and scientific systems up to the present time, and the most evident merit of Logical Positivism is to be discovered here. That is why I have been content with a minimum of criticism on such matters as pertain to purely syntactical problems.

The nature of verification, the solution of the problem of intersubjectivity, and, in general, all questions which concern the connection between discourse and empirical reality, have principally occupied my attention in the present essay, because I believe that further investigations are required here, and because it seems to me that the questionable doctrines of Logical Positivism are involved.

Chapter XIV

THE POSSIBILITY OF AN ALTERNATIVE THEORY
OF LANGUAGE

In the earlier version of Logical Positivism the conception of proposition led to a kind of solipsism which rendered the expression of methodological principles impossible. In Radical Physicalism the conception of the content of sentences seemed to abandon any univocal criterion of truth. The question remains whether a somewhat different theory of language is possible which effectively avoids these difficulties.

The theory which I have to propose is not essentially different from doctrines advanced by Carnap as far as the nature of general sentences and the form of a scientific system are concerned. I shall have a rather different view, however, to propose concerned the nature of the basic empirical sentences of a system.

It would have been possible to advance other and perhaps rather stock arguments against the view that a distinction between discourse and empirical reality is unnecessary, but I have preferred to remain within the limits set by Carnap's doctrine in criticizing the adequacy of the formal idiom.

The difficulty with the formal idiom lies in the fact that it is impossible to express the relation between protocol-sentences of the object language and the empirical data to which these sentences refer. The syntax-language consists of sentences about the expressions of the object-language and about expressions of the syntax-language itself. The object-language contains, *inter alia*, reference to empirical data. It also contains reference to such data as protocol-sentences outside the system-language. The syntax-language of descriptive syntax may contain reference to the physical properties of expressions, and to the physical association of sentential expressions and human organisms. But the formal idiom prohibits mention of a relation between the terms of a protocol-sentence and the data of experience mentioned by it. This prohibition is made because the separation of psychological subjects makes an intersubjective correlation of sentences and empirical data impossible, and because correlation of sentences and data allegedly involves an inexpressible realm. Hence sentences can only be compared with sentences.

It will be conceded that an intersubjective comparison of sentences with empirical data is impossible granting the separation of subjects. But this does not imply the meaninglessness of sentences expressing such a comparison. For we may recall Hume's argument [1] that the existence of perceptions not occurring among the perceptions of a given subject is not logically impossible (although it is likely that the assertion that perceptions occur apart from *any* subject contradicts the scientific axioms). Moreover, the assertion that a given subject has some specified kinds of perceptions is not metaphysical in terms of the " liberal requirement of testability ", because such assertions are falsifiable. (I shall attempt to demonstrate this presently.)

The inexpressibility of the structure and constituency of empirical data only obtains on the terms of Wittgenstein's absolutistic and finitist theory of language. If we permit the use of ostensive definitions, a functional hierarchy of types, unlimited operators, and syntactical categories, whatever is inexpressible in Wittgenstein's finite language becomes expressible. For example, Russell and Whitehead, in the *Principia Mathematica*, define similarity of structure and properties of relations, and Carnap, in his syntax-language, very adequately expresses the syntactical categories (*Gattungen*). The use of ostensive definitions

[1] Hume, David, *Treatise of Human Nature*, book i, part iv, § 2 and book i, part iii, § 16.

makes it possible to characterize in discourse all constituents of the empirical data. The fact that every term of the object-language and the syntax-language may be discursively explained, given a sufficiently rich language-system, eliminates the possibility that the mysticism of the inexpressible will be reintroduced.

It would therefore seem possible to construct significant sentences about the correlation of perceptions and discursive entities. Although this would violate the formal idiom I cannot see how it would reintroduce metaphysical pseudo-sentences. Thus, if I write :—

(a) The syntactical designation of the word " red " is $^1pr^1_e$ (i.e. " red " is a one-place predicate of the first logical type), of the word " apple " is $^\circ ind_a$.

(b) $^1pr^1_r$ ($^\circ ind_a$) represents : the apple is red.

(c) $^1pr^1_r$ ($^\circ ind_a$) is true $\equiv$ There is a correlation between the datum, red apple, and the sentence $^1pr^1_e$ ($^\circ ind_a$), such that certain specified conditions of isomorphy, etc., are fulfilled ;

I do not see how any metaphysical pseudo-assertion is involved. It may be objected that " datum " is a pseudo-category, but I believe that this may be overcome by regarding " datum " as a class name for the categories " colour ", " sound ", etc. (when these terms are categories definable within the object-language). Moreover, if in descriptive syntax, sentences of the form " $\mathfrak{S}_1$ is uttered by John Smith " are allowed, it is not plain that sentences of the form : " $\mathfrak{S}_1$ is correlated with the datum $\mathfrak{D}_1$ via a co-ordination of $\mathfrak{A}_1, \ldots \mathfrak{A}_n$ which constitute $\mathfrak{S}_1$ and $\mathfrak{C}_1, \ldots \mathfrak{C}_n$ which are the constituents of $\mathfrak{D}_1$ " should be disallowed.

As a consequence the circumstances that (1) every characteristic of empirical reality is discursively specifiable via ostensive and nominal definitions, (2) the sentences about specific perceptions of psychological subjects (other than oneself) are unilaterally testable, and (3) the connection of discursive and extra-discursive entities is characterizable in discourse, allow for a non-metaphysical determination of the direct test of protocol sentences.

One further objection to a distinction between discourse and the empirical realm will be encountered. It will be said, perhaps, that, even though no unanswerable questions of meaning can arise granted the possibility of unlimited analysis and unlimited testing of sentences, the question " what essentially is the datum over and above its expression in sentences ? " always remains. On the one hand, the analysis of the content of sentences admits of a theoretically unlimited delineation, on the other hand, something remains to separate data from discourse such that this something is essentially unexplained. But this, I think, is the result of a misunderstanding both of the nature of expression and of the character of data. The expression of the characteristics of the empirical datum cannot effect an identification of data and the sentences which express the characteristics of data. On the other hand, if the characteristics of data are completely explained or are explicable in discourse, no question of *meaning* will finally remain unanswered. The autonomy of the data of observation, moreover, is not an occasion for questions about existence. *These* questions arise in connection with hypotheses, i.e. in respect of the truth of sentences ; observation is a method of answering these questions, but introduces no questions in turn, because *truth* and *falsity* are terms wholly inapplicable to data.

The larger problem of intersubjectivity remains. I have suggested that Physicalism as an assertion is at least a tenable hypothesis if the protocol-sentences can be physicalized with a minimum of convention and arbitrariness. The possibility of a failure to physicalize protocol sentences remains. Is it possible to test sentences about the perceptual data of others without a complete physicalization of protocols ? Is it possible, that is to say, to establish intersubjectively valid sentences without a physicalistic system-language ? Is it possible to have a univocal criterion of truth in such a system ? In what follows I shall try to indicate that this is the case.

I have tried to show that the solipsistic language of Positivism is forced upon us by an unacceptable doctrine about the atomic nature of the data of experience. And it was also shown that the relativism of Neurath's theory depends on another unacceptable doctrine which identified discourse and fact. A theory of language which does not make these assumptions cannot force us to accept solipsism or relativity in the criterion of truth *as a deductive necessity*.

There is, of course, no question of *deducing* our way out of solipsism. We can only avoid the absurdity of a system which logically implies it. For the hypothesis of intersubjectivity has an existential import which makes it impossible to prove the existence of a common world in the sense of deductive demonstration. I turn, therefore, to the specific problems at hand, namely the analysis of meanings which will afford a method of escaping from solipsism.

In the construction of the language of a scientific system I agree with Logical Positivists that we must distinguish basic sentences from non-basic sentences. The former had the character of singular statements about individual observations ; the latter are of the nature of hypotheses, general laws, prescriptions for the use of basic sentences, rules of transformation (deductive formulæ), and the like. In the Positivistic and Physicalistic systems all non-basic sentences are reducible or translatable into basic sentences through the use of explicit definitions and transformation formulæ. I believe I have shown that such analytic reduction is impossible. This is because the meaning of sentences, i.e. the method of verification, requires formulæ which determine their meaning over and above the data. The basic sentences and the non-basic sentences stand in another connection than that of the opposite poles of analysis and synthesis. In particular the connection of prescriptions for the use of basic sentences cannot be finally separated from these sentences. This is because the directions for the use of concepts enter explicitly into the meaning of the concepts. What I shall try to show in what follows is (1) that this interconnection of basic sentence and directive formulæ (resp. hypotheses) allows for a univocal criterion of truth, and (2) involves a public character of meaning which saves us from solipsism.

When I say that the meaning of a sentence is the *method* of its verification, and when I say that this *method* explicitly requires the application of certain rules and/or the assumption of certain hypotheses over and above the data *qua* data, I mean that these rules or hypotheses enter explicitly into the meaning of the sentence in question. Prescriptions and conventions are necessary in establishing a univocal criterion of truth, while hypotheses are used in establishing intersubjectivity of meaning and verification.

The necessity for a definite and univocal criterion of truth is a consequence of the nature of scientific systems. This may be seen as follows. A scientific system is a set of hypotheses usually axiomatized; and the axiomatization consists in constructing the system of scientific concepts so that the hypotheses are either axioms or deductions from axioms. Theoretical physics exemplifies this process of axiomatization. Now the axiomatic part of the system is purely deductive, and no question of verification is involved, but when the consequences of the axioms are applied to the prediction or description of data there arises the question of the criterion of truth. In order, therefore, to determine whether the consequences of a system of science are true, it is necessary to have a univocal criterion of truth.

It has frequently been said that if data do not have an absolutely definite structure, the sentences describing them will likewise suffer from indefiniteness and will therefore be unverifiable, since indefinite sentences cannot be univocally verified. This argument is not valid, for to insist that indefinite data necessarily imply indefinite sentence is like saying that we cannot call a man a thief unless we know exactly how many people he has robbed. However, since the question is important, I shall discuss it in greater detail.

It must be noted that the argument depends on inferring indefiniteness in sentences from indefiniteness in the data which they are devised to describe. It is therefore proposed that since the data and the sentences are necessarily indefinite a multi-valued truth-system must be employed. A univocal criterion of truth will then be out of the question. I wish to show that this whole argument fails to be convincing. A consideration of the claims put forth by the supporters of the multi-valued systems will bring out all the important points.

That multi-valued truth-systems are mathematically rigorous developments is unquestionable. If they have any fault it is, as has been frequently noted, in their interpretation. But this is not, as is usually supposed, a consideration external to their mathematical properties. While it is true that we can give names to sentences and then fictively proceed as if we operate on these names alone, the whole validity of the procedure depends on the possibility that the sentences themselves can always be reintroduced. Otherwise antinomies can be manufactured, and it is noteworthy that such antinomies can occur in multi-valued systems as well as in the ordinary two-valued system. But, with the proviso that sentences can always be reintroduced, the interpretation of a multi-valued system is not separable from its mathematical aspect as a pure calculus.

If we assume that the names " p ", " q ", etc., are to denote any kind of sentence, e.g. either elementary or non-elementary, the question of the interpretation of multi-valued systems must be subdivided into questions relating to these various kinds of propositions. Thus " If ' p ', ' q ', denote *non-elementary* sentences, what interpretation can be given to the n-valued system in which p and q are operands ? " is to be distinguished from the question " If ' p ', ' q ', etc., denote *elementary sentences*, etc. . . . ? " In order to show that multi-valued systems are non-interpretable, it is necessary only to reintroduce the elementary sentences into the system and then to ask what meaning can be given to the assertion " 'p' is either 1 or 0 or ? "[1] The question becomes " ' $\phi(x_1, x_2, \ldots x_n)$ ' is either 1 or 0 or ? ". Let ϕ mean " red " and " x " mean " spot ", so that " ϕx " means " the spot is red ". Then " ϕ " denotes a range within which " ϕx " can vary without being false, outside of which " ϕx " can vary without being true. We need not assume that " ϕ " denotes an absolutely specific shade of red. All that it is necessary to assume is that the _boundary_ of the range of variation be definitely fixed. We may imagine that the spectrum is arbitrarily divided by vertical bars of definite thickness. Then " ϕ " will denote the colours lying between a certain pair of these bars. The question of the truth or falsity of ϕx is then absolutely determinable and the so-called " third value " loses significance. With such determinations, arbitrary as they are, the two valued system is always interpretable and the many-valued systems never. It is to be noted that a sufficiently fine method of determination of ranges is a sufficient condition of the adequacy of the two-valued system. But it is also a necessary condition, for assuming that there was a limit to the refinement of range-determination, then there could be a ϕ such that ϕ was neither true nor false but (?). Now the method of determining ranges depends on the use of real numbers in conjunction with physical instruments. Hence, since there is no initial difficulty in using the real numbers in conjunction with physical instruments (i.e. conventional and physical factors do not present insurmountable problems), the whole question depends on the assumption of the consistency of the real numbers. But this assumption lies also at the foundation of the multi-valued systems. Hence, without making any further assumption than those assumed by the founders of the multi-valued systems, we can eliminate the " third value " and _a fortiori_ any n value from the system, thus reducing it to the ordinary two-valued logic.

It might be said that the application of ranges and the

[1] $1 =$ true, $0 =$ false, ? $=$ some intermediate value.

determination of ranges have an arbitrary character which weakens the force of the argument. Whenever there is an indeterminacy we change the proposition ϕx in such a way that *it* becomes determinate, whereas the original indeterminacy was due to the indeterminacy in the fact itself. It is this latter indeterminacy, it will be said, that occasions the introduction of multi-valued systems. But this is merely an after-thought which can easily be eliminated. Indeterminacy, a relative term, is applied to the *means* of describing facts. We can only have indeterminacy where there is a determinacy and this last *only where a method of description is in question*. Indeterminacy comes in question only in connection with our conceptual apparatus.

It seems, of course, to be indifferent whether we choose to make our sentences more exact and to speak only of true and false sentences, or whether we continue to retain inexact formulations of sentences and introduce new truth-values whenever our sentences become indeterminate. But two considerations militate against the latter view. First the progress of science has undeniably been in the former direction, namely that of the refinement of concepts. Second the actual result of dealing with inexact concepts is usually a permanent indeterminacy, whereas the refinement of concepts by, e.g., range-determination tends to reduce the indeterminacy. The description of the world by scientific methods requires this.

To summarize : The two-valued logic is interpretable given a sufficient degree of refinement of concepts, whereas the reverse is true of multi-valued systems. Multi-valued systems must admit of interpretation, i.e. the " p's, q's ", etc., must be replaced by the sentences which they denote, in order to avoid antinomies. When this is done, however, the multi-valued systems are always reducible to the two-valued system, and hence lose the special significance that is sometimes claimed for them.

From these considerations it is clear that we can retain the univocal criterion of truth which science requires. The

CONCLUSION

indeterminacy in data does not imply an indeterminacy in sentences. We can and should make sentences definite. Since the definiteness cannot be fixed by the data the only recourse is the method of constructing the language in which the sentences occur.

The method of verifying sentences thus depends on two factors, (1) the rules for fixing the meanings of concepts which are relative to the whole system of concepts constituting the language and (2) the data which the sentences describe.

The solution of the problem of intersubjectivity involves the hypothesis that there are distinct sets of experience which may have common parts, i.e. parts structurally identical in some respects. This hypothesis is admissible because there is no *a priori* reason for rejecting it as nonsense as the Logical Positivists did. Sentences used for communication or for corroboration will therefore contain this hypothesis as an explicit part of their meaning. There is no possibility of demonstration here for one of two reasons : (1) either such a demonstration would be formally invalid, or (2) it would be fallacious as being an alleged proof for an existential assertion. (1) If we said that the consequences of the hypothesis such as, for example, similar behaviour of various individuals, implied the truth of the hypothesis we would be guilty of affirming the consequent. (2) If we attempted to say, e.g., that the similar behaviour of individuals implied the existence of experiences with a common structure we would be guilty of inferring the existence of one fact from that of another wholly or partially different from it. In either case proof is evidently out of the question.

On the other hand, we can say, a necessary but not a sufficient condition for establishing communication is a method of discovering misunderstanding. This is due to Ajdukiewicz.[1] His criterion for discovering misunderstanding is applicable to assertions about facts and assertions

---

[1] Ajdukiewicz, K., " Sprache und Sinn," *Erkenntnis*, Band iv.

of pure logic. On the assumption that there are distinct sets of experiences, we can say :—

A. If S understands " P " = " S has a pain " then S cannot fail to assert " P " when S feels pain unless S is prevaricating.

B. If S understands " Q " and " $Q \supset R$ ", then S cannot affirm " Q " and " $Q \supset R$ " and deny " R ".

Converting by denying the consequents of these sentences we have :—

A. S feels pain and denies " P ", implies S does not understand " P " (excluding the cases in which S prevaricates) or S does not feel pain and asserts " P ", implies S does not understand " P ".

B. S affirms " Q " and " $Q \supset R$ ", and denies " R ", implies S does not understand " Q " and/or " $Q \supset R$ ".

This criterion provides a necessary condition for mutual understanding. It is impossible to give the totality of sufficient conditions for mutual understanding. The likelihood of it, however, can be increased beyond a mediocre limit, given an increasing number of cases of exclusions and positive conditions of the subject's behaviour. This is the case because there are necessary conditions of understanding on the basis of which to erect the hypothesis " S understands ' P ' " with initial finite probability.

Now we may take the condition of objective (or intersubjective) verification. If :—

(1) S and S_1 are in a certain position, L,

(2) S observes E (= an event),

(3) S and S_1 understand " P " which is verified by E, and

(4) S_1 denies " P ", then S_1 does not observe E.

Under these conditions we may say that an objective verification by S and S_1 does not occur. A necessary condition of objective verification is, then, that S and S_1 understand " P ", and that S or S_1 in position L observes E which would verify " P ".

Again, since the necessary condition of verification has been given, the probability of the hypothesis "S and S_1 verify 'P'" can be increased beyond a mediocre limit as the number of exclusions and positive instances of similar behaviour increase.

The intersubjective conditions on the basis of which verification of a sentence may occur may then be stated somewhat as follows :—

Given the following assumptions :—

(1) The existence of different sets of experiences which do not overlap (i.e. contains no numerically identical elements in common) but which may be structurally identical in some respects is a significant hypothesis ;

(2) The singular (basic) sentences of any scientific language contains explicit conventions required for their application to the data with which they are concerned ;

(3) The necessary condition of understanding a basic sentence by several subjects is contained as an hypothesis in the meaning of the basic sentence ;

(4) The necessary condition of corroborative verification by several subjects is contained in the methodological rules by which verification occurs ; We can say that the meaning and truth of a basic-sentence (and of any sentence). may be called intersubjective in so far as the necessary conditions have been fulfilled, and in so far as the sufficient conditions give a likelihood superior to a mediocre limit.

There is, as has been insisted, no possibility of absolute certainty in the case of basic sentences. We must be satisfied with three things :—

(1) It is sometimes possible to determine when we have not been understood and when our observations have not been corroborated.

(2) It is sometimes possible, given the assumptions, to determine to a degree of probability that our sentences have been corroborated.

(3) There is no *a priori* reason why the conditions of inter-subjectivity should not be assumed. The theory of language given here explicitly allows for these conditions.

It may, after all, be asked why one should make these assumptions. They are not capable of verification in the Positivistic sense. The only replies to these objections are :—

(1) The hypothesis of intersubjectivity tends to be confirmed to a high degree of probability and this is all that can be asked of a good hypothesis. It is, in fact, the assumption which is always made by persons communicating and mutually corroborating sentences.

(2) The contrary hypothesis (which is an inevitable consequence of Wittgenstein's doctrine) makes it utterly impossible to explain the appearance of communication. If communication is meaningless on the basis of a theory of language, then the *appearance* of communication will for-ever be an enigma to the exponents of that theory.

(3) Hence either we assume a hypothesis of intersubjectivity which cannot be demonstrated logically but which can be given a high degree of probability, or we are left with a connection of facts (apparent communication and corroboration) which cannot be explained.

It is clear that an antimetaphysical doctrine cannot admit of unsolvable riddles. As a consequence, the Positivistic position cannot be made self-consistent even within its own limits. We are obliged to *assume* intersubjectivity if we are to explain the world of science at all, and if we do in fact *assume* it the consequences of the hypothesis are confirmed with a high degree of probability.

That language is used for communication and that corroborative verifications occur is and must be an assumption. It is, however, the assumption that is almost universally made in scientific practice and everyday life ,

And we end up with good old fashioned horse-sense.

INDEX OF NAMES

INDEX OF SUBJECTS

Logic is not a psychological description of the way we
actually think, but a method of determining the
correctness or incorrectness of inferences....